T0355731

Saving New Sounds

Saving New Sounds

*Podcast Preservation
and Historiography*

Jeremy Wade Morris and Eric Hoyt,
editors

University of Michigan Press • *Ann Arbor*

Published in the United States of America by the
University of Michigan Press
Printed and bound by CPI Group (UK) Ltd, Croydon, CR0 4YY
First published July 2021

A CIP catalog record for this book is available from the British Library.

Library of Congress Cataloging-in-Publication data has been applied for.

DOI: https://doi.org/10.3998/mpub.11435021
ISBN: 978-0-472-05447-3 (Paper : alk paper)
ISBN: 978-0-472-90124-1 (OA ebook)

Contents

Revisiting Podcasting's Histories

Analyzing Podcasting's Now

Imagining Podcasting's Future

Digital materials related to this title can be found on the Fulcrum platform
via the following citable URL: https://doi.org/10.3998/mpub.11435021

Acknowledgments

Is this thing on? Part microphone check, part technical support query; the question seems a fitting way to start this collection, which is not just the book you hold in your hands (or the PDF you see on your screen) but also a vibrant, growing, and slightly temperamental database that indexes millions of podcasts. We grab the mic then to say thanks to the many individuals and institutions who had a hand in helping this project go from mic check to showtime.

The publication of this book, as well our work in building and sustaining the PodcastRE archive, was made possible thanks to a UW2020 Discovery Initiative grant. Support for this research was provided by the University of Wisconsin–Madison Office of the Vice Chancellor for Research and Graduate Education with funding from the Wisconsin Alumni Research Foundation. Additionally, further research and the development of PodcastRE's data analytics tools were supported through a Digital Humanities Advancement Grant from the National Endowment for the Humanities. We would like to thank these institutions for their generous support and for believing in us and our work.

Within our home institution, there are many people we need to thank for their expertise, creativity, kindness, and contributions to the underlying database from which this collection stems. PodcastRE would not exist without the engineering brilliance of Peter Sengstock, who manages the large-scale technical needs of this highly demanding project with grace and patience. Similarly, Samuel Hansen's incomparable efforts in coding, scripting, and problem solving almost the entire back-end infrastructure deserve more recognition than this paragraph allows. Our thanks also go to UW Libraries' digital team—Lee Konrad, Peter Gorman, Cameron Cook, and Scott Prater—for their guidance and contributions to the AV Data Core.

We are fortunate to work in UW–Madison's Department of Communication Arts with an extraordinary group of colleagues and students. We would like to thank the Media and Cultural Studies and Film faculty—Jonathan Gray, Michele Hilmes, Derek Johnson, Lori Kido Lopez, Jason Lopez, David Bordwell, Kelley Conway, Erik Gunneson, Lea Jacobs, Ben Singer, Jeff Smith, Darshana Mini, and Aaron Greer—for the intellectual community that makes this work possible (and fun). We especially want to call attention to the graduate students, past and present, who have contributed immeasurably to the PodcastRE project and this book: JJ Bersch, Andrew Bottomley, Dewitt King, Jackie Land, Nick Laureano, Jacob Mertens, Lesley Stevenson, Tom Welch, and Susan Noh (with a special nod for her impressive design and implementation of the PodcastRE visualization and analytics tools).

Beyond Madison, we are grateful to belong to a vibrant community of scholars working at the intersections of media studies, sound studies, and the digital humanities. Many of these scholars generously contributed chapters and their voices to this book. We would especially like to thank the organizers and participants of the 2018 GLASS (Great Lakes Association of Sound Studies) conferences, including Neil Verma, Jacob Smith, Marit MacArthur, Mara Mills, Robert Ochshorn, and Mack Hagood. Thanks also to Josh Shepperd and the Radio Preservation Task Force, Sarah Florini, Dana Gerber-Margie, Craig Eley, Wendy Hagenmaier, Elana Levine, Troy Reeves, Reginold Royston, Shawn Vancour, Lia Wolock, and others who have contributed ideas, advice, and podcast recommendations as the database has grown in scope and scale. Our advisory board—Jonathan Sterne, Tanya Clement, and Adam Sachs—also provided much-needed support during the funding stages of the project.

In bringing this book to completion, it was a pleasure to work with the University of Michigan Press, a publisher that shares our commitments to open access and digital preservation. Thank you to Mary Francis, Sara Cohen, Flannery Wise, Mary Hashman, and Anna Pohlod for guiding us through the process and Pilar Wyman for the great index.

The final stages of the editing process occurred as we sheltered in place during a global pandemic—something we never imagined we would be living through. We could not have done it without the love, laughs, and care of our families.

Jeremy would like to thank Leanne for a lifetime of listening (to podcasts, music, each other, etc.). To Lucas, Rachel, and Justine, thanks for making podcasts with me and for all the noise you bring to my life.

Eric thanks Emily, Rumi, Liam, and Esme for their love, inspiration, and creativity. Thank you for showing me how to be mindful and present, through the good and the bad. You are my best teachers.

Is this thing on? Let's find out.

Introduction

The Inseparability of Research and Preservation Frameworks for Podcasting History

ERIC HOYT AND JEREMY WADE MORRIS

In March 2014, podcaster and comedian Adam Carolla initiated a crowd-funding campaign designed to "save" podcasting. A company called Personal Audio LLC was suing Carolla for infringing on a patent—a "system for disseminating media content in serialized episodes" (Nazer 2018)—that it claimed gave the company exclusive rights over the very practice of distributing audio via a podcast. Carolla's campaign called on podcast listeners and podcast creators to band together to offset the legal fees it would cost to pursue the case, a case that would save podcasting by ensuring it remained a practice anyone could do rather than become a licensable technology exclusive to one company. In the end, Carolla raised close to half a million dollars from over twelve thousand supporters, and his cause was featured in dozens of podcasts and hundreds of other media outlets. The Electronic Frontier Foundation (EFF)—a nonprofit digital rights group that promotes internet civil liberties—also began challenging the patent through the patent office, in support of Carolla and other podcasters. Although Carolla was the highest-profile podcaster at the center of the infringement suit, with many other podcasters out there and millions of avid listeners who regularly download and use podcasts, the threat that Personal Audio might go after a much wider swath of podcast producers was enough to galvanize a disparate community of listeners, users, media producers, and tech activists.

Through the EFF's work, the overly broad claims related to the patent were invalidated in 2018 (Nazer 2018). Yet the dispute highlights how fragile new media formats can be and how vulnerable new industries are when the protocols, norms, and conventions of production, circulation, and consumption have yet to settle (Gitelman 2006).

As we write this in 2020, podcasting has moved past the existential threat of a patent troll. By many measurements, the medium is flourishing—with the quantity of podcasts, listeners, advertising revenue, and nonprofit funding increasing sharply year after year, including an "explosive" 2018, which saw the number of US people over the age of twelve who have ever listened to a podcast climb above 50 percent for the first time (Edison Research 2019; *Podnews* 2019). While it's tempting to conclude that podcasting has been "saved," there are many other related issues and threats that demand attention. The challenges span the technical and the cultural, the mundane and the complex. Podcast feeds end abruptly, cease to be maintained, or become housed in proprietary databases, like iTunes,[1] that are difficult to search with any rigor. Many podcasts get put behind paywalls as they get popular or as back catalogs become a potential source of revenue. Then there's the precariousness of the very platforms that help make up podcasting's diffuse and sometimes DIY infrastructure. All it took was a minor change in Dropbox's features and terms of service for a number of podcasts to disappear from their regular feeds (Morris 2017; *Dropbox* 2017), while other platforms have their own intricacies about how much content they'll keep and for how long.

It's not just the audio recordings that can disappear, either. Carolla's call to save podcasting was more about preserving cultural practices and values than it was about the technology or content. Podcasting's origins as a relatively open and accessible format—one built on highly usable and adaptable technologies like RSS, one that was platform agnostic, and one whose associated technologies for making and consuming the format—were certainly enough to fuel hopes that the format could represent a democratic form of media and communication with low barriers to entry and the promise of amplifying a diverse multitude of voices.

Yet it's also worth reflecting on what it means that Carolla had the loudest voice in this campaign. While most podcasters share the stated values of openness and free expression Carolla was pushing, few possess the audience, advertising base, reputation, and thus privilege that Carolla developed through his career working in traditional radio and television. His perspective and identity—as a cis-gendered white heterosexual male most publicly visible as one of the creators and hosts of Comedy Central's *The Man Show* from 1999 to 2004—represents just one perspective present in the podcasting ecosystem. If podcasting is saved in a manner that reproduces the structures of power and privilege from traditional media industries (and society at large), then the innovative and diverse potential of the form runs the risk of being lost.

To confront these issues and the dynamic audio landscape that podcasting affords, this book brings together contributions from a number of leading and emerging scholars in podcasting and digital audio with the hope of taking stock of podcasting's recent history and imagining future directions for the format. We trace some of the less amplified histories of the format and offer discussions of some of the theoretical and cultural hurdles podcasting faces nearly twenty years into its existence. The questions our authors ask are sometimes technical or aesthetic: What sonic practices are unique to podcasts? What does a shift away from RSS feeds to streaming services mean for podcasting? What is the production quality of various shows, and how does this affect the overall aesthetic of individual podcasts? But they are also cultural and social: What voices are highlighted or silenced in podcasts versus other media? What reconfigurations between producers and audiences are taking place in podcasts? What are the economics that underpin this largely unmonetized circulation of audio content?

No collection will likely be able to answer all of these questions satisfactorily, but we hope that by asking them, and by providing tools and examples for how we might go about responding to them, researchers will be better equipped to evaluate how audio production is changing in light of new technologies, and how listening and speaking, as cultural practices and modes of being, are also undergoing a renegotiation. We hope the collection will help reexamine accepted histories of the format and consider possible future developments as well as offer methodological models for future research. We are particularly interested in questions related to how we, as media historians and cultural researchers, can save and preserve the booming audio culture currently emerging from podcasting. Though we, like Carolla, are certainly also limited by our own perspectives and identities, and relative privilege as university professors far removed from many of the communities and voices our collection aims to address, we hope that the perspectives we've been able to gather here from our contributing authors help broaden the scope and scale of the project. Even then, the project still largely focuses on histories of podcasting in the United States, and English-language podcasts more generally, which certainly means there are many other regional and cultural histories of this form in need of preservation. There's also the fact that there are likely unforeseen consequences that emerge given that, in our case, the preservationists and the scholars are one and the same. The two coeditors (along with many, though not all, of our contributors) are media historians first and accidental archivists second. We hope including the ideas of the archivists involved in the Preserve This Podcast initiative (Dana Gerber-Margie, Mary Kidd, Molly Schwartz, and Sarah Nguyễn) helps mitigate this, but our project is still fundamentally built, and therefore colored, by the perspectives of media and cultural studies scholars. Still, despite these limitations, we believe that the explosion of new perspectives and voices echoing through the podcasting industry is culturally worthwhile and politically significant. We also believe that if sound and sonic objects are going to play a greater role in humanities-based research, this depends on ready access to historical, current, and (eventually) future sounds.

If there is a single intervention and argument that we hope readers take away from this book, it is that the work of preserving podcasts is inseparable from how we conceptualize the medium's histories, meanings, and definitions. By this we mean that the way we think about podcasting's histories, either its cultural past or technical past, end up affecting decisions that archivists and media historians might make regarding how to go about "saving" podcasts. If, for example, we conceptualize podcasts as MP3 sound files found on the internet, then we might focus our collection efforts on gathering audio files and building a technical infrastructure that can find and house those. If instead we treat podcasts as MP3 files plus their accompanying RSS feeds, then a different kind of search index and technical infrastructure is needed. Similarly, if we accept the standard history of podcasting as starting with the *Daily Source Code*, an early podcast produced by former MTV star Adam Curry that earned him the nickname "Podfather," then the focus of a collection becomes different from how it would be if we believed there were dozens, if not hundreds, of other Podparents out there during the early years of the format whose work needs to be uncovered. Working on the archive/ database project we describe in the next paragraph has prompted us to think through discovery strategies for finding podcasts, curation strategies for determining which podcasts to save, and technical strategies for how to physically and computationally do the work of gathering files and metadata. Each decision has confirmed the inseparability of theoretical frameworks and preservation practices.

We have come to understand the inseparability of digital media's research and preservation programs through working on the development of PodcastRE—a database we have built that is hosted at the University of Wisconsin–Madison with over 2.5 million archived podcasts and that provides tools for searching and analyzing these audio files. The chapters that follow include dispatches from individuals working closely with the database and its search and analytics tools (e.g., JJ Bersch on advertising and versioning challenges; Samuel Hansen on RSS; Eric Hoyt on new collection development policies; Jeremy Morris on the preservation risks of paid subscription services; Susan Noh on metadata analysis; Jacob Mertens, Hoyt, and Morris on the digital analysis of podcasting vocal performances). Yet an equal number of chapters might be better classified as *dispatches to* the PodcastRE project. By sharing their research on the history of audioblogs (Andrew Bottomley), sound documentaries (Michele Hilmes), the true crime genre (Amanda Keeler), and the role podcasting can play in pedagogy (Mack Hagood), these four authors insist that efforts to save, study, and teach podcasts place the medium within a larger historical frame. Similarly, the chapters from Jennifer Hyland Wang and Sarah Florini and Briana Barner write both amateur women and Black podcasters into media history and demand that PodcastRE and administrators of other archives think critically not only about biases and erasures that traditional histories enshrine but also about how to broaden and expand collection policies so that a greater diversity of voices are available when the time comes for future histories to be written.

A Brief History of the PodcastRE Project

Before assessing the scholarly landscape on research into podcasting, sound studies, digital humanities, and digital preservation that informs our work, and before outlining the book's various chapters, we first offer a brief description of the project that sparked the creation of this collection. As we write this in the spring of 2020, the PodcastRE database has grown to over 2.5 million podcast episodes from over 16,000 unique feeds. They occupy 100 terabytes of space on multiple hard drives—which, in more technical terms, is called a RAID (Redundant Array of Independent Disks) storage array—that are housed in our university's AV Data Core. The collection has expanded beyond what any individual could listen to within a lifetime, and it only keeps growing.

Like many collections, however, PodcastRE began with more modest ambitions (Morris et al. 2019). Interested in studying podcasts and writing a follow-up to an earlier history he had worked on (Sterne et al. 2008), Morris realized in early 2014 that there were few searchable databases of podcasts and thus few ways of studying and analyzing the booming audio culture taking place in podcasting. Since the ability to study media history depends heavily on the preservation of media artifacts, the accessibility of those artifacts, and the tools to analyze them, it is worrisome that the most comprehensive podcast databases currently existing are corporate databases like iTunes, Stitcher, or Podbean. These platforms contain millions of podcasts, but they are generally geared toward discovery and playback of podcasts rather than exploring the wider landscape of digital audio or promoting preservation. More public archives, such as the Internet Archive, have smaller and more eclectic holdings, and the web interface and user-driven nature of the site's collection are not as robust as scholarly researchers might want, despite the critical role in audio preservation that the Internet Archive plays. Pop Up Archive's AudioSear.ch tool provided a more user-friendly search tool, but it indexed only a fraction of the most popular podcasts, and in 2017 it was purchased by Apple and ceased operating as a stand-alone search database (Leswing 2017). PodDb, PodChaser, and other similar services provide rich databases of metadata about podcast hosts, producers, and other production credits (like IMDb), but they leave the preservation of files and data out of the equation.

Worried about the vulnerability of digital audio files, and excited about the increased interest in the podcast industry in the wake of *Serial*'s surprise success in 2014, Morris and contributor Andrew Bottomley began downloading audio files from podcasts that were being talked about and referenced in the press (Adams 2015). Along with our in-house information technology specialist, Peter Sengstock, we added RSS feeds manually in an iTunes account and saved as many audio files as we could to a local hard drive on an aging Mac Pro. RSS feeds are, in our minds, an essential characteristic of podcasts. As described further in Hansen's and Morris's chapters, RSS—or Really Simple Syndication—is the technology that lets users "subscribe" to a podcast through the click of a button and ensures that when new podcasts are released, they will be instantly available for subscribers on their devices (be it computers, phones, tablets, etc.). RSS is the same technology that powered the blogging trend of the early 2000s, and its relative openness makes it possible for a wide range of users to easily broadcast a message to a much larger public than they could otherwise. In this way, RSS feeds are a technical standard, lines of code that stipulate how podcasts are distributed. But they also contribute to podcasting's cultural meaning, lines of code that stipulate that anyone can and should have the ability to share their perspective sonically. Given the historical importance of RSS feeds for podcasting, both technically and culturally, we felt it was important to center on this technology while building our database. It is worth noting here that our steps of appraisal (determining whether a podcast merits preservation) and acquisition (adding it to the database) always take place at the level of RSS feed and not the level of the individual episode, the creator, the podcasting network, or any number of other ways archives might organize their record groups.

Indeed, the articulation of a coherent collection policy and our methods of appraisal became increasingly important as the project's data storage needs expanded and we began applying for funding. "You can't save everything" was a line repeated to us so often that it ultimately became a cliché. True, we can't save everything. However, in our era of relatively compressed digital files and ever-expanding storage, we were wary of making choices based on our assumptions of present and future value that would eliminate large groups of podcasts from our project. Artificial constraints, such as limiting the collection to only the podcasts in a certain region (e.g., Wisconsin), genre (e.g., true crime), era (e.g., early podcasts between 2004 and 2008), production (e.g., amateur), or cultural or demographic groupings (e.g., podcasts created by queer producers), would be a disservice to researchers looking to study the full breadth and excitement around podcasting's emergence and current popularity. We came to align our approach with the *archival multiverse* perspectives shared in the influential, lengthy book *Research in the Archival Multiverse*, edited by Anne J. Gilliand, Sue McKemmish, and Andrew J. Lau (2017). We came to understand the importance of appraisal and collecting policies while simultaneously recognizing that such methods are always culturally and historically contingent, and as Gilliand (2017) shows, have shifted across national, cultural, and political contexts.

In addressing this web of opportunities and challenges, the question for us quickly became, How could we index and save as much as possible while working within the constraints we faced through the technology, resources, and our own cultural positions? The questions of what to save are not just theoretical, then—What content to seek out and preserve? What policy guides the collection?—but also technical. For example, in an environment of dynamic advertising insertions, what instance of the show do we save (a question JJ Bersch explores in chapter 5)? What version of the metadata do we save and use to power the searches the site facilitates (issues that Susan Noh and Samuel Hansen address in their chapters)? And what material in addition to the audio file should we save to give context to the text (a topic Eric Hoyt explores in chapter 14)? Ultimately, we recognize that any act of collection is also an act of power, and being clear and transparent about cultural and technical factors that shape any collection is key.

In the spirit of blending research and preservation frameworks, our project took on dual tasks: saving the podcasts that were being included in discussions of podcasting's "golden age" as well as interrogating what podcasts were being left out of that discussion and saving representative works from those podcasters. We've navigated the need to preserve the "popular" by automating the collection of a particular index of what's popular: the iTunes charts. Using Python and other computer scripting tools, we index and save podcasts on the top 100 lists for several large podcast markets every twenty-four hours. We began by collecting just the lists for the US market, but as the stability of our ingestion process improved, we were able to add other "pilot" markets. We added the UK and Australia because we wanted two other English-speaking countries with robust podcasting ecosystems that might have some overlap with the United States but also their own original shows and podcast networks, and we added France to test ingestion in a different language (though one still based on the same alphabet). We plan to continue to add other markets if these pilot tests are successful, and we continue to work on improving the ingestion process so that it better handles different alphabets and characters (e.g., Chinese). All the files in the database are backed up regularly to physical media—magnetic tapes. To facilitate fast playback access while complying with copyright laws, PodcastRE's interface allows users to play the files from the locations in which they were publicly hosted or were indexed. This algorithmic approach toward collecting embraces both the affordances of the digital media and the MPLP (More Product, Less Process) model proposed by Mark A. Greene and Dennis Meissner (2005). Rather than immediately narrowing our collecting mission or attempting to achieve fully standardized object descriptions, we cast a wide net and accept that because podcasters enter their own metadata, their descriptive information arrives to us imperfect and incomplete.

The idiosyncrasies of podcasting metadata are something that we discuss in depth in other publications (Morris et al. 2019) and that Susan Noh and Samuel Hansen address in their chapters. Here, we want to emphasize that the Apple Podcast charts (which we save on a weekly basis) are also complex indexes of culture that require interpretation. They provide some sense of what's currently being promoted and potentially listened to on the world's largest platform for podcast distribution. But Apple's charts are also notoriously prone to manipulation, with entrepreneurial podcasters stuffing popular keywords into their metadata (contributing to the above-noted idiosyncrasies) and sometimes hiring the services of questionable third-party vendors that promise to elevate the ranking of a given podcast, regardless of whether or not any human beings are actually listening to it (Carman 2018; Cridland 2018). Rather than trying to separate the wheat from the chaff—the truly popular shows from the hucksters and posers—we accept that all of these coexist in our current moment of podcasting and will continue to coexist in our archive moving forward. Our efforts are better spent describing and analyzing the charts rather than trying to vet them and kick out podcasters who have supposedly gamed the system.

Realistically, the hucksters and posers probably need more preservation help with their podcasts than the iTunes chart toppers from WNYC, WBEZ, and other National Public Radio (NPR) affiliates. Many of the top shows come from large media organizations, and, as a result, we may be saving duplicate copies of audio files that may reside in more professionally preserved private and public radio station archives. In preservation efforts, however, redundancy is a safeguard, and our database opens up these texts to new forms of research and analysis. Many of these shows are also popular independent podcasts that succeed on the iTunes charts, such as *Limetown*, *Welcome to Night Vale*, and *36 Questions*, but that may not have as robust or well-thought-out preservation plans as NPR or the resources of the top commercial podcast networks.

If even popular podcasters are not always safely preserving their own material, then there's even more vulnerability at the other end of the spectrum. There are a huge number of independent, amateur, and off-the-iTunes-radar podcasts and an equally sizeable number of hosts, producers, and engineers without the foresight, budgets, or means to properly label, store, and archive their audio. Strides are being made in this regard, such as the Preserve This Podcast project, which Dana Gerber-Margie, Mary Kidd, and Molly Schwartz report on in their chapter. However, because of the mundane nature of numerous podcasts, many podcasters probably do not realize the audio they are making is shaping the early stages of this emerging format and doing so in a way that media historians, scholars, and hobbyists might later want to analyze, research, teach, and reference.

In our efforts to identify and collect significant podcasts that remain uncharted on the iTunes top 100, we have pursued collaborations with scholars who are researching independent podcasts produced by women, indigenous peoples, and people of color. Additionally, we have benefited from working with historians studying forms of internet-delivered audio that preceded the term "podcast." These researchers have served as curators, sending us lists of significant, neglected podcasts and sharing analyses that situate the contributions of those podcasters. PodcastRE's collection of 2.5 million podcast episodes has thus been built by a combination of algorithmic methods and informed selections made by hand. There's also a "submit a podcast" feature on the project's website that allows individuals to add their own choices for podcasts they'd like preserved. The fifteen thousand podcast feeds don't come close to representing the over seven hundred thousand podcast feeds that, according to estimates, are currently being distributed (Podnews 2019). But the PodcastRE collection does offer a valuable and diverse cross-section of English-language podcasts from the past several years, from the United States, Australia, and the UK. The database also provides a growing collection of French-language podcasts from France and some African countries, with, hopefully, additional languages being added in the years to come, although languages that use non-Roman alphabetic or character-based alphabets still pose a challenge (and thus a blind spot) for the database's search features.

In parallel to our efforts to curate and preserve podcasts, we have sought to develop new methods for studying and analyzing these media files. Our efforts toward these ends have been generously supported through funding from the NEH Office of Digital Humanities and the University of Wisconsin–Madison's Office of the Vice Chancellor for Research and Graduate Education. PodcastRE's web interface allows users to search the database (e.g., by keyword, title, description, etc.) and stream podcasts from their original location online. It also allows users to conduct advanced searches filtered by date, length, category, and publisher. We have built visualization tools—a keyword/word cloud search feature and a keyword frequency line graph—so that users can further investigate the prevalence of their chosen keywords across the entire corpus. The resulting data analytics features can be accessed at http://podcastre.org/analytics. We have also been working with frequency and pitch tracking tools to examine patterns within the sonic files (and not simply the keywords and metadata). These digital tools and methods are discussed in the book that follows, alongside other chapters that address the broader histories and theoretical frameworks that inform our ongoing work and that, we anticipate, PodcastRE's users will find equally valuable.

Interdisciplinary Approaches to Studying and Saving Sounds

Our collection is most immediately informed by the growing research in podcasting as format and phenomenon but also by work in sound studies, the digital humanities, and digital preservation. While academic interest in podcasting has renewed since the launch of the highly successful true crime podcast *Serial* in 2014, scholarship on podcasting, like the medium itself, has grown slowly and steadily since the mid-2000s. Early articles from media and cultural studies scholars (Berry 2006; Crofts et al. 2005; Menduni 2007; Moscote Freire 2007; Sterne et al. 2008) track the emergence of the format, its possibilities and problems, and place podcasting in its historical context in relation to radio and broadcasting more generally. Some early research also looked at the motivations of independent podcasters and provided the statistics on the imbalances in podcasting hosts/producers with respect to class, race, and gender (Markman 2011; Markman and Sawyer 2014; Madden and Jones 2008). In addition, researchers provided ethnographies of listeners and producers (Millette 2010; McClung and Johnson 2010), giving greater insight into the production cultures that helped fuel this new medium, even as they revealed that many of podcasting's earliest promises to disrupt traditional radio's power dynamics had yet to be realized. Early scholarship on podcasting also came from the field of education and technology studies (Campbell 2005; Harris and Park 2008), though this work was, and remains, primarily focused on podcasting's potentials and challenges for teaching and learning. It is, on the whole, less concerned with the form and content of podcasts as a medium for everyday use, the imbalances of who is hosting and producing them, what new voices may be emerging, or which traditional structures of power still govern the medium.

Newer work on the subject—research written after or about what Tiziano Bonini (2015) has called the "second age" of podcasting—has begun to approach podcasting less as a new medium and to focus more on the details of the form, be it podcasting's continuity with traditional, web, and satellite radio (Bottomley 2015; Berry 2015; Bonini 2015; Cwynar 2015; Fauteux 2015; Markman 2015); the "long tail" economics of the format (Berry 2016); aesthetics of podcasting (McHugh 2016; Verma 2017); practices and techniques of recording and sound production (Heeremans 2018); or the specific communities, genres, and formats that podcasting networks and connects (Florini 2015; Copeland 2018). There have been two special issues on the subject in leading journals—*The Journal of Radio and Audio Media* and *Radio Journal*—and a recent one on the theme of "Podcasting, the Popular, and the Public Sphere" in *Popular Communication: The International Journal of Media and Culture* (Sienkiewicz and Jaramillo 2019). The recent collection *Podcasting: New Aural Cultures and Digital Media* (Llinares et al. 2018) combines critical and practitioner perspectives as it explores the meanings of the term "podcasting" (e.g., as medium, as cultural industry, as praxis, etc.), the evolution of new industry structures (e.g., podcast networks, new genres and shows, etc.), as well as analyses of specific podcasts. Martin Spinelli and Lance Dann's *Podcasting: The Audio Media Revolution* (2019) also makes a valuable contribution by employing a range of research methods—including practitioner interviews, social media data collection, and close listening—to test out assumptions about podcasting and assess the medium's significance.

Notably, both *Podcasting: New Aural Cultures and Digital Media* and *Podcasting: The Audio Media Revolution* include companion podcasts that feature the authors reflecting on their work. Rather than merely serving as promotions for the books, the companion podcasts are examples of using podcasts and sound as *a method* for exploring media and culture. In the first episode of *New Aural Cultures*, Dario Llinares emphasizes the "possibilities of using the medium to work through particular research areas and then distribute them outside those traditional trajectories" and calls attention to the benefits of "sitting between being a theorist and a practitioner" (*New Aural Cultures* 2019). Similarly, Mack Hagood's call in our collection to foreground sound-based scholarship—along with the companion audio interviews we have provided in the online edition of our book (https://doi.org/10.3998/mpub.11435021) with three researchers who generally share their work in print (Jonathan Sterne, Tanya Clement, and Reginold Royston)—are attempts to use sound as another format to further the study of media and culture.

Even with all the emerging work in the area, there remains much research to be done on the communities and networks of practicing podcasters and their production cultures in a way that would build on and extend Kris Markman's early work (Markman 2011; Markman and Sawyer 2014). There are helpful studies of individual podcasters, podcasts, and their audiences (Tran 2019; Salvati 2015), and some scholar/podcasters have helpfully detailed their process and purposes for turning to podcasts to put their research into practice (Tiffe and Hoffman 2017). Sarah Murray (2019) provides an analysis of the independent podcasters who band together as podcasting collectives to explore how independent and precarious audio producers negotiate the tensions of working as individuals within a larger group. She finds that while podcasting holds the potential to be a space for new voices and new listening publics, these potentials are often limited or hampered by entrepreneurial demands and expectations. This is precisely why studying podcasts, including the history of the format and the industries emerging around it, is important: we need to trace both the potentials for public expression and public reception of a diverse set of perspectives that this emerging format represents and how those potentials are under threat or were maybe always flawed from the beginning.

Beyond research on podcasts and the podcasting industry, our work is also indebted to contributions from the field of sound studies, a multidisciplinary mode of inquiry that asks questions about sound that are both perceptual (i.e., How does how we hear affect how we are?) and cultural (i.e., How is what we hear conditioned by who, where, and when we are?). A slew of publications from interdisciplinary anthologies, including *The Sound Studies Reader* (Sterne 2012), *Sound Studies* (Bull 2013), *The Auditory Culture Reader* (Bull and Back 2015), and *The Oxford Handbook of Sound Studies* (Pinch and Bijsterveld 2012), and journal special issues, including *differences* (2011), *American Quarterly* (2011), and *Radical History Review* (2015), have helped scholars reconceptualize the role that sounds play in everyday life (and in media studies research). Collections dedicated to methods for studying with and through sound, such as *The Bloomsbury Handbook of Sonic Methodologies* (Bull and Cobussen, 2020), offer practical tools for sound-related research that we hope will complement the intentional reflections on methods by many of the authors in this current collection and will further conversations around sound as method.

While the tradition of using sound as a meta-method is clearly growing, there have been fewer attempts to use the digital properties of podcasts as a method for research exploration in a manner that employs true digital methods, akin to those presented in, say, Richard Rogers's *Digital Methods* (2013). Susan Noh's chapter in this collection makes progress in this direction, using methods of metadata analysis to study how podcasters select keywords to describe their shows. The audio files of podcasts have similarly been underutilized for methods of computational sound analysis. This is part of a broader lack of attention that the digital humanities have given to tools for studying sound and audio media. There has certainly been a flourishing of digital humanities projects in the last decade, many of which apply large datasets to reveal new insights about questions long facing the humanities (see, for example, projects described in Berry and Fagerjord 2017; Burdick et al., 2012; Schreibman et al., 2016). Many of these projects, however, focus on literature and visual media. There have been a few attempts to analyze sound (Clement 2016a; Clement 2016b; Foka and Arvidsson 2016; MacArthur 2016; MacArthur et al. 2018; Mustazza, 2018), though as Tanya Clement and Stephen McLaughlin (2016) note, "Humanists have few opportunities to use advanced technologies for analyzing large, messy sound archives," meaning many researchers have shied away from using sound objects like podcasts in their research. Our coauthored chapter with Jacob Mertens in this collection acts as encouragement in this regard, then, promoting the benefits of combining digital tools with more traditional listening skills to study the vocal performances of podcasters.

The final area of scholarship that *Saving New Sounds* engages with is studies of archiving and digital preservation. We should acknowledge up front that neither of us pursued our graduate training in the field of library and information sciences. In working on PodcastRE and the Media History Digital Library, we have been consistently inspired, assisted, and humbled by moving through the literature of these fields and, even better, sitting down for coffee with trained archivists and librarians. There is much, to put it mildly, that most humanities scholars don't understand about the archival profession. Just as dining out frequently doesn't necessarily lead to any insights about the inner workings of a restaurant kitchen, historians can use archives extensively for research and still fail to understand the theories of appraisal, accession, arrangement, and description that led them to the record boxes that they are "discovering." In surveying the development of history and archives as professions, Francis X. Blouin Jr. and William G. Rosenberg (2011) emphasize the ways their conceptual frameworks have increasingly diverged over the past few decades. Together, Blouin (an archivist) and Rosenberg (a historian) reflect upon this trajectory:

A sense of partnership joined by shared assumptions about historical authority and the evidentiary power of archival documentation has given way to radically different ways of understanding the past.

The various linguistic, cultural, and other "turns" that have recently shaped new historical understanding have been complemented in the archival community by a sharp turn from historiographically based authorities themselves, in a variety of forms, to those more strictly archival or based on the practices of records management. Historians now ask important questions not easily answered or understood through an examination of archival documents alone. Archivists now confront an almost unimaginable mass of documents both in paper form, typically measured in linear feet, and in new and unstable digital forms whose very nature seems to dissolve any limits on what might be preserved. (2011, 6)

Despite the large-scale divergences noted above, however, we have found that both recorded sound and digital media are areas of study in which there is a great deal of fruitful collaboration and cross-pollination between the research and archivist communities. It may help that both the researchers and archivists who work with sound generally feel like outsiders within their home disciplines, which remain visually and textually oriented. An article titled "Listening to the Archive: Sound Data in the Humanities and Sciences," in a recent issue of *Technology and Culture*, explores these collaborations in partnership with a European sound archive in Berlin (Birdsall and Tkaczyk 2019), while within the United States there has been a major multi-institution effort to bring sound archivists, sound scholars, and state and industry representatives together through the Library of Congress and the Radio Preservation Task Force (RPTF). A massive preservation effort led by Josh Shepperd, the RPTF is trying to locate and digitize radio broadcasts from before 1975, noting that a significant portion of broadcasting history—possibly 75 percent of all recordings between the 1920s and 1980s (Shepperd 2016)—has already been lost through neglect, decay, or destruction of historical materials (in the United States, primarily, but in other countries as well). While podcasts are generally outside the mandate of the RPTF's mission, our efforts in preserving and studying emerging digital audio objects hold potential to contribute to the RPTF's wider discussions surrounding audio preservation and sonic research more generally.

The PodcastRE project started as a modest, and mostly individual, effort to collect enough podcasts to provide a decent sample for a research project. It grew somewhat accidentally into a much larger sample than was originally intended, and in the process it became a project that was more closely aligned with digital archives and audio preservation. Thankfully, there is significant commonality between work on preserving digital audio and the conceptual frameworks for archiving and historicizing the internet. Media studies scholars researching the internet have long employed techniques such as walkthroughs, interface analysis, bots, screenshots, and screencasts to capture and hold on to website designs, aesthetics, and user experiences that are subject to change at any moment (Brügger 2009; Brügger 2018; Rogers 2013; Stanfill 2015; Light et al. 2016; Ankerson 2018; Milligan 2019). Digital archivists now champion many of these same practices, increasingly eschewing expensive, labor-intensive attempts to build software emulators in favor of the more low-tech screenshots and videos that media studies scholars have been using for two decades. Digital archivists are also anticipating the potential needs of media researchers as they seek to save the "significant properties" (Stepanyan et. al. 2012) or "contextual metadata" of digital objects (a topic that Eric Hoyt explores in more depth in his chapter).

Drawing on scholarship from the field of internet history and on the work of digital archivists, we tried to design PodcastRE in a way that fused ideas from *what* we saved (audio files, metadata, and other "significant properties") and from *how* we saved and presented it (for example, visual analytics and advanced search features). Ultimately, the question of how to preserve any given digital media format will always depend on how we conceptualize the object in question. Take, for example, Trevor Owens's (2018) thought experiment on what it would mean to save the online game *World of Warcraft*. A purely technical approach—saving the installable software for personal computers and attempting to replicate Blizzard Entertainment's proprietary server environment—would prove costly and ultimately not tell us much about the game's cultural meanings and social dimensions in the early twenty-first century. To capture the social and cultural meanings of the game, archivists would be better off saving user-generated videos of gameplay and ancillary fan websites (81–82). Owens uses the example to highlight the importance of heritage organizations clarifying their preservation intent. Because preservation intent often anticipates questions that researchers will want to ask, this represents an important juncture in the process for media scholars to contribute their ideas (and possibly the data they have gathered in their work, too).

Despite the above-noted convergences between the practices of media scholars and digital archivists, media scholars should not assume that the framing of good research questions and recording of screencasts represent the totality of digital preservation. They do not—not even if those screencasts are backed up to the cloud on a daily basis. We have done our best to build redundancies and put protocols in place for restoring the PodcastRE database when it crashes. We have worked with archivists, librarians, and scholars to design features and tools that will meet the needs of a variety of communities. But we also know how quickly both technologies and needs change, let alone the fact that podcasting itself, as a format, is still emergent and dynamic. Digital preservation requires many additional steps, including managing copies, describing objects, and formulating access policies. And these stages are not a checklist that can ever be fully completed. "The work is never finished," explains Owens. "Nothing has been preserved, there are only things being preserved" (7). The statement demands a paradigm shift for media scholars like ourselves. We were trained to publish books and articles, list them on our CVs, and then move on to more books and articles that we can list on our CVs. We were actively discouraged from starting projects that, by nature, are never finished. And yet, as we've discovered from our foray into media history and preservation, this is exactly what we did when we started PodcastRE.

Book Structure and Chapter Overviews

We have organized this book around three thematic groupings that are meant to frame the collection's main arguments: that saving and studying podcasting as a vital emerging media format go hand in hand, and in order to effectively accomplish these tasks, we need theoretical and methodological tools to explore its rise, its contemporary relevance, and its possible futures. In laying out our three sections, we aimed to provide a balance between chapters that present broader arguments about podcasting's rise and possible futures and chapters that use specific case studies to detail particular ways to use the PodcastRE database in order to advance the study of recorded audio. All chapters, at their core, share a concern with the importance of studying audio cultures and, thus, with issues of audio preservation and the methodological challenges of saving, studying, and teaching with audio. They aim to intervene in theoretical debates about studies of sound and in methodological debates about how best to save, study, and preserve digital sonic artifacts. They each, in their own way, emphasize how the technical (e.g., RSS feeds, MP3s, metadata, etc.) and structural (e.g., podcatching apps, portable media devices, hosting platforms, etc.) elements of sound—in this case podcasts—are essential to understanding how researchers conduct historiographies of emerging formats.

The first section, **Revisiting Podcasting's Histories,** critically questions some of the more popular origin stories around podcasting and its contributory antecedents. Rather than take podcasting's accepted history for granted, the authors in this section explore alternate beginnings, technologies, and ideologies that shaped podcasting. In the first chapter, Andrew Bottomley reflects on his experience researching the history of audioblogs and other forms of internet radio that preceded podcasts, emphasizing the challenges that these forms pose both to digital preservation and conventional narratives about podcasting. Next, Jennifer Hyland Wang interrogates the roles that gender, professionalization, and production cultures play in podcasting, highlighting the ways early amateur women podcasters have been pushed out of the medium's history. In the third chapter, "Reality in Sound: Problem Solved?," Michele Hilmes places nonfiction podcasts within a much longer tradition of sound documentary practices and radio storytelling. All of the three first chapters contribute to ongoing definitional debates about what constitutes podcasting as a medium and the stakes for one definition over another. Similarly, and to avoid repeating the cycles of neglect and erasure that have omitted Black media producers from the histories of many media forms, Sarah Florini and Briana Barner use their chapter to call attention to the significant contributions of the Loud Speakers Network and the late podcaster Combat Jack to early podcasting culture. In the final chapter of this section, JJ Bersch examines the important role that advertising has played within the podcasting industry and the challenges it creates for podcasting preservation.

The second thematic section, **Analyzing Podcasting's Now,** brings together the work of scholars who are carrying out research on specific podcasts, genres, or collections of shows, in order to explore current issues that the format and its technologies raise. Drawing on the work of scholars who are using both quantitative and qualitative methods to explore podcasting, this section shows how sonic media objects, audio archives, and sound collections present particular challenges for media and cultural studies researchers while also presenting possible solutions for addressing those challenges. In "Podcasting the Donald Sterling Scandal," Jacob Mertens models how the searchable PodcastRE database can be used to dig deep into a particular controversy from our recent past, retrieving and comparing perspectives on sports and racism from both independent and corporate podcasters. Whereas Mertens uses the

PodcastRE database to explore a particular moment, Amanda Keeler's chapter applies the PodcastRE collection to explore a popular genre— true crime—and the way that the ethics of journalism come into conflict with the norms of documentary filmmaking in the making of true crime podcasts. Susan Noh considers issues of sound, race, ethnicity, and identity but does so with big-data methodologies using PodcastRE's metadata analytics software, which she helped to develop, reminding us that metadata—which may sound dry, objective, and purely descriptive—are loaded with cultural meaning and can be harnessed in novel ways. Our coauthored chapter with Jacob Mertens further explores digital methods by utilizing the sonic analysis tools Gentle and Drift to study pitch inflections and vocal performances among podcasters, focusing especially on the norms developed in public radio and measured expressions of emotion.

The final section, **Imagining Podcasting's Futures,** concludes by looking forward to future developments in podcasting with respect to technological and industrial changes, shifting production cultures, growing cultural relevance, and other factors, again with an eye toward preservation. It considers the ongoing changes taking place with the back-end infrastructure of podcasts (from RSS feeds to streaming); the challenges they present for researchers trying to preserve audio, ratings, and discovery mechanisms; and the influence these have on what counts as "worthy" of preservation, as well as the increased use of podcasts as tools for teaching. This section also examines other current efforts to increase awareness of the importance of preserving podcasts (and their contexts) and the massive amount of work that remains to be done. In his chapter, "The Scholarly Podcast," Mack Hagood assesses the growing trend of researchers using podcasting as a tool to communicate and share their work. Next, Samuel Hansen discusses the outsized influence that RSS has had on podcasting as a medium and the PodcastRE database and looks ahead to technologies and metadata standards that may eventually supersede RSS and change the podcasting format as we know it. Walking this same idea in a different direction, Jeremy Wade Morris takes stock of the "Spotification of Podcasting" that is already underway and evaluates what the move toward a subscription-based, streaming model of podcasting will mean for both contemporary sound culture and future preservation. The last two chapters further take up the questions of preservation central to this book and PodcastRE's mission. Dana Gerber-Margie, Mary Kidd, Sarah Nguyễn, and Molly Schwartz share their work on "Preserve This Podcast," an initiative to better educate independent podcasters in methods for archiving their digital files. Meanwhile, Eric Hoyt appraises and surveys the range of podcasting artifacts, beyond the digital audio and metadata files, that cultural heritage institutions should consider collecting; how-to manuals, crowdfunding websites, and listener oral histories are all sources that would allow future media historians to answer questions about podcasting's cultural significance that the sounds alone cannot.

There are, of course, overlaps across the three sections of this book. Some of the chapters that look backward at podcasting's origins inevitably need to consider its possible future directions (e.g., Bersch's chapter on podcast advertising), just as chapters that analyze current podcasts also need to reference historical factors that led to the contemporary moment (e.g., Noh's chapter on podcasting, metadata, and analytics). The individual chapters also have varying levels of engagement with the PodcastRE database, which is at the heart of this project. By showcasing several chapters in this collection that make use of the PodcastRE database and its tools, we aim to reflect on the processes and challenges of collecting and preserving audio using a real-life (and ongoing) preservation project. By also including chapters from scholars who are not directly active in the project—those written and audio dispatches *to* PodcastRE—we hope to highlight some of the theoretical frameworks and media histories that are informing our work.

Given that this book is openly accessible on the web, we also wanted to include sounds from the podcasts under discussion and voices from contributors whose perspectives might amplify key themes in our collection. We have accomplished the former by providing links to sonic reference materials in PodcastRE.org where possible. We've accomplished the latter through four brief audio dispatches that can be found at https:// doi.org/10.3998/mpub.11435021. In the first, which adds industrial context to the "Revisiting Podcasting's Histories" section, Adam Sachs, former CEO of Midroll Media, reflects on the growth and formalization of podcasting as a new media industry. In the second, Reginold Royston reflects on his research into studying podcasting cultures in Africa and the African diaspora and extends our collection's discussions of race, identity, and digital tools beyond a US perspective. The third dispatch features a leading sonic digital humanities expert, Tanya Clement, discussing the links between digital tools for sound analysis and the ways they shape how we research and understand sound. The final audio dispatch comes from sound historian Jonathan Sterne, who reflects on where podcasting may fit within the longer trajectory of recorded sound history and sound studies as a discipline.

Podcasting is a conversational medium, and the dialogue between saving and studying podcasts runs throughout this book. Just as the work of preserving podcasts is inseparable from how we conceptualize the medium's histories, the ways researchers imagine audio archives are intimately tied to the tools and models available to search and analyze them. It is our hope that bringing these frameworks and practices together can serve as a starting point for better understanding our recent past and for anticipating and acting upon the sonic future that awaits.

Note

1. At the time of writing, iTunes was the name of Apple's podcasting and music software. It has since become Apple Podcasts and Apple Music, though this collection continues to refer to the original iTunes.

Works Cited

Adams, Dan. 2015. "After 'Serial,' Sponsors Pour Money into Podcasts." *Boston Globe*. February 13.

Ankerson, Megan Sapnar. 2018. *Dot-Com Design: The Rise of a Usable, Social, Commercial Web*. New York: NYU Press.

Berry, David, and Anders Fagerjord, eds. 2017. *Digital Humanities: Knowledge and Critique in a Digital Age*. Cambridge, Eng.: Polity. https://search.library.wisc .edu/catalog/9912336945502121.

Berry, Richard. 2006. "Will the iPod Kill the Radio Star? Profiling Podcasting as Radio." *Convergence: The International Journal of Research into New Media Technologies* 12 (2): 143–62. https://doi.org/10.1177/1354856506066522.

Berry, Richard. 2015. "A Golden Age of Podcasting? Evaluating *Serial* in the Context of Podcast Histories." *Journal of Radio & Audio Media* 22 (2): 170–78. https://doi.org/10.1080/19376529.2015.1083363.

Berry, Richard. 2016. "Podcasting: Considering the Evolution of the Medium and Its Association with the Word 'Radio.'" *Radio Journal: International Studies in Broadcast & Audio Media* 14 (1): 7–22. https://doi.org/10.1386/rjao.14.1.7 _1.

Birdsall, Carolyn, and Viktoria Tkaczyk. 2019. "Listening to the Archive: Sound Data in the Humanities and Sciences." *Technology and Culture* 60 (2): 1–13.

Blouin, Francis X., Jr., and William G. Rosenberg. 2011. *Processing the Past: Contesting Authority in History and the Archives*. Reprint ed. Oxford: Oxford University Press.

Bonini, Tiziano. 2015. "The 'Second Age' of Podcasting: Reframing Podcasting as a New Digital Mass Medium." *Quaderns Del CAC 41* 18 (July): 21–30.

Bottomley, Andrew J. 2015. "Podcasting: A Decade in the Life of a 'New' Audio Medium: Introduction." *Journal of Radio & Audio Media* 22 (2): 164–69. https://doi.org/10.1080/19376529.2015.1082880.

Brügger, Niels. 2009. "Website History and the Website as an Object of Study." *New Media & Society* 11 (1/2): 115–32. https://doi.org/10.1177/14614448080 99574.

Brügger, Niels. 2018. *The Archived Web: Doing History in the Digital Age.* Cambridge: MIT Press.

Bull, Michael, ed. 2013. *Sound Studies.* 1st ed. Abingdon, Oxon: Routledge.

Bull, Michael, and Les Back, eds. 2015. *The Auditory Culture Reader.* 2nd ed. London: Bloomsbury Academic.

Bull, Michael, and Marcel Cobussen, eds. 2020. *The Bloomsbury Handbook of Sonic Methodologies.* New York: Bloomsbury Academic.

Burdick, Anne, Johanna Drucker, Peter Lunenfeld, Todd Presner, and Jeffrey Schnapp, eds. 2012. *Digital Humanities.* Cambridge: MIT Press. https://sear ch.library.wisc.edu/catalog/9910275767102121.

Campbell, Gardner. 2005. "There's Something in the Air: Podcasting in Education." *EDUCAUSE* 40 (6): 33–46.

Carman, Ashley. 2018. "Gaming the Apple Podcast Charts Is Cheaper and Easier Than You Think." Tech News. *The Verge.* November 29. https://www.theve rge.com/2018/11/29/18097381/apple-podcast-charts-click-farm-advertiser -revenue.

Clement, Tanya E. 2016a. "Towards a Rationale of Audio-Text." *Digital Humanities Quarterly* 10 (2).

Clement, Tanya E. 2016b. "When Texts of Study Are Audio Files: Digital Tools for Sound Studies in DH." In *A New Companion to Digital Humanities,* edited by Susan Schreibman, Ray Siemens, and John Unsworth, 348–57. Chichester: John Wiley & Sons. https://search.library.wisc.edu/catalog/991222087630 2121.

Clement, Tanya E., and Stephen R. McLaughlin. 2016. "Measured Applause: Toward a Cultural Analysis of Audio Collections. *CA: Journal of Cultural Analytics* May 23. DOI: 10.22148/16.002.

Copeland, Stacey. 2018. "A Feminist Materialisation of Amplified Voice: Queering Identity and Affect in the Heart." In Llinares, Fox, and Berry, *Podcasting,* 209–26.

Cridland, James. 2018. "Placings on Apple's Podcast Chart Can Be Bought." Tech News. *Podnews.* May 13. https://podnews.net/article/rotten-apple-podcast -charts.

Crofts, Sheri, Jon Dilley, Mark Fox, Andrew Restsema, and Bob Williams. 2005. "Podcasting: A New Technology in Search of a Business Model." *First Monday* 10 (9): 1–20.

Cwynar, Christopher. 2015. "More Than a 'VCR for Radio': The CBC, the Radio 3 Podcast, and the Uses of an Emerging Medium." *Journal of Radio & Audio Media* 22 (2): 190–99. https://doi.org/10.1080/19376529.2015.1083371.

Dropbox. 2017. "The Public Folder." Corporate Blog. Dropbox.com. September 1. https://help.dropbox.com/files-folders/share/public-folder.

Edison Research, "The Podcast Consumer 2019," April 5, 2019, https://www.edi sonresearch.com/the-podcast-consumer-2019/.

Fauteux, Brian. 2015. "Blogging Satellite Radio: Podcasting Aesthetics and Sirius XMU's Blog Radio." *Journal of Radio & Audio Media* 22 (2): 200–208. https:// doi.org/10.1080/19376529.2015.1083372.

Florini, Sarah. 2015. "The Podcast 'Chitlin' Circuit': Black Podcasters, Alternative Media, and Audio Enclaves." *Journal of Radio & Audio Media* 22 (2): 209–19. https://doi.org/10.1080/19376529.2015.1083373.

Foka, Anna, and Viktor Arvidsson. 2016. "Experiential Analogies: A Sonic Digital Ekphrasis as a Digital Humanities Project." *Digital Humanities Quarterly* 10 (2): 16.

Gilliand, Anne. 2017. "Archival and Recordkeeping Traditions in the Multiverse and Their Importance for Researching Situations and Situating Research." In *Research in the Archival Multiverse,* edited by Anne J. Gilliland, Sue McKemmish and Andrew J. Lau, 31–73. Melbourne: Monash University Press.

Gitelman, Lisa. 2006. *Always Already New: Media, History, and the Data of Culture.* Cambridge: MIT Press.

Greene, Mark, and Dennis Meissner. 2005. "More Product, Less Process: Revamping Traditional Archival Processing." *American Archivist* 68 (2): 208–63. https://doi.org/10.17723/aarc.68.2.c741823776k65863.

Harris, Howard, and Sungmin Park. 2008. "Educational Usages of Podcasting." *British Journal of Educational Technology* 39 (3): 548–51.

Heeremans, Lieven. 2018. "Podcast Networks: Syndicating Production Culture." In Llinares, Fox, and Berry, *Podcasting,* 57–80.

Leswing, Kif. 2017. "Apple Buys Pop Up Archive, a Sign It's Getting Serious about Podcasting." *Business Insider.* December 5. http://www.businessinsider.com/apple-buys-pop-up-archive-signals-getting-serious-about-podcasting-2017-12.

Light, Ben, Jean Burgess, and Stefanie Duguay. 2016. "The Walkthrough Method: An Approach to the Study of Apps." *New Media & Society.* https://doi.org/10.1177/1461444816675438.

Llinares, Dario, Neil Fox, and Richard Berry. 2018. *Podcasting: New Aural Cultures and Digital Media.* London: Palgrave Macmillan.

MacArthur, Marit. 2016. "Introducing Simple Open-Source Tools for Performative Speech Analysis: Gentle and Drift." *Jacket2.* June 6. http://jacket2.org/commentary/introducing-simple-open-source-tools-performative-speech-analysis-gentle-and-drift.

MacArthur, Marit J., Georgia Zellou, and Lee M. Miller. 2018. "Beyond Poet Voice: Sampling the (Non-) Performance Styles of 100 American Poets." *Journal of Cultural Analytics.* https://doi.org/10.22148/16.022.

Madden, Mary, and Sydney Jones. 2008. "Podcast Downloading 2008." PEW Research Center for Internet and Technology. August 28. http://www.pewinternet.org/2008/08/28/podcast-downloading-2008/.

Markman, Kris M. 2011. "Doing Radio, Making Friends, and Having Fun: Exploring the Motivations of Independent Audio Podcasters." *New Media & Society* 14 (4): 547–65. https://doi.org/10.1177/1461444811420848.

Markman, Kris M. 2015. "Considerations—Reflections and Future Research. Everything Old Is New Again: Podcasting as Radio's Revival." *Journal of Radio & Audio Media* 22 (2): 240–43. https://doi.org/10.1080/19376529.2015.1083376.

Markman, Kris M., and Caroline E. Sawyer. 2014. "Why Pod? Further Explorations of the Motivations for Independent Podcasting." *Journal of Radio & Audio Media* 21 (1): 20–35. https://doi.org/10.1080/19376529.2014.891211.

McClung, Steven, and Kristine Johnson. 2010. "Examining the Motives of Podcast Users." *Journal of Radio & Audio Media* 17 (1): 82–95. https://doi.org/10.1080/19376521003719391.

McHugh, Siobhán. 2016. "How Podcasting Is Changing the Audio Storytelling Genre." *Radio Journal: International Studies in Broadcast & Audio Media* 14 (1): 65–82.

Menduni, Enrico. 2007. "Four Steps in Innovative Radio Broadcasting: From QuickTime to Podcasting." *Radio Journal: International Studies in Broadcast & Audio Media* 5 (1): 9–18.

Millette, Mélanie. 2010. "Le Podcasting Indépendant Montréalais, un Cas Significatif au Sein d'une Culture Participative en Émergence." In *Le Web Relationnel: Mutation de la Communication?*, edited by Serge Proulx, Florence Millerand, and Julien Rueff, 125–43. Québec: Presses de l'Université du Québec.

Milligan, Ian. 2019. *History in the Age of Abundance?: How the Web Is Transforming Historical Research.* Montreal: McGill-Queen's University Press.

Morris, Jeremy Wade. 2017. "Saving New Sounds: Podcasts and Preservation." *Flow: A Critical Forum on Media and Culture* (blog). October 30. https://www.flowjournal.org/2017/10/saving-new-sounds-podcasts/.

Morris, Jeremy Wade, Samuel Hansen, and Eric Hoyt. 2019. "The PodcastRE Project: Curating and Preserving Podcasts (and Their Data)." *Journal of Radio & Audio Media* 26 (1): 8–20. https://doi.org/10.1080/19376529.2019.1559550.

Moscote Freire, Ariana. 2007. "Remediating Radio: Audio Streaming, Music Recommendation, and the Discourse of Radioness." *Radio Journal—International Studies in Broadcast and Audio Media* 5 (2/3): 97–112. https://doi.org/10.1386/rajo.5.2&3.97/1.

Murray, Sarah. 2019. "Coming-of-Age in a Coming-of-Age: The Collective Individualism of Podcasting's Intimate Soundwork." *Popular Communication: The International Journal of Media and Culture* 17(4): 301-316, DOI: 10.1080/15405702.2019.1622117

Mustazza, Chris. 2018. "Machine-Aided Close Listening: Prosthetic Synaesthesia and the 3D Phonotext." *Digital Humanities Quarterly.*

Nazer, Daniel. 2018. "EFF Wins Final Victory over Podcasting Patent." Tech Advocacy. *Electronic Frontier Foundation.* May 14, 2018. https://www.eff.org/deeplinks/2018/05/eff-wins-final-victory-over-podcasting-patent.

New Aural Cultures Podcast. 2019. "Introducing *New Aural Cultures.*" Anchor.fm. March 15. https://anchor.fm/newauralcultures.

Owens, Trevor. 2018. *The Theory and Craft of Digital Preservation.* 1st ed. Baltimore: Johns Hopkins University Press.

Pinch, Trevor, and Karin Bijsterveld, eds. 2012. *The Oxford Handbook of Sound Studies.* New York: Oxford University Press. https://search.library.wisc.edu/catalog/9910542611502121.

Podnews. 2019. "The Total Number of Available Podcasts Is Now 700,000." Tech News. *Podnews.* March 29. https://podnews.net/update/700000.

Rogers, Richard. 2013. *Digital Methods.* Cambridge: MIT Press.

Schreibman, Susan, Ray Siemens, and John Unsworth, eds. 2016. *A New Companion to Digital Humanities.* Second edition. Malden, MA: Wiley-Blackwell.

Shepperd, Josh. 2016. "Radio Preservation Task Force Conference: Sound History and the Logistics of Social Recognition." *Sounding Out!* (blog). February 26. https://soundstudiesblog.com/2016/02/26/radio-preservation-task-force-conference-sound-history-and-the-logistics-of-social-recognition/.

Spinelli, Martin, and Lance Dann. 2019. *Podcasting: The Audio Media Revolution.* New York: Bloomsbury Academic.

Stanfill, Mel. 2015. "The Interface as Discourse: The Production of Norms through Web Design." *New Media & Society* 17 (7): 1059–74. https://doi.org/10.1177/1461444814520873.

Stepanyan, Karen, George Gkotsis, Hendrik Kalb, Yunhyong Kim, Alexandra Cristea, Mike Joy, Matthias Trier, and Seamus Ross. 2012. "Blogs as Objects of Preservation: Advancing the Discussion on Significant Properties." In Proceedings of the 9th International Conference on Preservation of Digital Objects:218–24. Toronto: Digital Curation Institute. https://www.researchgate.net/publication/233935527_Blogs_as_Objects_of_Preservation_Advancing_the_Discussion_on_Significant_Properties.

Sterne, Jonathan. 2012. *The Sound Studies Reader.* New York: Routledge.

Sterne, Jonathan, Jeremy Wade Morris, Michael Brendan Baker, and Ariana Moscote Freire. 2008. "The Politics of Podcasting." *Fibreculture*, no. 13. http://thirteen.fibreculturejournal.org/fcj-087-the-politics-of-podcasting/.

Verma, Neil. 2017. "The Arts of Amnesia: The Case for Audio Drama, Part One." *RadioDoc Review* 3 (1). https://doi.org/10.14453/rdr.v3i1.5.

Revisiting Podcasting's Histories

ONE | Podcast Archaeology

Researching Proto-Podcasts and Early Born-Digital Audio Formats

ANDREW J. BOTTOMLEY

Chuck Palahniuk was in a panic. It was September 2003 and the *Fight Club* author, who was a closeted gay man, feared an *Entertainment Weekly* reporter was about to out him. Rather than let the press divulge his personal secret, he issued a frenetic rant to the public in which he revealed he was in a decade-long relationship with a man and, in the process, lashed out at the *EW* reporter. It was a desperate effort to control his own narrative by speaking directly to his loyal fans, with whom Palahniuk was known for maintaining a warm relationship. But it is notable that Palahniuk's angry rant was not delivered in the form of a press release or even a blog post—this was 2003, after all, the height of the blogging phenomenon. Rather, it arrived via an audio recording uploaded to the author's fan-run website, *The Cult* (https://chuckpalahniuk.net/). There, since July 2003, Palahniuk had been using the nascent phone-to-blog web service Audblog to record short-form audio messages known as "aubioblogs"—the progenitors of what we now call podcasts.

Palahniuk's audioblog posts were each a minute or two long, consisting primarily of messages from the road while on a book publicity tour for his novel *Diary*. Always beginning genially with "Hey, this is Chuck," Palahniuk adopted a chatty tone for his fans. He would announce upcoming public appearances, give rundowns of previous events, thank fans for showing up at readings, and encourage them to introduce themselves in person or to mail letters. The audioblog in which Palahniuk outed himself—and trash-talked reporter Karen Velby while threatening a member of her family—was quickly deleted by *The Cult*'s webmaster at the request of Palahniuk and his publisher (Dundas 2003). And here lies the first in a number of challenges that arise when researching "born-digital" audio formats: content can be easily deleted by its host, erased from existence with the push of a button (Striphas 2010). Web publishing lacks the permanence of commercial print or sound recording, where even a recalled text still circulates via initial retail sales or advance promotional copies that reside in people's personal collections and exchange hands in secondary markets like eBay and secondhand stores. Palahniuk's audioblogs were available only through his website; they were not redistributed through a podcatcher like Apple iTunes, and there is no sign of them recirculating on file-sharing sites. The deletion of the September 22, 2003, audioblog source file from *The Cult* website effectively removed it from the internet entirely.

Silences like this one are an all-too-common occurrence for researchers investigating podcasting's past. In the case of a traditional broadcast radio network, a media historian trying to uncover these lost sounds might reliably turn to libraries and archives where sound recording collections are gathered. Or in the absence of sound artifacts, they may at least locate paper records such as scripts and program logs from the broadcaster, regulators, or production personnel. However, this is rarely the case for born-digital soundwork, since it was mostly produced independently by individuals or small startups (Hilmes 2013, 60; 2014, 20). Internet audio is not regulated like broadcast, and thus government agencies like the Federal Communications Commission (FCC) or trade associations like the National Association of Broadcasters (NAB) do not keep public records on their activities. Chuck Palahniuk is a popular public figure, and thus there is a chance his personal records might end up in an archive someday—but he is relatively young and still engaged in an active writing career, and his papers remain private. Since these audioblogs were independently made, there is no radio station or podcast network that distributed them and that might, therefore, retain recordings or official documents related to their creation. There is only the fan-run *The Cult* website—and as is the case with most websites, it has not actively preserved its own past. Created in September 1999, *The Cult* website today remains online at the same domain. An example of the dynamic and unstable nature of the web, however, the current website contains none of the content from its early 2000s existence, including no trace that the "Chuck's AudioBlogs" feature ever existed. The site retooled in the mid-2000s; the "News Archive" currently contains nothing prior to April 2007. More often than not, web media historians in search of sound and other multimedia artifacts must rely on the web itself as a historical source. And despite the sense of permanence that the web has inculcated in the popular mind—the notion that every podcast or song or video is at the user's fingertips and will always be there waiting—it is in actuality a largely ahistorical medium that is constantly updating itself and, in the process, shedding content on a massive scale.

There are methods for recovering lost audio from the World Wide Web, even if it has been deleted or the original web page is offline. The most reliable resource is the Internet Archive's Wayback Machine digital archive. Yet, Wayback Machine "snapshots," or "crawls," are sporadic. For example, *The Cult* website was saved by the Wayback Machine only 1,209 times in the two-decade span between November 1999 and June 2019.[1] On average, then, the site has been crawled about 60 times per year. Those crawls are not evenly distributed, however; some years *The Cult* was crawled hundreds of times, other years only a dozen times. In 2003 the Wayback Machine took a total of nineteen snapshots of *The Cult* website's main page. Coincidentally, the software actually crawled *The Cult* on September 22, 2003—the date Palahniuk posted the deleted audioblog—however, it only captured the home page, which at that time was a static front page that contained just an image and an "enter here" link. None of the subpages, including the audioblog sound recording, were collected. The next crawl capturing any content beyond the front page occurred on October 1, 2003, at which point all traces of the controversial audioblog post had been removed from the site. Luckily, there are a number of blog entries from the site's webmaster, Dennis Widmyer, that provide context around Chuck's audioblog and its removal. After navigating through incomplete captures and broken links, it is possible to recover twenty-two of Palahniuk's audioblog posts from the year 2003 via the Wayback Machine.[2] However, there is audio accessible for only nineteen of them; the other three are accessible as text transcripts only. (Contributors to *The Cult* started transcribing Palahniuk's audio messages in September 2003 for fellow fans who lacked internet connections capable of streaming or downloading the MP3 audio files.) That is, the Wayback Machine captured the text pointing to the multimedia content but not the actual MP3 linked object. That nineteen of the twenty-two Palahniuk sound recordings are accessible is a remarkably high number for the era; there are many other early audioblogs where no linked audio exists, or at best maybe one in five audio files are recoverable. And the fact that there are transcripts for the missing audio is exceptionally rare. Still, this case points to the ephemerality of web audio and the hit-or-miss nature of web archives, plus the labyrinthine efforts that media historians must go through to excavate these emergent forms of born-digital soundwork.

Revisiting podcasting's early history is a primary focus of my research, which I situate more broadly in the areas of sound studies and digital media history. For nearly a decade, I have been investigating the cultural history of internet radio beginning in the 1990s, including the emergence of streaming audio, podcasting, and precursors to podcasting like audioblogging. This research began with my PhD dissertation, completed in 2016, and it has extended through to my recent book, *Sound Streams: A Cultural History of Radio-Internet Convergence* (Bottomley 2016; 2020). This chapter draws attention to some of the methodological issues I have encountered during my research with very early forms of born-digital audio on the internet. These materials predate the 2005 rise of podcasting as a popular medium, and, importantly, they are highly ephemeral: most of the content and the physical infrastructure has disappeared, as have the communities of producers and users involved with their creation. After summarizing some of the firsthand lessons learned from my research experiences, I discuss two types of audio media—audioblogs and internet-only radio programs distributed via RealAudio—including the challenges of using the Internet Archive's Wayback Machine to research them. I also point to some of the other extant source material to which digital sound scholars may turn in order to fill the silences left by missing audio artifacts, from press materials and blog posts to oral histories and even public records like SEC company filings. Finally, I comment on some of the ways my work connects with the PodcastRE project, observing how PodcastRE is capturing many of the sonic traces absent in other web archives while offering suggestions for how PodcastRE can possibly grow to accommodate other nontraditional web audio archives.

The Wayback Machine, Web Audio, and the Web as a Historical Source

Researching internet radio and the online media industries presents distinct methodological challenges, especially when attempting to access material from the World Wide Web's first decade (the 1990s into early 2000s). Streaming audio and podcasts are converged media that merge two types of content, both of which are notoriously difficult to archive:

sound and web objects. Ephemerality has been a major problem across radio's more than a century long history: as a live broadcast medium, much radio programming was never recorded—a fact that still remains true of many radio broadcasts being made today (Hilmes 2013, 44–48). Even in cases where recordings exist, there has been little in the way of systematic or sustained methods, institutions, and infrastructures for the preservation of radio materials as exists in other media fields like film (Birdsall 2015).[3] The internet has similar—if not more vexing— problems of impermanence. Audiovisual materials on the web present archivists and historians with challenges in scale, content, description, discovery, and expectations of access when compared to traditional film and media archives (McKernan 2017, 35). Media historians studying the internet and the World Wide Web, such as Lisa Gitelman (2008) and Megan Sapnar Ankerson (2018), have previously outlined these methodological dilemmas of web historiography. Websites are dynamic entities by design, characterized by constant change. Both the content and the software are updated frequently—not to mention the many different experiences generated when users access the same content across different apps, devices, and platforms—resulting in there being constant instability for the media objects under study. Much of the web is also incredibly difficult to archive; while text and images of static web pages are relatively simple to capture, multimedia and linked content—such as streaming audio, animated images and video, interactive chat rooms and instant messages, social networking content, games and virtual worlds, plus their associated metadata—are much more difficult to preserve, particularly all together in their original context. As Ankerson (2011) alerts us, what is saved is almost inherently incomplete. Thus, web audio sits in an especially precarious position.

The Internet Archive (https://archive.org/), which preserves "snapshots" of older versions of web pages via its Wayback Machine (https://archive.org/web/), is a tremendous resource for web historians. To use the Wayback Machine, users type a web page's URL into a search box, which generates a list of dates when snapshots were taken. Users then choose which archived version of the web page to access. Yet, the Wayback Machine tool did not launch until 1996 (half a decade into the web's life), when Brewster Kahle set up the project as essentially a DIY archive in his attic. The publicly accessible version of the Wayback Machine was not activated for another six years, in 2001 (Crockett 2018, par. 5). The service's archival snapshots, or "crawls," can be very sporadic—especially those gathered during its initial alpha phase from 1996 to 2001. It is also significant that the service's automated software programs take snapshots of web*pages* (usually only the home page and main parent pages) rather than websites as a whole. The Wayback Machine's archival approach is premised on a "single URL" access model, an approach that is not particularly well-suited to the modern search interface–based web (Ben-David and Huurdeman 2014, 107). This approach is effective for "flat" web pages but much less so for complex websites with voluminous subpages, or "child" pages, and lots of frequently updated content, as well as dynamic website structures like sequential or matrix models. For instance, according to director Mark Graham, the Wayback Machine often prioritizes breadth over depth, the crawls performing only one "hop" of many websites (quoted in Crockett 2018, par. 27)—meaning it archives only one URL and all the links on that page but not the links within those links nor the live linked content. Thus, the subpages containing individual radio programs, podcast episodes, or audio clips often evade capture. The Wayback Machine works best at cataloging standard HTML pages. However, there are many cases where it does not catalog all content within a web page, and a web page may appear incomplete. Images that are restricted by a robots.txt file appear gray. Dynamic content such as Flash applications or content that is reliant on server-side computer code may not be collected. Most relevant for sound archaeology, the linked objects of audio files (e.g., MP3 files) are omitted more often than not.

While the Wayback Machine is the closest thing researchers have to a permanent web archive, web historians like Ian Milligan have described the web archive tool as "relatively circumscribed" due to its lack of full-text search (users need to know the exact URL they are looking for) and the absence of contextual information (2016, 81–82). Niels Brügger reminds us, too, that the process of web archiving may change the web object being archived; what is accessed via a resource like the Wayback Machine is not necessarily identical to what was once online (2012, 108). Generally speaking, the web is constantly changing and far less permanent than most users presume. Despite its many strengths, the Wayback Machine presents at best a rough sketch of web pages from even our immediate past. Kalev Leetaru has pointed out the various oddities and shortcomings of the Wayback Machine's holdings, such as how the data that is archived can be "extremely bursty," capturing a large number of snapshots of one (seemingly random) website for a short period while ignoring other (often very popular) sites for significant time spans (2015, par. 16). Crucially, it is unclear how the Wayback Machine is constructed;

the Internet Archive's crawlers are constantly changing their behavior in unknown ways, which can have particularly profound effects on research that uses the service's data longitudinally.

In my anecdotal experience, attempting to use the Wayback Machine to access web content prior to 2005 is extremely hit-or-miss. For most pre-millennium radio web pages, there might be a handful of snapshots at best, and none of those are from earlier than 1996. The first Wayback Machine snapshot of NPR.org, for example, dates from October 17, 1996, even though the website launched on April 10, 1995. There are only about a dozen other snapshots available before the year 2000.[4] And keep in mind that the Wayback Machine's crawls are based largely on a site's popularity: NPR was an established national broadcaster attracting a sizeable amount of web traffic; smaller sites and services were lucky to be crawled at all. It is not uncommon, too, for those limited snapshots to display only a partial image of the web page or nothing other than an error message. To the point, the Wayback Machine is especially lacking for the study of internet *radio* (and other convergent multimedia), since it rarely captures associated media content like audio files or JavaScript display images and graphics. A snapshot might capture the text version of a radio station website with schedules or program descriptions but none of the actual recorded sound. There are other sites offering archived web pages, such as *Screenshots* (www.screenshots.com); however, few of these hold archives dating back any earlier than 2004, and they often capture only a static image of the page without any dynamic elements. In other words, the sound studies researcher is hard-pressed to find much *sound* with these tools.

Reconstructing Podcasting's Histories without Podcasts

With a few exceptions, the materials I have needed for my research are not available in public archives. Many of the institutions involved in early internet radio were small private corporations (i.e., "startups"), modest nonprofits, or DIY amateurs. Most of these entities either went out of business or were bought up by much larger media conglomerates, typically to be scrapped for a few key assets. Even the corporate-backed initiatives mostly failed or were absorbed into other platforms and apps, the records of the original entities presumably jettisoned in the transition. This has meant that accessing the usual primary archival sources for a media history project—program recordings, scripts and transcripts, internal memos and correspondence, listener letters, promotional materials—requires approaching each individual directly. Most internet audio companies of the 1990s and early 2000s were small startups that existed for all of a year or two and now have been out of business for almost two decades. (This situation persists in podcasting today, where many independent podcasters come and go after only a few years or even just a few episodes—a phenomenon so common it has a name: "pod-fade" [Niemeyer 2018, par. 8]. These gradual disappearances have been the case with well-established podcast networks, too, such as The Heard indie podcast collective and the independent network/production company Feral Audio; even major networks like Slate's Panoply Media have shut down in recent years, while in-house production teams at BuzzFeed and Amazon's Audible have either been terminated or significantly scaled back.) In pursuing the 1990s–2000s proto-podcasters, frequently I have been unable to track down a company's principal actors, or if I can locate them, I have been unsuccessful in securing their cooperation. Therefore, I must assume that whatever archives they once had are now lost. In the case of major media corporations, such as Progressive Networks (makers of RealAudio) and Yahoo! (which purchased Broadcast.com and numerous other webcasting services and software providers), I could not even so much as get through to management to ascertain whether or not they have corporate archives to which they would be willing to grant me research access.[5] This was not entirely surprising, as such access is a problem that many contemporary media scholars face: commercial media corporations today keep their archives closely guarded for legal and financial reasons. Moreover, capitalist and presentist ideologies mean past business ventures, especially financially unsuccessful ones, are deprioritized; they are quickly forgotten—even purposefully buried, out of fear of embarrassment and bad publicity—and not worth the staff's time.

To complicate matters further, when it comes to internet radio and podcasting, there is often little in the way of trade press coverage to fall back on. Other media industries, such as film, television, and popular music, have robust trade publications covering new developments, to which historians can turn to reconstruct the past. Internet media in the 1990s and early 2000s received some coverage in broadcast trade publications (e.g., *Broadcasting & Cable*, *Variety*, *Current*), computer and software industry publications (e.g., *PC Magazine*, *Macworld*, *UNIX Review*), advertising trade publications (e.g., *Mediaweek*, *Business Week*, *Advertising Age*), and occasionally the business section of mainstream newspapers like the *New York Times* or the *Wall Street Journal*. This coverage was spotty at best, however, and often limited in scope to technological innovations and financial transactions. There were some nascent trade publications and blogs covering the internet economy (e.g., *Silicon Alley Reporter*), though these were mostly online-only affairs that are not institutionally archived and thus subject to the same preservation and access issues mentioned previously about the Wayback Machine.

In a few instances, I was granted special access to an institution's archives or an individual's personal records. These opportunities produced only limited results, however. For example, New York Public Radio and its flagship network, WNYC, gave me access to their archives, yet the network's holdings for the late 1990s and early 2000s (when it developed its first websites) consisted of little more than a few file folders of program guides, annual reports, and press clippings. Any materials like memos and correspondence still resided with individual staff members, and it was unclear if or when they would ever be turned over to the archivists. (Indeed, many staffers had since left the organization, and presumably their business records went with them or have disappeared into a file cabinet or hard drive stashed somewhere in the building.) From what I observed, WNYC's archives for the 1930s and 1940s are, ironically, more robust than they are for the 1990s. In fact, the program guides and annual reports ceased to be printed after 2000—at which point that information was published on the web only, with access to it limited to the Wayback Machine's unreliable snapshots. I ran into similar problems with multiple college radio stations I investigated; the executive management team of student volunteers at these stations typically turns over every year or two, and even if the previous staff's records remain in the office somewhere, there is typically no system in place to preserve them for longevity. Also, as student organizations, their records could or should find a home in the university's archives; however, at most I found a lone folder in a university archive's collections containing a half-dozen press releases and newspaper clippings spanning an entire decade of a college radio station's existence.

This brings to light another significant problem for historical research in the digital age: the quantity of documents being generated are vast—a multitude of daily emails, countless drafts of presentations or scripts, and so on—but the lack of a paper presence makes them all the more likely to end up locked away on a hard drive, abandoned in a closet, accidentally erased or deteriorating, or otherwise made inaccessible to researchers. I have spoken with numerous individuals who were interested in providing me with materials but responded with some variation of "I think I have some of that stuff in a box in the basement." More than a few times, the data ended up being corrupted or simply unrecoverable because it was on a format for which the owner no longer had the hardware to access it, such as floppy disk or MiniDisc. Just as often, the person looked and could not find it, or they said they would look but I never heard from them again despite multiple follow-up attempts. A few times I was able to get very useful archival records directly from individuals, though even in these cases, it was abundantly clear that what remained was a mere fraction of what once existed—and that it survived more by luck than plan.

All of this is to say that you need to get rather creative when doing internet history research, drawing upon unconventional sources and methods. A large amount of my research comes from the (limited) industry trade press and popular press articles I could scrounge up. This is a standard approach in production studies today: advertising, marketing materials, and popular newspaper and magazine reports have been widely used in discourse analyses of new media in society—for example, in Lynn Spigel's canonical *Make Room for TV* (1992). For the period covered in my study, I located press releases through databases like PR Newswire and Business Wire. For companies that went public on the stock market, Securities and Exchange Commission (SEC) prospectuses are fascinating documents that contain a wealth of hard data as well as strategic discursive framing. While these are all ideologically loaded texts that also occasionally feature blatant factual inaccuracies, by synthesizing multiple sources, the real sequence of events can usually be sussed out.

Podcast Production Studies and PodcastRE's Interventions

A publicly available resource that is unique to internet history research is, of course, the internet itself. While the web as a research tool is not without its shortcomings, there are plenty of materials relevant to my research that are still accessible online. Some of the historical actors I cover in my study, such as the software developer and entrepreneur Dave Winer, were regular bloggers who wrote about their technologies or programs and the motivations driving them to create.[6] These texts can be read like journals or memos in historical print-based research. Occasionally, old online message boards and email listservs have been archived on the web by dedicated community members, and these texts can be read like letter correspondence.

I also turned to interviews that took on qualities of oral history and ethnography. The process of tracking people to access their personal records sometimes led to my conducting original, open-ended interviews with them. Often the interviews enabled me to fill in gaps I identified in the primary texts and to fact-check sources. For instance, there was a particular dearth of primary documentation on the college radio stations that were the first to develop streaming internet audio (WXYC, WREK, and KJHK), and the few available trade and popular press articles offered incomplete or contradictory information. Speaking directly to multiple individuals involved in the development of those stations' simulcast streams enabled me to determine the who, what, when, where, and how of the situation and to ask questions about the *why* (the ideological motivations). That latter question of why is the most crucial for media historians, yet it is one that press accounts rarely address. Oral history–style interviews like these can also get at the experience of audio production and performance, context that is especially important when relatively few recordings of these creations exist to be heard.

While I do conduct textual analysis of radio programs and podcasts in my research, I was often limited in my ability to perform close readings of specific audio texts without access to audio of many of the earliest internet radio productions. Indeed, the methodological challenges of internet radio historiography are remarkably similar to broadcast radio in its first few decades (1910s–1940s), when much of the content that went out over the airwaves was live and unrecorded. Even when early radio was recorded, the recordings frequently ended up being destroyed or lost. As a result, broadcast historians studying the content, aesthetics, and cultural milieu of early radio texts are forced to take a production-oriented approach that recreates programming through transcripts, production scripts, program logs, newspaper reviews, producer autobiographies, professional journals, and other surviving texts that describe the programs and the creative practices shaping them. Shawn VanCour calls this "sound historiography without the sound" (2018, par. 2). In my study of internet radio and podcasts, discourse analysis and oral history often have to stand in for traditional textual analysis.

Too often research into sound media, especially the current boom in podcasting, focuses principally on economics, technology, social context, and reception, with the specifically aural nature of sound getting lost (Hilmes 2005). However, there are numerous reasons why it is important to hear the sound that is the basis of our sound history. Some reasons should be obvious, especially if a researcher is focused on conducting a formal analysis of radio/podcast style and aesthetics. It is one thing to read the transcript of what was said during a radio program or to read a podcast editor describe their sound mixing approach, but it is something else entirely to actually *hear* the soundwork. The aurality of radio and podcasting carries a whole subtext of affect and meaning: tone, stress, volume, speed, pitch, accent, dialect, and other emotional elements of speech and the ways in which the words are spoken, not to mention how the sound is mixed or the music is arranged and performed. To analyze sound's function within narratives or its modes of representation, we must be able to listen to and understand it as a *sound* medium. From a preservation standpoint, however, web archives like the Wayback Machine approach the web as a textual medium, focusing on capturing the printed word—and some rudimentary, static visual images—as they appear on the web *page*. The PodcastRE project is rather unique in treating the web as a multimedia platform, prioritizing the collection of digital audio artifacts.[7] Moving forward, PodcastRE's archive will be an indispensable resource for sound studies scholars seeking to analyze elements of podcasting that are specifically aural.

Audioblogging and Locating Proto-Podcasts in the Web Archive

Turning now to the specific example of researching the proto-podcast form of "audioblogs," and in particular using digital archive tools like the Internet Archive's Wayback Machine, I will skip the full history of online radio and podcasting, except to point out that the commonly accepted origin story of podcasting emerging circa 2005 is perfunctory. Podcasting began well before 2005—at least a few years and as much as a decade earlier, depending on one's definition of a podcast. If your definition of podcasting is along the lines of "downloadable radio programs available for personalized, mobile consumption," then such things existed as early as 1993. The Internet Multicasting Service (also known as Internet Talk Radio) was started in 1993 by Carl Malamud, a technologist and Washington, D.C., political insider. He founded the Internet Multicasting Service as a nonprofit organization, and it produced programming about internet technology and regulatory politics, along with other public affairs and entertainment programs in an NPR style. In the early to mid-1990s, accessible live streaming technology did not exist, so content was distributed on demand: users had to download sound files, decompress them, and play them back on their computer on primitive audio players. (Files were formatted in .au and .gsm formats—.au developed by Sun Microsystems and common on NeXT systems, and .gsm short for Global System for Mobile Audio, originally designed for mobile phones.) Luckily, we still have access to a fair amount of this early internet radio programming because Malamud is a committed open source advocate; he preserved the material himself and has continued to keep it accessible online.[8]

That is not the case with other more fringe born-digital content like audioblogs. Basically, audioblogs are exactly what they sound like: audio versions of personal weblogs (or blogs). These existed in the early 2000s (circa 2000–2005), and they are the direct antecedents to podcasts. Audioblog posts were short, personal audio recordings. These were not full-fledged radio programs, nor were they produced by media professionals. Like the earliest blogs, they consisted of user-created content made by ordinary web users (i.e., amateurs). Whereas a written blog post runs on average a couple hundred words, the audio equivalent contains only a couple minutes of an individual monologizing on a topic. In totality, an audioblog featured a succession of these brief posts, most of which were one-off dispatches that did not directly connect to each other apart from the fact that they came from the mind of a single individual. The main thing uniting the posts together was the audioblogger's personality. These recordings were very much presented in the vein of the "first-person-singular" audio storytelling mode described by Hilmes (this volume), albeit de-professionalized and much less controlled. An individual audioblog post was, in effect, the expression of a single thought from start to finish, unscripted and unedited, warts and all. In this way, it would be akin to a telephone answering machine message or a voice memo broadcast via the internet.

An audioblog post is more like a sound clip, an almost random fragment. The length of recordings was usually restricted to a maximum time of five minutes per post. Notably, this is very similar to what early Anchor. fm app clips sounded like circa 2016–2017, before the "audio social network" pivoted to its current podcast hosting service model (Shieber 2016). Therefore, this format traces both backward and forward. Interestingly, many audioblog posts not only sounded like telephone voicemail messages; they actually *were* telephone voicemail messages. Recording, formatting, and uploading digital audio for the web was still a burdensome undertaking for average internet users in the early 2000s. As a result, a number of phone-to-blog services sprung up that allowed users to call up a phone number and record an audioblog post over the phone; then it automatically converted the recording into an MP3 that was uploaded to the user's blog. This early approach to podcasting was highly ephemeral, as the audio recordings were dispersed across individual blogs rather than centrally located in podcatcher apps like iTunes (that can be relatively easily scraped by the likes of PodcastRE). Small blogs like these were not often crawled by the Wayback Machine and few remain intact on the live web today. The audioblog service providers that facilitated and often did the actual server hosting of the audio files mostly went out of business after only a few years.

One of those audioblog services was the San Francisco–based Audblog. The company was launched in February 2003 by young entrepreneur Noah Glass, and it quickly became the most widely used platform in the audioblogging space. Audblog formed a partnership with the Google-backed blog publishing service Blogger to offer a co-branded service, audioBLOGGER. Audblog was short-lived; it lasted for only a couple of years. And in an odd twist of fate, it morphed into a podcast company called Odeo that then turned into Twitter. From an archival perspective, what is significant about a company like Audblog and the broader practice of audioblogging is that we have an entire audio form here that is effectively orphaned. These are in essence home recordings, albeit made publicly available (for a time). They were not the products of professional media institutions with content libraries. It is certainly possible that some users saved their personal files, stashing them away on an old hard drive, but they are inaccessible to the public and to researchers like myself and certainly at risk of data loss (if they have not been lost already). This audioblog example is prescient of our current social media era, where a considerable amount of media content is user-generated and not distributed through professional media organizations. While broadcast networks and the like have not always proven to be the best guardians of their own content historically, today there is at least a strong likelihood that these institutions will store, if not formally archive, their content in a systematic manner—for legal and economic reasons, if anything else. In contrast, much of today's online content is produced by individual "produsers" on a massive scale and an irregular schedule, which creates deep challenges for archiving. And the platforms hosting the material typically position themselves as service providers (facilitating storage) and explicitly *not* as content providers (Hart 2011). In practice, this means that social media platforms are not just unreliable for archiving and preservation purposes, but they also deliberately avoid these activities. Yet, users often treat them as permanent repositories for their content, and there is a significant risk that if the platform removes a user's material for any reason or the platform shutters completely, then the content is gone forever—a recent example being MySpace's "accidental" deletion of twelve years' worth of user-created music, videos, and photos in 2019 (Krukowski 2019).

Platforms like Audblog were private startups that failed and went out of business. If the platform owners kept copies of their users' data, there is no way of knowing. For years I have tried locating Audblog's former owners, along with its corporate successors (Google and Twitter), without luck. It is possible to recover some of these recordings via the Internet Archive's Wayback Machine, but more are unavailable than available. Typically, text and images were captured by the crawlers while audio files were not. In cases like these, the Wayback Machine is hardly a long-term preservation plan. We are lucky to have the few traces it captured, yet these fragments are inadequate source material to build a rigorous academic study. Again, access to the sound artifacts matters here for a variety of reasons. For instance, in these audioblogs there was an emphasis on witnessing: people documenting their personal experience, their speech rife with individual self-expression and affective disclosure. Even though these recordings were time-shifted (they were never broadcast or streamed live), they were nevertheless posted online within minutes of being recorded. The aural nature of the audioblogs best captures the characteristics of presence and immediacy that make these consequential cultural artifacts. Moreover, audioblogging is notable for the plurality of voices it brought to the web media environment, something that cannot be sufficiently captured through only a few isolated audioblogs. Access to large collections of content is needed if we are to truly understand the structure of feeling this media form encapsulated.

One other significant obstacle I have encountered relates to obsolete or incompatible formats. Up until the early 2000s, most internet radio content was distributed through proprietary audio formats like RealAudio rather than open source formats like MP3. As a result, even if audio files are recovered online today, they are usually not playable. RealAudio was developed as a streaming media format, meaning the complete audio file was not posted to the web page; rather there was only a small text file that contained a link to the audio stream (usually a .ram file, standing for RealAudio metadata). Clicking the link would launch the user's media player, which would then initiate a real-time download from RealAudio's servers. In other words, what appears to be an audio file is in actuality a shortcut to an audio file located elsewhere on the internet. Recovering one of those links today proves useless; it is a partial seed file and a dead link. The connection to RealAudio's streaming servers has expired. This is a problem with a site like Pseudo.com, which was one of the first internet-only radio networks centered on its own original content. Pseudo produced a ton of content in the late 1990s, but then the company shuttered during the dot-com bubble burst. You can recover some of Pseudo's program archives via the Wayback Machine but none of the actual audio, since it is in the RealAudio format and the servers are disconnected. Even in instances where you are able to locate a complete RealAudio file somehow, the newer versions of the RealPlayer software do not support early iterations of the RealAudio audio codec (coder-decoder). You would need to locate an untouched, un-updated version of RealPlayer from at least fifteen years ago in order to play back RealAudio files from the 1990s (this is software that is no longer distributed; finding a copy is much more difficult than one might think).

The bottom line is that a tremendous amount of early internet radio content from the 1990s and early 2000s distributed in audio formats like RealAudio is inaccessible to us today because those formats are obsolete. And if the audio is not there, it is effectively silent, incapable of being considered; if we cannot hear it, we cannot analyze its content and form. These texts are important for a whole variety of reasons; the mere existence of a text tells us very little about its social, cultural, or political significance. For instance, say a researcher is attempting to trace the aesthetics that informed modern podcasting. Being able to hear Pseudo's "ChatRadio" programming is the primary way they would be able to determine the strategies of sonic representation, musical instrumentation, and sound mixing that were used, along with the performance styles early internet radio listeners heard. Moreover, these silences mean that the history of internet radio pioneers like Pseudo have been almost entirely left out of popular press narratives about web audio and the emergence of podcasting.

Based on my research, I have found original internet radio programming made between 1993 and 2003 to be extremely difficult to locate. It is possible that individual producers or webcasting institutions have their old audio saved, but these personal ad hoc archives nevertheless remain inaccessible to researchers. And few internet radio producers seem to regard their content as historically significant and worth saving to donate the material to a public archive or established a media library online (e.g., the Internet Archive). I hope this changes in the near future, with institutional efforts like the Radio Preservation Task Force (https://radiopreservation.org/) or archivist-led podcaster-focused initiatives like Preserve This Podcast (see Gerber-Margie et al. in this volume). Nonetheless, few seem to regard the recent past of the 1990s–2000s as "historical," and every year that goes by puts this born-digital material at risk—formats continue to change and older formats become more difficult to access, digital storage media decay, people clean out their spaces and trash their old files, and so on. Shawn VanCour addresses the need among sound preservation efforts to avoid privileging the distant past and to pay equal attention to the present and recent past of born-digital content (2016, 400). Despite being digital, and thus relatively easy to record and archive, then, I would venture that less audio programming exists from this time period than from just about any other period in broadcast radio history.

Conclusion

All of this raises a number of questions that I invite readers to explore. First, what can we do about audioblogs and other types of orphaned independent or fringe radio and podcast content? Such content is scattered around on different personal blogs and websites, most of which are long disconnected from the web. PodcastRE's digital archiving efforts are impressive, though its tools and protocols are designed to capture only podcasts that are released in the present, along with older materials that remain accessible in apps like Apple Podcasts. It is not capable of recovering what has already disappeared from the web. Audioblogs and other early podcast materials mostly do not belong to a radio broadcaster like NPR, a podcast network like Gimlet Media, or other established sound culture institutions that might save them. The companies that hosted the files (like Audblog) were service providers that long ago went out of business, their servers disconnected and most likely destroyed. It seems the best option is to hunt down these companies or the individual audiobloggers and hope they saved the content themselves. Yet, that is much easier said than done. And even if an independent researcher like me accumulated a personal collection of such materials, that does not make it publicly accessible to others. We need an established library or archive to step up and gather these materials in a systematic manner. One promising recent development is the US Library of Congress's Podcast Preservation Project, news of which began to emerge in January 2020 (reports also suggest that the British Library Sound Archive is undertaking a similar initiative). Though, based on the currently available information, the LOC's approach seems similar to PodcastRE's in that it is collecting only podcast audio that is currently available (Waits and Klein 2020).

Second, we should urge more libraries and archives to preserve old versions of software like web browsers and media players, enabling researchers to play back obsolete and proprietary audio, video, and multimedia files. This may require maintaining older computers, the way many motion picture archives keep Steenbeck machines for playing 16mm and 35mm film materials. Indeed, media archivists point out that while digital technology permits easy transmission, storage, and duplication of media, preserving digital artifacts can actually be much more expensive and resource-intensive than analog materials (Wollard 2015, par. 8). This is because computer software and hardware change so rapidly, and formats can become obsolete in mere years. Sound files formatted in proprietary, non-open file formats—like the RealAudio audio codec—are becoming increasingly difficult to access as fewer and fewer machines contain the software to play back the files. Likewise, sound files may exist on a floppy disk or CD-R, but most modern computers do not contain drives that support these formats. Even if the physical storage media are intact, they are inaccessible if there is no equipment to play or transfer them. Preservation costs increase as files need to be repeatedly transferred to current formats. Digital media is also incredibly vulnerable to damage and destruction (e.g., hard drive failure and disc rot), meaning they need to be stored with redundant backups. To properly save early born-digital radio and podcasts from the 1990s and early 2000s, archivists and media historians should be hoarding whatever audio files still exist along with older versions of the software and devices with which these files and formats are compatible.

Third, a valuable resource that readers—and scholars involved with projects like PodcastRE and the Radio Preservation Task Force—could help initiate is the development of a directory of digital media archives, including companies with standing corporate business archives. In my area of soundwork research, these corporations range from more traditional media producers such as iHeartRadio (formerly Clear Channel), SiriusXM, ESPN, and CNN, to nascent podcast networks such as Gimlet Media, Radiotopia, Wondery, and Earwolf, as well as technology companies, social media platforms, and service providers such as RealAudio, Pandora, Soundcloud, Amazon, Spotify, Stitcher, Google/YouTube, Yahoo!, Twitter, and Microsoft. These companies rarely provide information about their corporate records online, and it can require a great deal of legwork for an individual researcher to even locate the contact information for the company archivist, historian, librarian, or records manager (if one exists), let alone gain access. If one researcher establishes a way in at a digital media company, there should be a forum for sharing that information with our community of scholars. Such a directory could list a description of the collection, the conditions of access, and contact information for the administrators (similar to the Directory of Corporate Archives maintained by the Society of American Archivists).

PodcastRE is already providing much-needed solutions to some of these born-digital audio preservation problems, though there is also room for expansion and improvement. Importantly, PodcastRE harnesses the decentralized, open source nature of internet technologies like podcasting. By using RSS (Really Simple Syndication) feeds as the basis of its collection mechanism, PodcastRE is developing a podcast archive with both breadth and depth. And it is able to do so without needing to rely on regulatory tools like mandatory archive deposit requirements, as is the case with popular music and other sound media. However, this reliance on RSS technology also has its shortcomings. For instance, how can PodcastRE track web audio that does not use RSS feeds? Or that once used RSS but the feeds are long gone? This includes most of the audioblogs and proto-podcasts described in this chapter, but it also includes an increasing number of new podcasts that are produced and distributed via walled garden platforms like Luminary or Spotify that eschew RSS. There is also a sizeable amount of online streaming radio that is never archived as podcasts and thus disappears into the internet ether the moment it is webcast. Hopefully, PodcastRE can evolve to allow for donations of old podcasts and proto-podcasts from individuals (fans/collectors and independent podcasters themselves) or defunct platforms (like Audblog), expanding its holdings of nontraditional web audio forms that shaped the podcasting of today. And, ideally, as PodcastRE's visibility increases, including through the publication of this very volume of essays, more of podcasting's early adopters will become aware of the PodcastRE project and also become conscious of the immense cultural value that their initial forays into internet audio hold for scholars seeking to understand podcasting's past.

Notes

1. Based on a Wayback Machine search accessed on June 17, 2019. https://web.archive.org/web/*/https://chuckpalahniuk.net/.

2. https://web.archive.org/web/20031204194132if_/http://www.chuckpalahniuk.net/blog.php.

3. In the United States, the Library of Congress's Radio Preservation Task Force (RPTF) is intervening to create a sustained field for archiving, restoring, exhibiting, and distributing historical radio.

4. NPR has undertaken considerable digital archiving initiatives in recent years, and their staff informs me they have some partial archives of their 1990s-era websites available on location at the National Public Broadcasting Archives (NPBA) at the University of Maryland in College Park. https://www.lib.umd.edu /special/collections/massmedia/about-us.

5. The Society of American Archivists (SAA) maintains a directory of North American corporate archives; few digital/new media companies are included. http://www2.archivists.org/groups/business-archives-section/directory-of-corp orate-archives-in-the-united-states-and-canada-introduction#.V3LsMJMrKls

6. Dave Winer has regularly blogged at his *Scripting News* site (http://scri pting.com/) since 1997, and at its precursor *DaveNet* since 1994. Other early audiobloggers/podcasters documented their experiences via personal blogs that remain online, such as Dave Slusher at *Evil Genius Chronicles* (http://evilgeniusc hronicles.org/), Christopher Lydon's *Christopher Lydon Interviews* . . . (http://bl ogs.harvard.edu/lydondev/), and Stephen Downes's *Ed Radio* (https://www.do wnes.ca/ed_radio.htm).

7. The Internet Archive certainly contains its share of audio collections; this is an immensely valuable resource for media historians, although these are overwhelmingly digitized versions of analog sound recordings rather than born-digital artifacts. Moreover, materials are collected in an unsystematic fashion, mostly subject to the whims of individual contributors.

8. When I first contacted Malamud in 2015, his digital archives were hidden away on an FTP (File Transfer Protocol) site that he personally directed me to. Subsequently, in April 2016, he uploaded some (but not all) of the Internet Multicasting Service documentation to the more easily accessible Internet Archive, located online at https://archive.org/details/RT-FM.

Works Cited

Ankerson, Megan Sapnar. 2011. "Writing Web Histories with an Eye on the Analog Past." *New Media & Society* 14 (3): 384–400.

Ankerson, Megan Sapnar. 2018. *Dot-Com Design: The Rise of a Usable, Social, Commercial Web.* New York: NYU Press.

Ben-David, Anat, and Hugo Huurdeman. 2014. "Web Archive Search as Research: Methodological and Theoretical Implications." *Alexandria* 25 (1/2): 93–111.

Birdsall, Carolyn. 2015. "Can We Invent a Field Called 'Radio Preservation Studies?'" *Flow: A Critical Forum on Media and Culture.* May 19. https://www.flowjo urnal.org/2015/05/can-we-invent-a-field-called-radio-preservation-studies/.

Bottomley, Andrew J. 2016. *Internet Radio: A History of a Medium in Transition.* PhD diss. Madison: University of Wisconsin–Madison.

Bottomley, Andrew J. 2020. *Sound Streams: A History of Radio-Internet Convergence.* Ann Arbor: University of Michigan Press.

Brügger, Niels. 2012. "When the Present Web Is Later the Past: Web Historiography, Digital History, and Internet Studies." *Historical Social Research* 37 (4): 102–117.

Crockett, Zachary. 2018. "Inside Wayback Machine, the Internet's Time Capsule." *The Hustle*. September 28. https://thehustle.co/inside-wayback-mach ine-internet-archive.

Dundas, Zach. 2003. "A Hazardous Outing: For Years, *Fight Club* Author Chuck Palahniuk Managed to Keep His Personal Life under Wraps. Whoops." *Willamette Week*. October 1: 9.

Gitelman, Lisa. 2008. *Always Already New: Media, History, and the Data of Culture*. Cambridge: MIT Press.

Hart, Terry. 2011. "Is YouTube a Service Provider or Content Provider?" *Copyhype*. April 7. http://www.copyhype.com/2011/04/is-youtube-a-service-provider -or-content-provider/.

Hilmes, Michele. 2005. "Is There a Field Called Sound Culture Studies? And Does It Matter?" *American Quarterly* 57 (1): 249–59.

Hilmes, Michele. 2013. "The New Materiality of Radio: Sound on Screens." In *Radio's New Wave*, edited by Jason Loviglio and Michele Hilmes, 43–61. New York: Routledge.

Hilmes, Michele. 2014. "The Lost Critical History of Radio." *Australian Journalism Review* 36 (2): 11–22.

Krukowski, Damon. 2019. "History Disappeared When MySpace Lost 12 Years of Music, and It Will Happen Again." *Pitchfork*. March 20. https://pitchfo rk.com/thepitch/history-disappeared-when-myspace-lost-12-years-of-music -and-it-will-happen-again/.

Leetaru, Kalev. 2015. "How Much of the Internet Does the Wayback Machine Really Archive?" *Forbes*. November 16. http://www.forbes.com/sites/kalevlee taru/2015/11/16/how-much-of-the-internet-does-the-wayback-machine-real ly-archive/#1f264d588d49.

McKernan, Luke. 2017. "Audiovisual Archives and the Web." *Journal of Film Preservation* 96 (April): 35–39.

Milligan, Ian. 2016. "Lost in the Infinite Archive: The Promise and Pitfalls of Web Archives." *International Journal of Humanities and Arts Computing* 10 (1): 78–94.

Milligan, Ian. 2017. "Welcome to the Web: The Online Community of GeoCities during the Early Years of the World Wide Web." In *The Web as History*, edited by Niels Brügger and Ralph Schroeder, 137–58. London: UCL Press.

Niemeyer, Liam. 2018. "How to Predict the Death of a Podcast: The What, How, and Why of the 'Podfade' Phenomenon." *Bello Collective*. October 12. https://bellocollective.com/the-death-of-a-podcast-the-what-how-and-why-of-podfade-568f6ae7322c.

Shieber, Jonathan. 2016. "Anchor Launches to Take Radio to the Next Level." *TechCrunch*. February 9. https://techcrunch.com/2016/02/09/anchor-laun ches-to-take-radio-to-the-next-level/.

Spigel, Lynn. 1992. *Make Room for TV: Television and the Family Ideal in Postwar America*. Chicago: University of Chicago Press.

Striphas, Ted. 2010. "The Abuses of Literacy: Amazon Kindle and the Right to Read." *Communication and Critical/Cultural Studies* 7 (3): 297–317.

VanCour, Shawn. 2016. "Locating the Radio Archive: New Histories, New Challenges." *Journal of Radio & Audio Media* 23 (2): 395–403.

VanCour, Shawn. 2018. "An Archaeology of Early Radio Production: Doing Sound Historiography without the Sound." *OUPblog*. September 11. https://blog.oup.com/2018/09/early-radio-production-sound-historiography/.

Waits, Jennifer, and Eric Klein. 2020. "Podcast #230—The Library of Congress Launches Podcast Preservation Project." Podcast episode. *Radio Survivor*. January 28. http://www.radiosurvivor.com/2020/01/28/podcast-230-the-library-of-congress-launches-podcast-preservation-project/.

Winer, Dave. 2018. "Podcasts Are Feeds." *Scripting News*. June 10. http://scripting.com/2018/06/10/192326.html.

Wollard, Matthew. 2015. "There Need Not Be a Digital Dark Age—How to Save Our Data for the Future." *The Conversation*. February 23. https://theconversation.com/there-need-not-be-a-digital-dark-age-how-to-save-our-data-for-the-future-37723.

TWO | The Perils of Ladycasting

*Podcasting, Gender, and Alternative
Production Cultures*

JENNIFER HYLAND WANG

In her profanely titled podcast *DTFD* (*Doing the F*ing Dishes*), Julia Barton mused on the connection between her work as a mother and the other subject of her podcast, talking about history. In an episode titled "Toy Assault," she picks up Legos, army men, and Playmobil figures from the floor while wondering aloud if "people who make sense of the world," the journalists, writers, podcasters, and history lovers, are also "tidying people" (*DTFD* 2014). She continues:

> We're tidying up things for the rest of you. History just happens and it's just a mess. Of course, it's a mess. When things are happening and it's just a shit storm, you know, especially cataclysmic things, wars and lynchings, and mobs and massacres. It doesn't happen, you know, usually by some sort of plan. It's just crazy and later on, you know, they start making up reasons why they did it depending on who wins. And then they're all dead and the real work of figuring it out can begin. That's what historians do. We're cleaning up the mess so it makes sense and we can function. (2:32)

Barton's musings resonated with me. The demands of neoliberal motherhood and the need to tidy up more than a century of historical narratives about American broadcasting are relentless. As a stay-at-home mother of three and a historian working (on and off) as an adjunct in the academy, I was comforted by Barton's understanding of the relevance of her and my various unpaid labors. I, too, work in a system where both the tidying in my house and in academia are unpaid. I write about broadcasting history in the interstices of my day, amid carpools, dentist appointments, and sinks full of dishes. At the same time, I mother in the margins, between publishing deadlines and conference presentations. I am paid for neither and feel compelled to do both. I write to have a voice in academia, to shape our understanding of the cultural and ideological practices of broadcasting, even though I have no guarantee that anyone will read what I write. I pick up after dogs and kids from morning until night in the hope that the housework I do in and around my family, as mundane as it is, is somehow meaningful.

Two dogs and three children create more clutter than I could ever have imagined. But they can't compare to the chaotic disarray of histories. The writing of history is messy. We pick up scraps of papers, recorded sounds, and faded photographs and try to make sense of a place and time. Built from what is available and accessible, we assemble a narrative that explains who, what, and why events occurred as they did. Based on assumptions that fill the evidentiary gaps, we, as historians, create stories about institutions, technologies, events, and practices that are inevitably incomplete. Particularly in histories of new media, as Lisa Gitelman eloquently argues in *Always Already New* (2008), how we sort the historical threads before us and produce stories about the origins of new media shapes that media and alters its future.

Not long after the term "podcasting" was coined in 2004, groups of "tidying people"—journalists, audiophiles, fellow podcasters, and scholars—began to assemble an origin story for this new media. Some of podcasting's more technologically savvy pioneers curated podcasting's recent history and cataloged the technological milestones and memories of the "podfathers" of this young medium: Dave Winer, Adam Curry, and Christopher Lydon. Quite quickly, the various and varied stories of podcasting's development coalesced into a dominant narrative, a techno-utopian tale that tied a small group of male audio pioneers to the commercial future only recently realized for podcasting (Hammersley 2004; Newitz 2005; Scott 2006; and Walker 2015). Thus, early in accounts of the origins of podcasting, I see evidence that creators who may have imagined uses of this emerging radio technology beyond its commercial potential, who may have labored under different production constraints, or who were not selected to appear in the "New and Noteworthy" section of iTunes have been overlooked in contemporary accounts. Specifically, these dominant narratives of podcasting's origins erase the stories, contributions, and voices of early podcasters—so many of them women—from the historical record.

In the context of the larger PodcastRE project, this chapter seeks to recoup and amplify some of those voices. Amid the evolving professionalization of podcasting, I examine the cultural divide emerging in the post-*Serial* podcasting world between public radio and commercial interests on one side ("pro-casters") and communities of independent audio producers ("podcasters") on the other. Looking specifically at a subset of female independent podcasters, I discuss the parameters of their distinctive production culture and the concerns of these producers as podcasting became commercialized. For these "stay-at-home" podcasters, I analyze how discussions about podcast production align with the demands of care work and family life for women as imagined within contemporary discourses of neoliberal feminism.

I argue that the stories we have told about podcasting in the early 2000s are not only incomplete but also potentially harmful. Compiled from the most accessible and popular podcasts and the existing traces of first-person narratives, academics and journalists alike disseminated tales of a normative podcasting world—white, male, professional, and with commercial potential—and an absence of female podcasters willing to operate in this world. Although NPR and other media partners attempted to grow the ranks of female podcasters, persistent barriers to access, the push for professional standards, and the industry's commercial expectations made it difficult to adequately support female-driven podcasts. Heather Ordover's "Podcaster's Manifesto" in 2015 alerted those who study podcasting to the presence and persistence of grassroots, female-led podcast productions that are largely invisible to platform gatekeepers. In light of these limitations, online groups like "She Podcasts" sought to empower women in the face of the industry's commercial expansion. While these efforts have allowed new voices to proliferate and provided much-needed community support for some independent female producers, they also implicitly reinscribe professional production standards as the norm, relegate indie producers to second-tier status, and acquiesce to the labor conditions under which these podcasters produce audio of women's lived experiences.

Through an analysis of one of many distinctive subcultures marginalized in early accounts of podcasting's origins, we can glimpse how the pursuit of perfect audio and commercial success influence the stories that journalists and scholars choose to tell about podcasting. "Tidying up" the histories of this young medium is thus essential work with material effects. The way we compose narratives privileges certain voices and mutes others. Refusing to interrogate the ideologies and contexts in which we produce histories, I argue, not only erases some women's voices in podcasting's past but may limit their possibilities in podcasting's future as well. A more comprehensive approach to archiving podcasts, as advocated by the PodcastRE project, which hand-curates lesser-known podcasts in addition to collecting popular podcasts from platforms, can help redress the faulty assumptions that academics and journalists have made thus far about the medium and point us toward a more inclusive history.

"Hey, Where Are All the Women At?": The Tales of Early Podcasting

Influenced by the groundbreaking work of Henry Jenkins, digital media, sound, and radio scholars first studied podcasting as a product of and participant in convergence culture. Some of the earliest published studies of podcasting (Berry 2006; Sterne et al., 2008) considered whether podcasting was a potentially emancipatory or disruptive technology in the media landscape. As compared to traditional radio, scholars saw in early podcasting examples of a "produsage" community, of user-generated content, propelled by accessible production hardware and software, circulated within user communities, and driven by its own amateur aesthetic (Bruns 2008). Thusly framed, Jonathan Sterne and his colleagues anticipated that podcasting would not only open up "opportunities for audiences to hear new kinds of content, or old kinds of content in new ways," but it might also offer "opportunities for people who could not easily broadcast to distribute their content online on what at least initially appears as a level playing field" (2008, 14).

Over the last decade, academics sought data about early podcasters to assess the techno-utopian potential of the medium (Millette 2011; Markman 2011; Markman and Sawyer 2014). Within this framework, scholars synthesized survey responses to classify podcasters as "produsers"—"a group of plugged-in, educated, older male professionals" (Markman and Sawyer 2014, 33; Markman 2011, 553). These podcasters were labeled "Pro-Ams," "a new breed of 'amateurs who work to professional standards,'" who were well-positioned to exploit podcasting's commercial potential (Markman and Sawyer 2014, 33; Markman 2011, 547). From the start, academic work established a normative independent podcaster (an older, white, technologically savvy man) and an intuitive commercial trajectory for podcasting as part of its origin story. Perhaps as a result of some combination of social bias, incomplete data, and the sheer volume of male podcasters experimenting in the medium, the narratives that emerged from scholars and journalists too often focused on the majority users and uses of the medium and obscured the various ways minority users may have experimented with podcasting.

As years passed, the gap between the utopian potential of the medium touted by scholars and the observed reality of podcast practice became more problematic. For the past decade and a half, much of podcasting has been a man's world populated by independent audio producers. Comprising 54 percent of the podcast audience and 70 percent of the hosts of the top 100 podcasts listed by iTunes in 2015, published data confirms "that podcasting in the U.S. is a white male thing" (Morgan 2016). Furthermore, the gender imbalance among podcast producers has been stubbornly persistent. The most commonly cited statistics by the industry and popular press suggest that women comprised somewhere between 12 and 14 percent of all podcasters (Escobar and Walch 2012). Radiotopia's Julie Shapiro argued that for all of its possibilities, the statistics

> point to a disappointing truth: that podcasting—hailed back in 2004 as a "revolutionary" new tool for freedom of expression and endless creative opportunity—quickly copied the same gender stereotypes and realities that traditional broadcasting environments have demonstrated throughout history. (2013)

Podcasting, imagined by scholar Richard Berry in 2006 as a "disruptive technology" capable of upending consumption, production, and distribution broadcast practices, more closely resembled traditional radio a decade later than a radical new form of media (144).

Although the gender imbalance in podcasting continued throughout its first decade, this lack of parity became a pressing industry issue only when it became possible to envision podcasting as a mass medium. In a 2007 article titled "Hey Where Are All the Women At?" Rob Walch and Elsie Escobar of the podcast hosting company Libsyn bemoaned the lack of women in early podcasting (in contrast to the relative gender parity among bloggers) (Escobar and Walch 2012). A follow-up article five years later confirmed that the disparity had endured (2012). The lack of female-hosted podcasts got more industry attention in the mid-2010s after the breakout success of *Serial* in 2014 (Madison 2015; Gloudeman 2015; Morgan 2016). Inspiring more than 175 million downloads by mid-2017, the popularity of *Serial* jolted the media industry and inspired articles in the popular and industry press to explain mass interest in a podcast (Spangler 2017). I argue that the gender imbalance (and unexpected success) of a female-led podcast became a much more important issue to discuss when the commercial prospects of the new medium hung in the balance. The bright commercial future of podcasting depended on the industry's ability to capitalize on the consumer interest in *Serial* and to attract mass audiences beyond those already cultivated by independent male podcasters. The impulse to woo larger and more female audiences to audio relied, in part, on the number of female-driven podcasts.

Public radio, more than any other entity, answered the call to cultivate more-diverse podcasting voices. With a stable of radio shows that could easily be repackaged as podcasts, public radio developed a veritable farm team for professional female podcasters in the emerging industry. As described by NPR's Ophira Eisenberg, "'the machine'"—the leadership at NPR and its member stations—"has been more visibly prioritizing gender parity in development and strategy decisions" in recent years (Madison 2015; Shapiro 2013; Gloudeman 2015). The "podcast girl gang" that found so much success in late 2014 and 2015, Alix Spiegel, Lulu Miller, and Sarah Koenig, all toiled behind-the-scenes at public radio—Spiegel and Koenig at *This American Life*, and Miller at *Radiolab*—before their shot at podcasting stardom. Public Radio Exchange's Radiotopia, a curated network of independent producers (many with public radio resumes), and Roman Mars, host of *99% Invisible*, intentionally sought funding to add more women's voices to the medium. Through its strategic initiatives, NPR and its flagship stations provided the training ground and the financial resources to support female creative teams behind and at the microphone to expand podcasts' reach into untapped markets (Shapiro 2013).

Despite these attempts to build a mass audience, a cultural skepticism about the commercial possibilities of female-produced content remained. One needs to go no further than contemporary discussions about vocal fry or "talking while female" to see how problematic it is for some to hear women's voices in public spaces. Criticized for upspeak and for its rough corrective, vocal fry, women on radio are truly "stuck between a rock and a high pitch" (Miller 2015). The culture's comfort with women as media consumers and discomfort with women as media producers is still pronounced. For example, *Invisibilia*'s Lulu Miller reported an online comment that said, "Interesting content, but they talk about [science] like they're talking about going shopping" (2015).

Despite their years as public radio journalists and audio producers, the listener could only hear their ability to consume, the "shopping in their voices," and not the tones of seasoned radio professionals (2015). The truth is, said journalist Jamila Bey, that "when we hear the spoken voice, we're still hearing men" (Madison 2015). Sadly, despite the belief that podcasting could be diversified, as discussed by Alexander Russo and myself, female voices and female bodies did not always feel universally welcomed in the corridors of National Public Radio (Russo 2019; Wang 2019).

Furthermore, when both scholars and journalists were searching for "where the women were at," it's not clear that we were looking in the right places. Truthfully, we have little hard data about the actual numbers of female podcasters (and even less about the numbers of people of color, of different classes, and of different sexualities who podcast) and the extent of the gender imbalance. There were women involved in podcasting from the very beginning; some of the pioneering podcasts like *Dawn and Drew, Keith and the Girl, Geek Fu Action Grip, Astronomy Cast,* and *Elsie's Yoga Class* were helmed fully or partially by women. The number of female inductees into the Podcasting Hall of Fame reaches to almost 30 percent of the class, a number much larger than the 12 percent often cited. I suggest that this is less likely a measure of the progressive attitudes of podcasters than that there were more women podcasting than the data recognizes (Academy of Podcasters 2018). So how do we account for the discrepancies in this data? Much of the answer may lie in the implied terms of being a "podcaster." For example, podcaster Lisa Rowan called "bullshit" on the media conversation that there were few women in podcasting (*She Podcasts* 2015a, Episode 45, 58:25). Rowan argued that in her research she "found plenty of women who were podcasting but very few in the top charts of iTunes" (58:33). Her experience suggests that the industry press paid little attention to podcasters below the radar of podcasting platforms. In a sense, if female podcasters podcast like male podcasters (more professional quality audio, more commercial in intent, and with more institutional backing), I suspect that they were more likely to be categorized as podcasters. In some sense, we (academics and journalists alike) found who we were looking for—men (and those women) who aspired to the commercial and professional trajectory prized by majority users. As I discuss in the following section, other users of the medium—specifically for this chapter, white, middle-to-upper-class women podcasting from their homes—produced podcasts that hovered below the top 100 in iTunes but were relatively invisible by the hegemonic understandings of the role and operation of podcasting in our culture.

The Podcaster's Manifesto: The Battle Cry of Podcasters as Bloggers

Public radio's interest in promoting women-hosted podcasts was not enthusiastically cheered in every corner of the internet. A decade into podcasting, mainstream publications seemed more interested in promoting the professionalization of the medium and its gender equity efforts than in publicizing growing tensions between public radio and commercial interests on one side, who were new to the medium, and communities of independent audio producers on the other, who had experimented with podcasting for years. Industry insider Nick Quah argued that the podcasting world was being divided in two during the mid-2010s, between "podcasts-as-an-extension of blogging" and "podcasts-as-the-future-of-radio" (2015). Although the two "share the same real estate," suggested Quah, they "are playing very different games" (2015). On one side, there were commercial producers who believed podcasting's future was professional and highly produced audio using podcasting as one of many distribution paths to get their products to market (2015). The launch of NPR One, public radio's mobile app, the rise of podcasting collectives like Radiotopia, and the emergence of podcast networks like Gimlet Media are evidence of mainstream media's heightened interest in this vision of podcasting.

On the other side, independent (and largely female) audio producers who had been experimenting in the medium for years, "the podcasts-as-extensions of blogging" camp, were concerned about the growth of corporate interest in spoken audio. For them, podcasting has been a platform through which hobbyists could speak to devoted listeners over RSS feeds (Kang 2014). In response to the commercial pressure unleashed by *Serial*'s success, Heather Ordover, the creator of *CraftLit* (2006–), a podcast offering spoken classic literature to accompany women while they sew or knit, responded publicly to the industry's prioritization of professionally produced female podcasting. On her website and on *She Podcasts*, a then newly formed podcast for women podcasters, Ordover delivered her version of the podcaster's "I Have a Dream" speech—the "Podcaster's Manifesto" (2016c, Episode 88, 46:34). Ordover claimed the term "podcasting" for independent producers like herself:

> *Serial* is radio, not podcasting . . . because we need to be honest, NPR is not getting into podcasting any more than I'm getting into a pri-

vate jet later today to go to the grocery store. Since 2005 NPR has used podcasting's distribution systems to repurpose radio audio for on-demand consumption. And that is not podcasting. (45:35)

Calling *Serial* a podcast, Ordover argued, "is like calling a Ferrari a go-cart. One, made with a lot of money and one, put together in your garage" (2015, 10:40). To podcast, she asserted, is to produce free audio that "lived on the Internet, delivered to your computer from someone else's computer, with no corporate intermediary, no delay, and no fee" (7:10). She argued that the products of professional podcasting networks should instead be called "pro-casts," not podcasts. The intent of podcasters is to do "what NPR can't," argued Ordover; "we build communities" (*She Podcasts* 2016c, Episode 88, 44:15). The mom-and-pop style of program production and social mission of some female audio producers thus suggested a production culture and medium use quite different from that described as the norm by many academics and journalists.

In an increasingly commercialized culture, veteran female podcasters feared that their time in podcasting was limited and that their contributions to the emerging medium would be overlooked. Referencing the early radio amateurs of the 1920s, Ordover argued that "what is happening to we, the podcasting pioneers, is exactly what happened to radio pioneers as well" (42:08). As private commercial networks drove radio amateurs off the air, so too, she feared, would "pro-casters" push podcasters off digital platforms. Partially driven by an algorithm that measures retweets, comments, and downloads, and partially curated by the app's moderators, platforms like iTunes and Stitcher serve as cultural gatekeepers to the public's access to podcasts. The system privileges podcasts with institutional support and commercial potential while obscuring independent voices, many of which are not readily visible on the platform and must be manually added via an RSS feed. To remedy this inequity, Ordover suggested that fellow podcasters should demand that platforms like Apple's Podcast list "pro-casts" and podcasts separately in their directory to make it easier for listeners to find independent audio (43:43).

Truthfully, their fears are not unfounded. As of October 2020, more than 1.5 million podcasts are available through the Apple Podcast platform (Winn 2020). Without the institutional support given by media entities or the requisite popularity of professionalized audio, independent female podcasters have been shoved aside by their better-funded, albeit female, rivals. Correspondingly, these women worried that the pioneering contributions of independent female podcasters would be ignored. Ordover recognized the gendered implications (and perhaps not the racial undertones of the gentrification of the podcast landscape) of "pro-casters'" eagerness to cash in on the medium's newfound popularity when she said:

> The insult is in the ways the pioneers are dismissed. That's so cute, or how sweet, or how nice that you have time for a hobby, you know, like building an entire neighborhood for me to barge in and take over once you've got it started or that's nice honey now you can let the grown-ups come in and make something of this. (2015, 42:45)

Identifying the same gendered discourses applied to them as had been applied to radio amateurs, these "She Podcasters" believed they would share the fate of amateurs almost one hundred years ago. Rumors that wikis of podcasting pioneers and independent audio producers had already been deleted fueled the fears of female podcasters, who imagined being erased not only from Apple's Podcast platform but from the history of podcasting itself (1:02:40). Despite overt attempts to diversify podcasting, certain kinds of female podcasters—those of hobbyists or stay-at-home mothers—and specific production cultures with their own aesthetics and stories were marginalized. Interestingly, it is also these accounts of this podcasting divide that exposed a strain of early female audio production to researchers and suggested other ways podcasts could be produced that were not legitimized by the mainstream media.

Keep Taking Care of That Lady Business—*She Podcasts, DTFD,* and the Woman's Way of Podcasting

When *Love and Radio* producer Nick van der Kolk wondered "why there are so few podcasts by women," the public radio journalist/stay-at-home caregiver Julia Barton had a simple, yet telling, response:

> I can't answer for the other ladies, but for me, it's because I'm doing the dishes. Of course, men do the dishes, too. Sometimes. But so as not to seem like a slacker, I've decided to podcast WHILE doing the dishes. Now I'm no longer muttering to myself in the kitchen, I am Podcasting. (2016)

Her podcast offering, *DTFD*, was the product of this clever conceit. Barton, working freelance as a journalist and audio producer while staying home with her two children, talks about history while she does the dishes, makes soup, or sorts bills. Because "the only way I'm going to podcast," Barton admits, "is if I can get the dishes done at the same time" (2016). Her response is not as sarcastic as it may seem. Radiotopia's Julie Shapiro suggested that the production requirements of podcasting made it difficult for women to participate in this field. "Unless born of already-existing media outlets," said Shapiro,

> most start-up podcasts bring in very little (if any) money, yet demand super-human efforts to be produced regularly. Many women who I spoke with mentioned they simply couldn't afford these terms—and if they could somehow manage not getting paid for tireless devotion to a project, they couldn't squeeze those hours needed into their already personally and professionally over-burdened days. (2013)

This is a challenge, argued podcaster Hillary Frank, that "affects women differently, and more tangibly, than men," because by the time women have gained sufficient production experience, they may have started families, which further discourages women to add one more thing to their busy lives (cited in Shapiro 2013). Unless explicitly funded by NPR, podcasting is a luxury for some female independent producers, adding to their unpaid labor and not subtracting from it. The demands of the "second shift" at home for working mothers, the neoliberal pressure to be relentlessly productive, and the considerable labor of podcast production have not been easily reconciled over the last two decades.

One homegrown initiative to address the obstacles to women's involvement in audio life is the *She Podcasts* community.[1] Elsie Escobar, a yoga podcaster since 2006 who works for Libsyn, and Jessica Kupferman, who began the podcast *Lady Business Radio* in 2013, joined forces to create online and offline spaces to nurture female podcasters. Escobar and Kupferman began a closed, woman-only Facebook group in 2014 that has grown today to over eighteen thousand "ladycasters" (*She Podcasts*, Facebook group, 2020). In addition to their solo podcasts and podcast consulting service, Escobar and Kupferman debuted *She Podcasts*, a podcast for women in podcasting, in 2014, and in 2015 they formed the Podcasting School for Women, an eight-week online course to teach women how to podcast. The explicit intention of the *She Podcasts* enterprise was to create an all-female online community where podcasters could seek support, advice, comfort, and technical expertise. The tagline on their website in 2016, "psst. you're home," had a dual function, acknowledging the reality of the environment in which many "she podcasters" produce audio and reassuring novices that they will find a nurturing space in this community of women (*She Podcasts*, website, 2016a). When Escobar and Kupferman talk about the stress and anxiety of juggling child care with podcasting, the comfort felt by those in the *She Podcasts* community is palpable. Amy Robles, host of the money management podcast *Think Enriched*, found solace in the camaraderie of the *She Podcast* community for those who wish to both parent and podcast, saying, "I thought I was the only one juggling Mom tasks of wiping noses, getting sippy cups filled up and wiping bottoms ALL WHILE podcasting." (Robles, online comment, 2015). As different from the training at NPR, this community offers support, advice, and understanding to surmount not only the technical but also the emotional barriers to female podcasting.

However, despite its best intentions, the messaging from the *She Podcasts* community is complicated. The initial promotional materials for the Podcasting School for Women (PSW) draw upon contemporary discourses of neoliberal feminism in its call to and lessons for novice media producers. Catherine Rottenberg suggests that neoliberal feminism produces a subject solely responsible for her own well-being, desiring both personal fulfillment and professional success and calibrating the two in "perfect equilibrium" (2018, 72). PSW sells podcasting to women as a means by which they can balance their personal and professional aspirations. Women should enroll in the Podcasting School for Women, not "because you want to 'fit podcasting in' to your already long to-do list" but "because you can't go another day without having a podcast" (*She Podcasts*, website, 2016b). The school offers beginners time-sensitive tricks to balance self-expression and daily obligations. "We know you already have a TON on your plate," but the Podcasting School for Women promises to "take you through how to fit podcasting into YOUR schedule, as well as how to organize, outsource and automate much of the grunt work" (*She Podcasts*, website, 2015b). Although PSW succeeds at creating a space for ladycasters to share information and to redress the industry's exclusiveness, PSW also schools ladycasters in the basic tenets of neoliberal motherhood. For example, the promotional video found on the *Lady Business Media* Facebook page includes an absurd inventory of expectations that contemporary women must navigate.[2] Imagine shots of attractive, multicultural women, a generic jazz score, and this narration:

> Whether you've just started to grow your business or you've been around the block and back, you're living the dream and there's no

looking back, darn it. We are going to change the world. We are going
to enhance our speaking careers, write our books, grow our email
lists, and guest host our ovaries off. We are going to take care of our
kids, our spouses, our significant others, our parents and our friends
and do it all while scheduling in a little me time. We're going to juice,
exercise, keep track of our expenses, travel the world, and give back
to society. . . . We are in it to win it. Every aspect of life. (*Ladybusiness-media* 2016)

And podcasting, PSW argues, is important to pull off the perfect balance of personal and career fulfillment recommended by contemporary
society. Although intended to encourage female podcasters, the promo's
laundry list of expectations is as exhausting as it sounds.

Simultaneously enticing women to podcast and to navigate the
multitasking, care-driven realities that make such an effort daunting,
the founders of PSW directed their pitch to the distracted female podcaster at home. For a woman based in the home, learning about optimal
recording settings or best podcast practices is laughable, says Escobar.
There are aspects of this female production culture—largely shaped by
the demands of care work—that distinguish it from other DIY production cultures. Escobar reports recording during stolen moments in front
of her bedroom dresser. Most of her postproduction work is done on
the go: "You see me do show notes in the car . . . and editing a lot in
the car, edit in the middle of doing laundry, in the middle of cooking"
(Jackson 2015, 23:37). Podcasting has to fit into her life of caring for
other human beings, and not the other way around. She said, "There is
no this is mommy time to record. . . . It doesn't matter if I'm recording,
[if one of the girls] needs her butt wiped, I'm the one that has to go do
this" (24:34). Escobar insisted that if she had learned to podcast "the
way that you're supposed to do it," in studios with expensive recording
equipment, she would not still be podcasting ten years later (22:41). For
podcasting production to become a habit for women, these pioneers
asserted, production must align with the demands of care work and
family life. Through the community cultivated by *She Podcasts*, Escobar
and Kupferman reveal a distinctive production culture—imperfect (or
unprofessional), aspirational, done piecemeal, at the hands of a distracted producer, and without priority or pay—far different from those
emerging from the offices of NPR or the garages of male amateurs.
Indeed, this specific audio subculture more closely resembles mommy
blogging—in both motivation and in its production process—than other

kinds of independent production described in the earliest accounts of podcasting (Lopez 2009; Friedman and Calixte 2009).

"Everyone Deserves to Be Heard": The Stakes of Perfect Audio

If producing podcasts is so difficult to fit into women's busy days, then why fight to podcast at all? Julia Barton of *DTFD* argues that the spaces offered by podcasting for women, while hard-won, are important to defend. Although it may be difficult to do a podcast without institutional support, you must balance that vulnerability, she says,

> against getting to say what you want, experimenting a little, and learning by mistake, and—with the right schtick—making household chores fun. I do think it's worth it. You have nothing to lose but some bandwidth and dignity, which is not all that anymore, I'm afraid.
>
> Furthermore, podcasting is the only way the audio world is going to hear how women really talk and think. We are still wearing corsets on broadcast radio. Someday that may change, and future generations of female producers will benefit from leaving behind our generation's strangely staid, "good girl" demeanor. But those female voices will find their listeners via podcast first. (Barton, online comments, 2013)

Corseted, suggests Barton, women's voices can't be fully expressed in commercial media or "pro-casts" of any kind (2013). Uncorseted in podcasting, women might speak full-throated to listeners.

The imperfect audio produced by these "stay-at-home" podcasters offers more than just the opportunity to hear women's voices; they also transmit the audio of women's unpaid labor at home and the emotional struggle of women trying to reconcile personal ambitions with family obligations. It sounds, argues Ordover, "more homegrown and . . . more real life" than the well-edited audio from professional studios (*She Podcasts* 2014c, Episode 30, 51:05). In *DTFD*, dishes clinking in a metal sink and running water underscore Barton's attempt to respond in real time to the insistent observations of her young child while simultaneously recording her podcast. In *First Day Back*, Tally Abecassis documents in Margaret Mead–like fashion the sounds of home; "I record my kids playing, I've recorded us eating supper, I do interviews with my husband, and I have even recorded my own rambling thoughts at 3 a.m. when plagued with insomnia," she says (Abecassis 2015). During *She Podcasts*, phones ring, doors open and close, and babies cry, and still, they record: "I know my program doesn't sound like NPR. I'm not Ira Glass or Terry Gross," Kupferman announces, but we keep going "because that's what chicks do" (*She Podcasts* 2014b, Episode 7, 10:15, and 2014a, Episode 1, 0:50). The cluttered audio, the "ums" and "ahs" of casual conversation, and the constant interruptions of life at home make visible the parts of women's lives that are often rendered invisible. Janicia Francis, cohost of the podcast *Tea with Queen and J.*, argues that she and her cohost intentionally don't edit their talk as ruthlessly as professionals do, because "there's a story in that sound" (Barner 2020). I argue that the story told by the audio of independent female podcasters is worth being heard.

Yet, the obstacles to producing this kind of audio are substantial. Nancy Fraser and Catherine Rottenberg remind us of the trap of contemporary feminist expectations for women (Gutting 2015; Rottenberg 2018). While it is all well and good to encourage women to juice, walk, and podcast in addition to their care work and/or paid labor outside the home, the structural inequities of the neoliberal capitalist system of the twenty-first century remain. No matter how much women "lean in," the production culture imagined for female podcasters is to just do more, at the expense of their leisure, their sanity, or both. The expectations placed upon female podcasters, a burden not shouldered by many male podcasters, are unsustainable. Podfading is the logical consequence of the clash between women's various workloads in and out of the house. As their voices and cluttered audio fade from digital platforms, so too does their place in podcasting history.

As of yet, there are few signs that the concerted efforts to woo women to podcasting, through either increased financial, institutional, or emotional support, have paid off. Although there have been some gains in the numbers of podcasters (anecdotally among white, middle-class women), it is unclear how much the number of female podcasters has risen from the 12 percent figure often cited by the industry, a number closer to the percentage of women with careers in broadcast radio than those who blog, and much lower than the numbers of men in podcasting (Shapiro 2013; Gloudeman 2015). As exposed by a series of harassment complaints made by the women of public radio, public radio's efforts at gender parity also did not radically shift the hierarchies that informed its workplace culture. Although there are a few female podcast startups emerging recently—most notably Stable Genius Productions and Unladylike Media—the needle is not yet moving as quickly as one might think. Fraser reminds us that because the "gendered, hierarchical division between 'production' and 'reproduction' is a defining structure of capitalist society and a deep source of the gender asymmetries hardwired in it," there can be "'no emancipation of women' so long as this structure remains intact" (Gutting and Fraser 2015). Although the lines between producer and consumer may be more easily blurred for men in convergence culture, the gendered logics that inform those definitions are not so easily distorted for many women. We, as a society, are much more comfortable with women as distracted media consumers than as distracted media producers.

The shifts in podcasting in recent years, from havens for DIY enthusiasts to commercial venues for professional audio, have significant implications for women's places in podcasting. Years of broadcast history recounting the rise of mass magazines, radio, and television have told the same tale, of how entrenched gender hierarchies shaped ideas about who are producers and who are consumers in American culture and influenced media participation. Despite its revolutionary potential, podcasting (like any other media technology) can't innately resist the power of these discourses. As podcasting becomes more professionalized, as we move from podcast production as unpaid labor to paid labor, those who want to use the medium commercially are prioritized by advertisers, critics, and platforms over hobbyists. And as these more professional programs multiply, the aesthetic standards—professional audio, studio spaces, and so forth—that so often accompany commercial media and public radio further marginalize the audio of women who may be unable to spare the time or money to craft professional-sounding podcasts. Soon we settle into a hegemonic paradigm—where professional audio and careful postproduction are prized—and those shows that feature professional aesthetics will be picked up by the Radiotopias or the Gimlets of the world and recognized by media scholars. Given the demands of neoliberal maternity, professionalization limits opportunities for women in podcasting and marginalizes their subculture. Thus, the pursuit of commercial possibilities sustains an aesthetic hegemony that slowly and gradually writes women out of podcasting's future. The power of these norms is revealed by a 2019 tweet cited by journalist Georgina Ustik that "a group of white men is called a podcast" (2019).

In composing stories of podcasting's past, we must be mindful of the necessity of, as Gitelman argues, a "critical reevaluation of production and consumption as either historically stable or mutually distinct terms of analysis" (2008, 61). In academic work, scholars must recognize the gendered ideologies and labor conditions that marginalize female podcast producers, that create their distinctive production cultures, that shape academic studies, and that influence the histories written about early media. Although it is essential that academics study the men who still dominate early podcasting, we must balance that impulse with the need to examine how other producers of different genders, races, classes, and sexualities may have imagined uses for this aural medium. As articulated by podcaster Kaitlin Prest:

> Currently, one demographic [white, straight, upper/middle class] has a monopoly on [feeling represented] and the power structures that provide access to it. There are so many other demographics whose experience is worth sharing. Whose stories are worth telling. (Gloudeman 2015)

PodcastRE's decision to curate podcasting sources beyond the most-talked-about podcasts offers the hope that the source material to fuel the necessary changes in podcasting's narrativization will exist. The urgent need to "tidy up" the history of podcasting, for journalists, media critics, and scholars, may preserve the audio work of independent female podcasters and the specific production cultures within which the founding mothers of podcasting shook off their corsets. As we begin to sort the complex and contested opportunities that audio offered women in the early twenty-first century, we give voice to forgotten female podcasters, a world of unpaid labor, and claim space for our own voices in assembling historical narratives. It's time to start. A woman's work is never done.

Notes

1. Journalist and podcaster Jamila Bey also began a Facebook group called "Women's Podcasting Network" in 2015 to support female podcasters of color. See *Women's Podcasting Network* 2015.
2. The *Lady Business Media* Facebook page and its members seem to have operated as a proto-*Podcasting School for Women/She Podcasts* community in the transition from Kupferman's solo projects into the *She Podcasts* community.

Works Cited

Abecassis, Tally. 2015. "What Podcasting Taught Me about Motherhood (and Life)." *Huffpost* (blog). March 8. https://www.huffingtonpost.ca/tally-abecas sis/motherhoodpodcast_b_6827668.html.

Academy of Podcasters. 2018. "Hall of Fame." *Academy of Podcasters*. Accessed on March 11, 2020. https://academyofpodcasters.pairsite.com/hall-of-fame/.

Barner, Briana. 2020. "Safe and Sound: How Podcasts Became Audio Enclaves for Black Women." *Bitchmedia*. February 26. Accessed March 6, 2020. https://www.bitchmedia.org/article/podcasts-audio-enclaves-black-women.

Barton, Julia. "Julia R. Barton." Accessed 2016. https://juliabarton.com/post/56 31632346/dtfd.

Barton, Julia. 2013. Online comments to "Women Hosted Podcasts." February 26. *Transom*. Last modified March 17, 2017. https://transom.org/2013/wom en-hosted-podcasts/.

Berry, Richard. 2006. "Will the iPod Kill the Radio Star? Profiling Podcasting as Radio." *Convergence* 12 (2): 143–62. doi: 10.1177/1354856506066522.

Bruns, Axel. 2008. *Blogs, Wikipedia, Second Life, and Beyond: From Production to Produsage*. New York: Peter Lang.

DTFD. 2014. Episode 6, "Toy Assault." Julia Barton. Podcast audio. August 7. https://soundcloud.com/bartona/dtfd-podcast-episode-6-toy-assault?in=bar tona/sets/dtfd-the-podcast.

Escobar, Elsie, and Rob Walch. 2012. "Where Are All the Women At? Part 2." *Libsyn* (blog). December 12. https://blog.libsyn.com/2012/12/12/where-are -all-the-women-at-part-2/.

Friedman, May, and Shana Calixte, eds. 2009. *Mothering and Blogging: The Radical Act of the MommyBlog*. Toronto: Demeter Press.

Gitelman, Lisa. 2008. *Always Already New: Media, History, and the Data of Culture*. Cambridge: MIT Press.

Gloudeman, Nikki. 2015. "Revolution Is Nigh: 8 Female Podcasters Changing the Game." *Ravishly*. February 26. http://ravishly.com/2015/02/26/revolution -nigh-female-podcasters-changing-game.

Gutting, Gary, and Nancy Fraser. 2015. "A Feminism Where Lean In Means Leaning on Others." *New York Times* (blog). October 15. http://opinionator.blogs .nytimes.com/2015/10/15/a-feminism-where-leaning-in-means-leaning-on -others/?_r=o.

Hammersley, Ben. 2004. "Audible Revolution." *The Guardian*. February 11, T1. https://www.theguardian.com/media/2004/feb/12/broadcasting.digitalm edia. Accessed June 25, 2019.

Jackson, Dave. 2015. Interview with Elsie Escobar and Jessica Kupferman. *School of Podcasting*. Episode 465: Women and Podcasting. "Are You Aware of the Women in Podcasting?" June 8. Podcast audio. http://schoolofpodcasting .com/are-you-aware-of-the-women-in-podcasting/.

Kang, Cecilia. 2014. "Podcasts Are Back—And Making Money." *Washington Post*. September 25. https://www.wapo.st/1ytdPL6

Ladybusinessmedia. 2016. "Ladybusinessmedia Facebook Page." *Facebook*. Accessed January 11, 2016. https://www.facebook.com/jesskupfermanpage/videos/10 151894657939829.

Lopez, Lori Kido. 2009. "The Radical Act of 'Mommy Blogging': Redefining Motherhood through the Blogosphere." *New Media & Society* 11 (5): 729–47.

Madison, Alex. 2015. "In the Male-Dominated World of Podcasts, More Women Are Claiming the Mic." *Bitchmedia*. February 23. https://www.bitchmedia .org/post/women-are-making-headway-in-the-male-dominated-world-of-podcasts.

Markman, Kris M. 2011. "Doing Radio, Making Friends, and Having Fun: Exploring the Motivations of Independent Audio Podcasters." *New Media & Society* 14 (4): 547–65. doi: 10.1177/1461444811420848.

Markman, Kris M., and Caroline E. Sawyer. 2014. "Why Pod? Further Explorations of the Motivations for Independent Podcasting." *Journal of Radio & Audio Media* 21 (1): 20–35. doi: 10.1080/19376529.2014.891211.

Millette, Mélanie. 2011. "Independent Podcasting as a Specific Online Participative Subculture: A Case Study of Montreal's Podcasters." October 10–13. Paper presented at the IR 12.0: Performance and Participation, the annual conference of the Association of Internet Researchers, Seattle, Washington.

Miller, Kelsey. 2015. "Why Do These Women's Voices Bother You So Much?" *Refinery29*. May 19. https://www.refinery29.com/en-us/2015/05/87351/female-podcast-voices-vocal-fry.

Morgan, Josh. 2016. "Data Confirm That Podcasting in the US Is a White Male Thing." *Quartz*. January 12. http://qz.com/591440/data-confirm-that-podcasting-in-the-us-is-a-white-male-thing/.

Newitz, Annalee. 2005. "Adam Curry Wants to Make You an iPod Radio Star." *Wired*. March. 111–13. https://www.wired.com/2005/03/curry/.

Ordover, Heather. 2015. "On Serial—Craftlit Bonus." January 26. *Craftlit*. https://craftlit.com/on-serial.

Quah, Nicholas. 2015. "Issue 48: Hot Pod: About a Year after Serial (and Hot Pod's launch), What Does the Future of Podcasts Look Like?" *Hot Pod*. Nieman Lab. November 10. https://www.niemanlab.org/2015/11/hot-pod-about-a-year-after-serial-and-the-first-issue-of-hot-pod-what-will-the-future-of-podcasts-look-like/.

Robles, Amy. 2015. Online Comment to Dave Jackson, *School of Podcasting*. "Episode 465: Women and Podcasting. "Are You Aware of the Women in Podcasting?" *School of Podcasting*. June 9. http://schoolofpodcasting.com/are-you-aware-of-the-women-in-podcasting/.

Rottenberg, Catherine. 2018. *The Rise of Neoliberal Feminism*. New York: Oxford University Press.

Russo, Alexander. 2019. "Possibility and Peril: Production Cultures of Public and Private Podcasters and Broadcasters." Paper given at the Society for Cinema and Media Studies Conference. March 17. Seattle, Washington.

Scott, John. 2006. "Your Moment of Audio Zen: A History of Podcasting." Paper presented at 2006 Notacon 3 Technology Conference. Cleveland, Ohio. https://archive.proxyof.pro/details/notacon-2006-scott-podcast.

Shapiro, Julie. 2013. "Woman Hosted Podcasts." *Transom*. February 26. https://transom.org/2013/women-hosted-podcasts/.

She Podcasts. 2014a Elsie Escobar and Jessica Kupferman. "Episode 001: OMG The *She Podcasts* Podcast!" Podcast audio. June 19. 41 min. https://www.shepodcasts.com/001-omg-the-she-podcasts-podcast/.

She Podcasts. 2014b. "Episode 7: The Low-Down on Podcast Interview Supah Skills, Tactics and Workflow." Podcast audio. July 14. 56 min. https://www.shepodcasts.com/007-the-low-down-on-podcast-interview-supah-skillz-tactics-and-workflow/.

She Podcasts. 2014c. "Episode 30: Podcasting in Education and the Skill of Listen-

ing." Podcast audio. December 22. 78 min. http://www.shepodcasts.com/30
-podcasting-in-education-and-the-skill-of-listening/.

She Podcasts. 2015a. "Episode 45: Podcasting Social Media Tips and New Podcasting Stats." Podcast audio. April 13. 63 min. https://www.shepodcasts.com/45
-podcasting-social-media-power-tips-new-podcasting-stats/.

She Podcasts. 2015b. "Home" Elsie Escobar and Jessica Kupferman. She Podcasts. Accessed November 4, 2020. https://web.archive.org/web/201512101
34719/www.shepodcasts.com/psfw.

She Podcasts. 2016a. "Home." Elsie Escobar and Jessica Kupferman. She Podcasts.
Accessed November 4, 2020. https://web.archive.org/web/20160119113739
/https://shepodcasts.com.

She Podcasts. 2016b. "Podcasting School For Women." Elsie Escobar and Jessica
Kupferman. She Podcasts. Accessed November 4, 2020. https://web.archive
.org/web/20160412064232/http://www.shepodcasts.com/psfw/.

She Podcasts. 2016c. "Episode 88: Calling Out Nick Quah and the Podcaster's
Manifesto." Podcast audio. March 14. 119 min. https://www.shepodcasts.com
/088-calling-out-nick-quah-and-the-podcasters-manifesto/.

She Podcasts. 2020. "*She Podcasts* Facebook Page." *Facebook.* November 5. https://
www.facebook.com/groups/shepodcasts/.

Spangler, Todd. 2017. "The 'Serial' Team's New Podcast, 'S-Town,' Tops 10 Million Downloads in Four Days." *Variety.* March 31. www.variety.com/2017/di
gital/news/s-town-podcast-10-million-downloads-serial-productions-1202020
302/. Accessed February 27, 2019.

Sterne, Jonathan, Jeremy Wade Morris, Michael Brendan Baker, and Ariana
Moscote Freire. 2008. "The Politics of Podcasting." *Fibreculture,* no. 13.
http://thirteen.fibreculturejournal.org/fcj-087-the-politics-of-podcasting/.

Ustik, Georgina. 2019. "Here Are the 11 Female-Led Podcasts You Should Be Listening To." *The Next Web.* February 27. https://thenextweb.com/distract/20
19/02/27/here-are-the-11-female-led-podcasts-you-should-be-listening-to/.

Walker, Benjamen. 2015. "Secret Histories of Podcasting." *Theory of Everything.*
Podcast audio. October 21. https://theoryofeverythingpodcast.com/2015
/10/secret-histories-of-podcasting/.

Wang, Jennifer Hyland. 2019. "The Sounds of Motherhood: Mediating Maternity in Podcasting's Golden Age." Paper given at the Society for Cinema and
Media Studies Conference. March 17. Seattle, Washington.

Winn, Ross. 2020. "2020 Podcast Stats and Facts." October 6. *Podcast Insights.*
https://www.podcastinsights.com/podcast-statistics/.

Women's Podcasting Network. 2015. "Women's Podcasting Network Facebook Page."
Facebook. February 9. Accessed on March 11, 2020. https://www.facebook
.com/WomenPodcastingNetwork/.

THREE | Reality in Sound

Problem Solved?

MICHELE HILMES

One of the most notable aspects of the growth of podcasting over the last decade is the revitalization of the sound documentary. Podcasting has given reality-based soundwork not just expanded reach, flexibility, and popularity but whole new expressive avenues that documentary producers have been quick to explore: extended serial investigations (like, yes, *Serial*, but also *S-Town* and *In the Dark* and their numerous kin); topic- and personality-driven factual series such as the pioneering *Radiolab, Invisibilia, Planet Money*, and *Revisionist History*; a host of print news sources transformed into sound by established outlets from the *New Yorker* to *National Geographic*; and many more. But perhaps most ubiquitous and innovative of all is the emergence of the reality-based "first-person-singular" storytelling podcast that interweaves intimate personal confession with exploration of factual experience in ways never heard before—or at least never before heard so widely and unconstrainedly.

I take the term "first-person-singular" from deep in radio's history—it was the original title of Orson Welles's spectacular venture into radio in summer 1938, continuing on as *The Mercury Theatre on the Air*. The singular person in question was Welles himself, and it was his mellifluous voice that led the audience through tales from *Dracula* to *The War of the Worlds* and beyond. From the beginnings of broadcasting, the intimacy of the voice, and radio's ability to bring the personal voice directly into each individual ear, had been recognized as a primary characteristic of the medium: one person speaking intimately to another, invisibly across vast distances, with nothing but air in between. For reasons discussed below, it was a capacity kept under tight control on broadcast radio, but it has found its full development in podcasting. From long-standing radio-based shows like *This American Life, StoryCorps,* and *The Moth,* to born-podcasts like *Love and Radio, This Is Actually Happening,* and *Terrible, Thanks for Asking,* to prizewinning documentaries like the Third Coast Audio Festival's 2016 top docs *Mariya* and *A Life Sentence: Victims, Offenders, Justice, and My Mother,* the first-person story told "from the inside," by someone deeply involved in the events, often focusing on subjects highly personal and deeply intimate, has become the signature form of the contemporary podcast. Even those that take on less personal topics, like history or science or sports, tend to involve one or more central narrators through whose unique sensibilities events unfold.

What contributed to this burgeoning sonic exploration of the realities of lived human experience, above and beyond what could be done on radio before? What does it owe to the tradition of the broadcast radio documentary of the past, and what is truly unique about podcasting's contributions? I ask this question almost rhetorically, since the fact is that broadcast radio's rich documentary past has become thoroughly forgotten today. "Telling true stories in sound," as audio producer and scholar John Biewen subtitles his groundbreaking book, *Reality Radio* (Biewen and Dilworth 2017), was baked into radio's fundamental creative and cultural intervention from its very beginnings, and early producers struggled with some of the same issues around sound's unique capabilities as podcast producers do today. Their experiences, successes, and failures have much to contribute to our understanding of podcasting's creativity and modes of expression and its potential impact on today's broader culture.

Yet the radio documentary remains one of the most persistently overlooked forms of broadcasting history, in media scholarship and in popular memory alike. Typically produced "live" in the studio, or transmitted live on location via temporary connections, few were deemed worthy of recording, even fewer have been preserved, and fewer still remain in the collective consciousness of scholars, producers, or audiences— effectively cutting off sound documentary's past from its burgeoning present. Even Norman Corwin, hailed in the 1940s as "radio's poet laureate" for his nationally broadcast radio features—and, not coincidentally, one of the few to have had his work preserved and sold on commercial LPs—had largely faded from cultural memory by the end of the century, until recently revived by a few notable, digitally inspired tributes (Smith and Verma 2016; Ehrlich 2011). Other documentary producers, working less prominently at local, educational, or nonprofit venues, found their work completely buried once network radio gave way to network television, as the power of the visual superseded the medium of sound.

Today's podcasters and broadcasters are feeling their way through the logistics of an incredibly diverse and vital medium with very little consciousness of the history and tradition of their art—as if today's film producers knew nothing of Hollywood's studio era, or as if novelists could read no further back than Hemingway to understand their creative forebears. On top of this, as I argue below, the rise of television documentary in the late 1950s, just as new audio recording technologies began to free radio from its technological limitations, created an emphasis on the truth-telling capacities of visual media that worked to cast their sonic counterpart into the deepest shade.[1]

However, archivists are made of sterner stuff than the general public of any given day, and though the bulk of predigital soundwork may have been forgotten—or in the worst cases, recorded over—it has not been completely destroyed. Many of those working in US public radio during its early years had roots in 1940s and 1950s educational and public affairs documentary production; many of the most important innovators in contemporary broadcast/podcast radio—such as Ira Glass, Davia Nelson and Nikki Silva, and Alan Hall, to name a tiny sliver—come from the public radio tradition. And public broadcasting organizations have been better than commercial ones for partnering with libraries and archival institutions to keep shelves of dusty transcription discs and boxes of unraveling reel-to-reel tapes in existence, even if their cataloging and preservation may have lagged behind more visually accessible media like film and documents.

Thanks to digital preservation and access, we are just beginning to unlock the radio archive, but such efforts also owe thanks to renewed public attention to sound's unique capabilities, demonstrated daily in the podcast universe and, thankfully, preserved and made accessible through projects such as PodcastRE. My purpose in this chapter is to consider what links today's reality-based storytelling podcasts to the way that sound documentary emerged in the pre–magnetic tape era, why it was forgotten as television arrived and radio faded as our national medium, and what is at stake for podcast producers, scholars, and listeners as digital initiatives like PodcastRE begin to overcome our collective audio-historical dead spot.

From Radio Feature to Sound Documentary

From its beginnings, reality-based radio struggled with enormous limitations: from an early lack of portable and editable recording devices, to later banishment to remote corners of the broadcasting schedule, to simple lack of permission to experiment in the days when limited spectrum capacity and large public organizations controlled sonic space. Radio was a public medium, heard "out loud" from sets pouring sounds into rooms, constrained by majority tastes and permissible topics in ways that effectively silenced large segments of lived human experience and all manner of topics deemed too intimate for radio.

Yet the urge to document and explore the world via sound goes back to radio's earliest days. Interviews, talks, discussions, and the occasional live event, such as FDR's "fireside chats," brought reality into yesterday's living rooms, though in stilted and highly controlled forms. To add a little life and action to reality radio, in 1932 the publishers of *Time* magazine introduced *The March of Time*, fifteen minutes of dramatized presentation of the news of the week, in which actors imitated figures in the news with such aural accuracy and compelling studio embellishments that NBC was forced to suspend the show's impersonations of the president and other key government figures for fear of misleading the public: sound could be untrustworthy in a way that the image was not. Norman Corwin's soaring productions like *We Hold These Truths*, reminding Americans of their democratic heritage just a week after Pearl Harbor, and *On a Note of Triumph*, which celebrated the Allied victory over Nazi Germany, both informed and inspired through sonic collages of music, verse, historical reenactment, and direct address to the audience in what Neil Verma calls a "kaleidosonic" evocation of the real (2012)— but this was understood as more "feature" than documentary (a term originated by the BBC to designate such creatively treated hybrids of fact and drama).[2]

In a similar vein, documentary filmmaker Pare Lorentz evoked the reality of Depression-era unemployment in his 1938 audio experiment *Ecce Homo*, broadcast on CBS's *Columbia Workshop* as part of a transatlantic documentary series commissioned by the BBC. Yet how "real" could a studio-bound, poetic style be, with its dependence on dramatic reenactments, manufactured sound effects, and evocative music? How could the actual voices of "real people," in particular those groups largely excluded from speaking on the air, be heard under these conditions?

In Britain, Manchester-based producers Olive Shapley and D. G. Bridson determined to address this issue, going out into northern coal towns and rural villages to interview workers, shopkeepers, and housewives, and then returning to the studio to turn those interviews into scripts performed by actors—as Corwin would later do in his famed *An American in England* series (NBC/BBC 1942). In 1937 Shapley and her crew perilously hauled the BBC's new "Mobile Recording Unit"—a 27-foot van carrying a double turntable apparatus, weighing over 7 tons with a top speed of 20 miles per hour—down twisting roads into coal towns and market villages, capturing the voices of "real people" on discs that could hold only four minutes of recording each. No editing was possible; however, sections could be played through skilled "needle drop" in the studio at appropriate moments in the broadcast (Scannell and Cardiff 1991, 345).

In the United States, two enterprising young producers at New York's city-owned station WNYC, Richard Pack and Nathan Berlin, announced in 1939 "a comparatively new and worthwhile idea in radio—'documentary radio' they call it"—possibly the first time this term appeared in print (Ranson 1939).[3] They planned to use "a mobile-recording unit and the editing and cutting methods of the movies."[4] The following year, the Library of Congress formed its pioneering Radio Research Project, which brought together a crew of talented young men including folklorist Alan Lomax, engineer Jerome Wiesner, playwright Arthur Miller, and two BBC-trained producers, Philip Cohen and Joseph Liss, to do the same across rural America (Gevinson 2002; Hilmes 2012). Their "Regional Series," recorded on location using a film-based editable process, resulted in only one nationally broadcast program—"Rebirth in Barrow's Inlet," written by Joseph Liss, aired on the *Columbia Workshop* in 1942—which was hailed in *Hollywood Quarterly* in 1949 as "one of the greatest documentaries we have ever had on the air." Today, however, it remains almost entirely unknown, a victim of radio documentary's historical erasure from our collective consciousness (Carson 1949).[5]

Then, as World War II broke out, a whole new genre of reality-based but highly dramatized radio feature series began to proliferate across the airwaves, intended to motivate, inform, reassure, and educate, produced by a wide range of government departments and private industries: *This Is War!, The Man behind the Gun, Report to the Nation, This Is Your Enemy,* and many more. Impact and emotion were now more important than preserving the reality of ordinary people's voices and experience; radio returned to the dramatized feature form with a vengeance. Wartime association with bombast and propaganda may be another reason that radio documentary disappeared from memory. Yet wartime radio also inspired the career of Edward R. Murrow, who may have had more influence on the evolution of the sound documentary form in the United States than any other person. Murrow broadcast from the BBC in London, which was hampered by the same technological limitations as other broadcasters. But he had an urgent need to convey the reality of war to listeners back in the States, and his development of what we might call the "first person singular" storytelling style of radio factuality had an enormous impact on what was to come. His vivid, first-person descriptions of wartime experiences, from the strange beauty of a bombing raid seen from a London rooftop to the horror of first entering a Nazi concentration camp, sometimes enhanced by location sound but more often recreated in the studio from memory and notes, gave not only the "facts" but also his own reactions, thoughts, and observations, with an attention to everyday detail and a low-key, intimate style that listeners found immediately compelling.

However, as the war ended and radio was slowly eclipsed by television, Murrow himself, now head of the CBS News division, led a transition away from the first-person intimacy of his earlier work to a less dramatic, more buttoned-down documentary style. This new style was based on location recording, using the new, highly portable and editable magnetic tape technology that would soon come to dominate both radio and TV. It was a style that would "place more emphasis upon the importance of the individual hearing and understanding what is said, rather than over-riding the voice with music or with sound effects of any kind" (Murrow 1947, 380). "Now the real reporter was the tape recorder gathering reality sound, to which narration as needed could be added," writes historian Lawrence Lichty (2004). Even though the postwar years were in some ways the heyday of the broadcast radio documentary, with well-known figures like Corwin and Murrow doing some of their most acclaimed work (Ehrlich 2011), they were also the years when television eclipsed radio. Attention shifted to the development of televisual documentary techniques while radio shifted to music, shunting sound documentaries to the margins of the dial and of public consciousness. As Lichty concludes, writing in the early 2000s, "There are now few stations where documentaries can still be heard" (2004, 474).

Redefining Documentary

However, this was about to change. Throughout the period of fact-based sound's primary transmission by public radio waves, from the 1930s into the 1990s, subjects that transgressed the boundaries of public acceptability by exploring private or marginalized realms of experience remained out of bounds. Beginning in 2004 and rapidly gaining traction, podcasting and online platforms broke open these silences by enabling a new kind of digital intimacy—not only allowing programs to be originated and distributed by a broader spectrum of producers than ever before, often working from personal experience uninhibited by corporate or public concerns, but also making listening choices truly individualized and received as a private experience, often via personal headphones. Intimacy now became not just a style of delivery but both a production and a listening practice. It's worth pointing out, too, that broadcasting's flow and ephemerality did not allow for stopping, starting again, going back to hear that bit, saving it to listen to once more, keeping it in your library—all things that podcasting and digital audio encourage, and all things that lead to the possibility of more complex narratives and deeper listening experiences.

Very quickly the new field of podcasting, alongside broadcast radio's transition to digital platforms, transformed what had been "radio" into an audio universe so rich and diversified it deserves a new word: sound-work.[6] Comprising both traditional broadcast radio, its digital platforms and archives, and original born-podcast work, contemporary soundwork is marked by a form of intimacy that places an emphasis on emotion and affect, often enhanced by music and creative uses of editing and sound effects, through an increasingly sophisticated deployment of what Andrew Bottomley calls a new kind of "poetics of sound" (2016, 311). This applies to fictional as well as documentary forms, leading to a revival of both. But in almost every list of "favorite" or "most popular" podcasts published each year, nonfiction forms dominate, many of them pioneering creative uses of the sonic storytelling tools at their disposal in ways that go beyond what was possible in the predigital era. Bottomley points to *Radiolab*—born on radio but finding its true niche as a podcast—as a leading illustration of the new poetics of sound in the reality genre.

So "sound documentary" has finally come into its own, but, I would argue, in a form that fundamentally disrupts and challenges traditional notions of what the very term "documentary" means, as developed in existing scholarship and critical analysis—most of which focuses on film and other visual media. Just as digital technologies and platforms challenged earlier expressive forms developed on radio, the intimacy of first-person-singular storytelling in sound disrupts the fundamental organizing premise behind the reality claims of both photography and the documentary film: the quasi-scientific authority of the visual image (Winston

1993). The documentary, as a concept and as a form, arose with the birth of image- and sound-capture technologies in the late nineteenth century: photography first, followed by sound recording and motion pictures, devices that were able to "document" reality in ways never before possible. Until the 1930s, documentary sight and sound remained more or less separate, marked by experiments like Robert Flaherty's pioneering *Nanook of the North* on the one hand and roaming "song-catchers" and audio ethnographers on the other, all hampered by the limits of their respective technologies, with little interaction between the two.

It wasn't until the evidentiary authority of the image, enlivened and made even more "real" by pictures that actually moved, met the added reality effect of synchronized sound recording in the 1930s that the term "documentary film" came into widespread use. John Grierson famously hailed documentary as "the creative treatment of actuality" (1933, 8) at a moment when the social and political tumult of the mid-twentieth century spurred the growth of reality-based forms, in both film and radio. Since then, we've had generations of both popular and scholarly attention to the documentary film. Yet even Erik Barnouw, himself a pioneering documentary producer in both audio and visual media, does not apply the term "documentary" to radio in his three-volume history until describing the advent of magnetic tape technology following World War II (1968, 238). This was the breakthrough that finally allowed radio to get out of the studio and reproduce reality directly by recording on location, the way that film had always been able to do, eventually leading to the "clips and commentary" NPR news style so familiar today.

Even more fundamentally, unlike the strong "visible evidence" provided by the image, sound has always had a complex and problematic relationship to reality. Sound is slippery: less definable or describable than the image, evanescent and unfixed, resistant to capture, and subject to "interference" when it comes to transmission of meaning. As sound theorist Michel Chion points out, our most immediate reaction to hearing a sound is to look around for a visual referent or source (1994, 69); take away a visible source and the evidentiary power of sound becomes problematic, its relationship to reality a matter of assertion and context—hence the discomfort surrounding early *March of Time* reenactments. The term "sound documentary" is still not widely recognized, and most books that claim to explore the entire field of "documentary" simply ignore its purely sonic forms, focusing only on the visual. This "slipperiness" even extends to sound documentary's historical persistence; locked away on decaying magnetic tape in the darker corners of archives, rarely revived and rebroadcast as radio drama might be, the tradition of radio documentary in the United States was largely forgotten, its history unwritten, its pioneers rendered as invisible as their medium. For decades, radio documentary slipped into silence.

Today documentary soundwork has reinvented itself in the new digital intimacy of the podcast era, at least in part by returning to the first-person-singular style pioneered by Murrow before the development of recording technology. Substituting the subjective authority of the individual voice for the "objectivity" of the image, exploring realities both public and deeply private through first-person experience, emotion, and human interaction, sound documentary leverages the unique qualities of the human voice to assert its claims to truth and validity, untethered to the visual and thus free to be absorbed on a private, highly subjective basis.[7]

So why worry about radio documentary's past when the present is so vital? Sarah Montague, an award-winning podcast and radio producer and a faculty member at the New School, has recently made a cogent and compelling call for the development of "a poetics of audio . . . a critical language and, with it, a critical culture" to move podcasting from its current status as a "craft" and a "club," shut out from the tradition of critical analysis and appreciation that other media enjoy, to a fully invested form of social and cultural expression (2017). She goes on to say, drawing on *New York Times* arts critic A. O. Scott's recent work *On Criticism*, "We are missing some of the important building blocks of a critical system: models from the past, and what A. O. Scott calls 'a pantheon'—artists about whose excellence there is some general agreement and whose influence can be clearly articulated and traced" (2017). I have made a similar argument in the pages of the *Australian Journalism Review* (2014), and along these lines it is encouraging to see critical efforts like the online journal *RadioDoc Review*, edited by Siobhan McHugh, offering consistently high-level review and criticism of international audio work, often bringing historical and contemporary documentaries into juxtaposition.

Thus, thankfully, we are now at a point when not only the contemporary poetics of sound but its historical roots are being liberated by digital technology through projects like PodcastRE, the Library of Congress's Radio Preservation Task Force, the American Archive of Public Broadcasting, the WNYC digital archives, *RadioDoc Review*, and many others. As this chapter has indicated, there is a rich, largely unexamined trove of historical soundwork out there, increasingly available to researchers, to the public, and to soundwork producers themselves, ready to reveal this long-hidden aspect of the American documentary tradition. Much of value to contemporary media culture is waiting to be discovered as the invisible but intensely, intimately real art of soundwork comes into its own.

Notes

1. Here I should make it clear that I am writing primarily about the American experience. Countries with more robust public service traditions kept the radio documentary alive, though not always with its past prominence. However, archival issues and lack of access to radio's past also inhibited scholarship around the world until the revival of radio studies as a field in the 1990s.

2. The BBC instituted a Features Department in 1936 under the direction of Lawrence Gilliam that persisted until the early 1960s, dedicated to the sonic representation of reality and the places where fact and expressive forms meet.

3. Thanks to Andy Lanset, WNYC archivist, for this reference.

4. Possibly the same one used by the LOC team: the Millertape (sometimes called Philips-Miller) system developed by James A. Miller, a Hollywood sound engineer, that etched sound waves onto coated film that could be optically read and edited.

5. They also released a six-part series called "This Is History!" on transcription discs that were syndicated to individual radio stations. See Gevinson 2002; Hilmes 2009, 131.

6. See Hilmes 2018 for an extended argument for the use of this term.

7. Meantime, the visual documentary has increasingly sought ways to interrogate and disrupt the authority of the visual through participatory and performative techniques that inject the personal experience of the filmmaker into the work, along the lines of Michael Moore and Marlon Riggs: the subjective becomes the marker of a greater form of objectivity than the detached exposition of Ken Burns can provide.

Works Cited

Barnouw, Erik. 1968. *The Golden Web: A History of Broadcasting in the United States*, vol. 2, *1933 to 1953*. New York: Oxford University Press.

Biewen, John, and Alexa Dilworth, eds. 2017. *Reality Radio: Telling True Stories in Sound*. 2nd ed. Chapel Hill: University of North Carolina Press.

Bottomley, Andrew J. 2016. *Internet Radio: A History of a Medium in Transition*. PhD diss., University of Wisconsin–Madison.

Carson, Saul. 1949. "Notes toward an Examination of the Radio Documentary." *Hollywood Quarterly* 4 (1): 69–74.

Chion, Michel. 1994. *Audio-Vision: Sound on Screen*. New York: Columbia University Press.

Ehrlick, Matthew. 2011. *Radio Utopia: Postwar Audio Documentary in the Public Interest*. Urbana: University of Illinois Press.

Gevinson, Alan. 2002. "'What the Neighbors Say:' The Radio Research Project of the Library of Congress. In *Performing Arts: Broadcasting*, edited by Iris Newson, 94–121. Washington, DC: Library of Congress.

Grierson, John. 1933. "The Documentary Producer." *Cinema Quarterly* 2 (1): 7–9.

Hilmes, Michele. 2017. "Sound." In *Keywords for Media Studies*, edited by Laurie Ouelette and Jonathan Gray, 180–81. New York: NYU Press.

Hilmes, Michele. 2015. "The Lost Critical History of Radio," in "Radio Reinvented: The Enduring Appeal of Audio in the Digital Age," special edition of *Australian Journalism Review* 36 (2): 11–22.

Hilmes, Michele. 2012. *Network Nations: A Transnational History of British and American Broadcasting*. New York: Routledge.

Lichty, Lawrence W. 2004. "Documentary Programs on U.S. Radio." In *Encyclopedia of Radio*, edited by Christopher H. Sterling, 474–75. Chicago: Fitzroy Dearborn.

Montague, Sarah. 2017. "Towards a Poetics of Audio: The Importance of Criticism." *The Sarahs*. April 3. http://thesarahawards.com/article/2017/4/3/towards-a-poetics-of-audio-the-importance-of-criticism.

Murrow, Edward R. 1947. "Preparation of the Documentary Broadcast." *Education on the Air 1947*. Institute for Education by Radio. Columbus: Ohio State University Press, 377–90.

Ranson, Jo. 1939. "Radio Dial Log: WNYC Marches On." *Brooklyn Eagle*. January 28.

Scannell, Paddy, and David Cardiff. 1991. *A Social History of British Broadcasting*, vol. 1, *1922–1939*. Oxford: Basil Blackwell.

Scott, A. O. 2017. *Better Living through Criticism: How to Think about Art, Pleasure, Beauty, and Truth*. New York: Penguin Books.

Smith, Jacob, and Neil Verma. 2016. *Anatomy of Sound: Norman Corwin and Media Authorship*. Berkeley: University of California Press.

Verma, Neil. 2012. *Theater of the Mind: Imagination, Aesthetics, and American Radio Drama*. Chicago: University of Chicago Press.

Winston, Brian. 1993. "The Documentary Film as Scientific Inscription." In *Theorizing Documentary*, edited by Michael Renov, 37–57. New York: Routledge.

FOUR | "I'm Trying to Be the Rap Oprah"

Combat Jack and the History of the Loud Speakers Network

SARAH FLORINI AND BRIANA BARNER

"Aye yo, internets!" was a frequent refrain of Reginald Joseph "Reggie" Ossé, better known as Combat Jack, on his podcast *The Combat Jack Show*. It became Ossé's unique way of addressing and connecting with his audience, whether as a greeting at the beginning of the show or to mark other moments of direct address. For example, unlike the advertisements heard on traditional radio, Ossé promoted products like the Bevel shaving system with his characteristic style, "Listen internets, let me tell you why you should fuck with Bevel" (Loud Speakers Network 2017). Between 2010, when *The Combat Jack Show* began, and his death from colon cancer in 2017, Ossé would become a trailblazer in podcasting, bringing his "internets" community along with him.

Ossé left behind a thriving podcast network, the Loud Speakers Network (LSN), and a legacy as a pioneer in podcasting. The Brooklyn-born son of Haitian immigrants, he graduated from Georgetown with a law degree and went on to have a successful career representing producers and artists in the music industry. In 2013, a year prior to *Serial* initiating the current podcast "boom," he partnered with Chris Morrow, a writer and radio producer, to found LSN. With *The Combat Jack Show* as its flagship podcast, by 2017 LSN's predominantly Black lineup of podcasts garnered 1.2 million listeners. Scouting talent from YouTube and Twitter, LSN created the first large and profitable podcast network built by foregrounding Black voices. Known for his carefully researched and in-depth interviews with the innovators, icons, and emerging artists of Hip-hop, Ossé produced an archive containing hundreds of hours of analysis and history of one of the most influential Black American art forms.

Black early adopters and innovators like Ossé are often forgotten as the histories of technology are assembled. The tales of new technologies, their emergence, and their early uses are commonly structured by the myth of Black nonparticipation in technology (Everett 2009, 1–20). However, the people of the African Diaspora have long displayed technophilia, rather than technophobia, and have often been among those at the forefront of new technologies. Because remembering is not a neutral process of recollection but a means of asserting power and legitimizing social relationships, the inclusion or exclusion of Black people in histories of technologies has important implications, as it both emerges from and reproduces notions that conflate technology, innovation, and whiteness and position them in opposition to Blackness.

The process of remembering transforms the past, extending it into the present and reimagining it (Casey 2000, xxii), reconstituting the past in ways that are socially conditioned and rooted in hierarchies of power and identity (Erll 2008, 7). We draw upon the past to construct patterns of self-interpretation that are, in turn, legitimized by the past. Past and present become mutually constitutive as versions of the past come to both reflect and justify the current values, needs, and concerns (Harth 2008, 91). People remember events "in ways that fit already familiar patterns and narrative structures," meaning that assumptions of Black nonparticipation in technology persist because they resonate with existing dominant racial discourses (Rosenberg 2003). This, in turn, perpetuates these beliefs in the present moment.

In cataloging Ossé's work and the rise of LSN, this chapter offers a twofold exploration of Black culture's contingent and contested place in accounts of media history. By performing our own intervention into the history of podcasting, we also detail how memory work was at the center of Ossé's priorities and practices. We briefly recount the origins of *The Combat Jack Show* and the creation of the Loud Speakers Network before explaining how Ossé used his show as oral history and archive for Hip-hop culture. We then conclude by reflecting on the need, and the challenges, for archives and databases like PodcastRE trying to preserve histories and media artifacts beyond those that are typically included in Top 10 charts or press accounts of "golden ages." Ossé's importance as both innovator and vernacular historian demonstrates the necessity for sites like PodcastRE to broaden their collection policies and to prioritize the inclusion of media by Black and other marginalized people that may not be typically credited in the standard histories of media formats. Using reference sites like *Podcasts in Color* (https://podcastsincolor.com) and through recommendations from scholars researching specific and integral podcasts, such as *The Combat Jack Show* or *This Week in Blackness* (Florini 2019), the PodcastRE database, at the time of this writing, has archived episodes from well over 100 Black podcasts, including six years of *The Combat Jack Show*, totaling 224 episodes. While there are certainly more voices to include, and doing so will always be in tension with the identities, positionalities, and whiteness of the lead researchers, we hope arguments such as those we make below show why histories like Ossé's depend on archives and databases that not only collect a wide range of media artifacts but also make them searchable and researchable. Initiatives like PodcastRE should play a role not only in preserving the early history of podcasting but also in aggregating an invaluable historical resource depicting the lived experiences of Black Americans in the early twenty-first century.

The Emergence of Combat Jack

Ossé was a digital pioneer in Hip-hop culture, consistently at the forefront of blogging, internet radio, and eventually podcasting. Following a successful law career in the music industry and serving as an editor for *The Source*, the world's longest-running Hip-hop periodical (Ogunnaike 2003), Ossé stumbled across blog communities while conducting research for his 2006 book, *Bling: The Hip-Hop Jewelry Book*. Hip-hop blogs were in their formative years, and Combat Jack, a pen name drawn from the book *Generation Kill*, was born in 2008, when Ossé began commenting on blogger Byron Crawford's site under the pseudonym. Combat Jack quickly made a name for himself in the Hip-hop blogosphere as someone with obvious insider knowledge of the music industry. Shortly after, Ossé launched his own blog, *The Daily Mathematics* (Cantor 2018). After the success of his blog, he was approached by PNC Radio program director Aaron "A-King" Howard about starting an internet radio show. After initially turning down the opportunity, in 2010 he and cohost Dallas Penn launched *The Combat Jack Show* as an online radio show available streaming and for download on iTunes.

The Combat Jack Show was characterized by the informal conversational style that characterized many other Black podcasts emerging in this period (Florini 2019). Ossé described the early days of the show:

"It was a circle of us talking nonsense. . . . But at the time I don't think there was a space where people of our culture could sit down and talk nonsense. . . . It was one of the few places where I could be as honest as I could be, as funny as I could be, as irreverent as I could be. It wasn't on-air radio. We had no censors; we had no restrictions" (Loud Speakers Network 2017). The show's conversation began to feature a series of regulars in addition to Penn—DJ BenHaMeen, Premium Pete, A-King, and Just Blaze.

Ossé admitted in retrospect that during some of those meandering discussions, the "nonsense" veered into problematic territory, including misogynistic and homophobic statements. For example, the hosts and guests frequently played the "pause" game, in which potentially homo-erotic statements are immediately followed with an emphatic "Pause!" as a means of marking the queerness of the statement and reifying the speaker's own straightness. Thus, when he partnered with Chris Morrow in 2013 to form the Loud Speakers Network, Ossé prioritized selecting and supporting a wider variety of voices and perspectives. Speaking frankly about the tone of the shows on LSN, Ossé positioned the network in opposition to NPR: "When we started *The Read*, we were looking at NPR as the gold standard, and it wasn't being urban. . . . When you hear NPR, everybody's so calm, and everybody's so measured. And it was like, 'Fuck that. We have different voices from our community, from our families, from our culture, that we wanted to promote'" (Loud Speakers Network 2017).

Morrow had a successful career in publishing, coauthoring with Russell Simmons, aka Rev. Run, and Tyrese Gibson, and in radio, working for Premiere Radio Networks. Ossé and Morrow launched the Loud Speakers Network as a way to speak to people who were raised in and have continued to be a part of Hip-hop culture into their thirties, forties, and fifties (Khan 2015). The first shows were *Reality Check with Jas Fly, NY Delight,* and *Sneaker Fiends.* But LSN had its first real hit with *The Read,* hosted by Kid Fury and Crissle, both of whom identify as queer. The following year, they added *The Brilliant Idiots,* hosted by Charlemagne Tha God and comedian Andrew Schulz. LSN recruited heavily from burgeoning Black social media celebrities, particularly Black Twitter. Both Kid Fury and Crissle were fixtures on Black Twitter, as were Freshalina, host of *Neck of the Woods,* and Taxstone, host of *Tax Season.* By 2015 LSN had 1.3 million followers on SoundCloud and its shows were garnering half a million listens a week (Khan 2015). By mid-2017, LSN shows drew a combined one million listens per month. However, despite these impressive numbers, LSN is rarely included in considerations of podcasting's history or cultural impact.

Remembering Ossé's contributions not only recognizes his place as a pioneer of podcasting, resisting the discourse that obscures Black technological innovation; it also mirrors his own prioritization of memory work throughout *The Combat Jack Show*. Ossé, sometimes referred to as a "Hip-hop historian," used his show to chronicle the history of Hip-hop as an art and a culture (Bossip Staff 2017). He not only explored contemporary Hip-hop music and culture, but he also chronicled the lives and music of some of Hip-hop's progenitors and legends.

The Combat Jack Show as Ad Hoc Archive

The Combat Jack Show was often devoted to discussions of Hip-hop music, culture, and history. Ossé's contacts in the music industry and established presence in Hip-hop circles allowed him to book guests ranging from legends to the newest up-and-coming talent. While *The Combat Jack Show* was innovative in its own right, Ossé's detailed and substantive interviews transformed *The Combat Jack Show* into an ad hoc archive of Hip-hop history. For example, he documented the earliest days of Hip-hop in the 1970s in his interview with DJ Kool Herc, one of the originators of the genre (Loud Speakers Network 2015). In "The Eric B. Episode," Ossé elicits detailed and little-known stories from Eric B., who rarely consents to interviews, about Hip-hop in 1980s New York, how he met Rakim, and the creation of their iconic album *Paid in Full* (Loud Speakers Network 2016). Ossé's interviews work to provide an extensive oral history of Hip-hop that might otherwise have been fragmented or lost altogether. Thus, Ossé's podcast stands as a resource with broad cultural implications, given the importance of music in Black cultural memory. The preservation and transmission of Hip-hop history is inextricably linked with broader issues of Black memory, culture, community, and subjectivity, and Ossé, with his professional ties to the music industry, was uniquely well-suited to undertake such work.

Music has historically served as a space for shared culture in Black American communities (Cruz 1999). Portia Maultsby argues, "Music is integral to all aspects of black community life" and, as a participatory group activity, serves to "unite black people into a cohesive group for a common purpose" (1990, 189). Black music has traditionally been a central arena in which Black American communities negotiate and embody group and individual identity (Ramsey 2003, 36).

In Black American communities, music has long played a role in maintaining and reconstructing cultural memory and positioning the contemporary community within that remembering. Samuel Floyd argues that all Black music making is driven by and permeated with the memory of things from the cultural past and that "recognition of the viability of such memory should play a role in the perception and criticism of works and performances of black music" (1995, 10). Cultural memories associated with music often "become standards against which many explore and create highly personal identities for themselves," making creative and innovative uses of the past for present needs (Ramsey 2003, 36). Hip-hop stands as the most recent in the lineage of Black American music, serving these functions for a "new" generation.[1] A large portion, if not the majority, of Black Americans under the age of fifty now identify as part of the "Hip-hop generation" (Rose 2008, 8). In her seminal book, *Black Noise*, Tricia Rose argues, "From the outset, rap music has articulated the pleasures and problems of black urban life in contemporary America" (1994, 2).

Hip-hop is both culturally important and deeply imbricated with memory. A defining characteristic of Hip-hop culture is its strong sense of historical identity. Indexes and intertextual references to the past are key to participation in Hip-hop culture and contexts. Hip-hop's historical consciousness is exemplified by the phrase "back in the day" (Boyd 2003, 88). The widespread use of sampling privileges traditional Black aesthetics that prize reuse, repetition, and recontextualization in the creative process (Rose 1994, 70–75). Imani Perry argues that the practice of sampling actually serves as a "montage of memory" that "creates a deep historical awareness" in Hip-hop culture (2004, 68). By constantly referencing previous forms and genres of Black music, Hip-hop makes memory part of the "musical experience" for Hip-hop listeners (Perry 2004). This relationship between Hip-hop, memory, and Black identities reveals the import of Ossé's preservation efforts and, by proxy, underscores the importance of preserving these efforts.

Motivated in part by his distaste for Hip-hop journalism that reads as if the writer has been "on safari," Ossé prepared for each interview with the explicit goal of uncovering new stories and information (*CJR* editors 2017). His attention to detail and dedication to extensive research for each interview is a nod to his careful construction of this archive and the importance he placed on Hip-hop history. Many of his guests were artists he already knew, including former clients from his time in the music industry, allowing Ossé to elicit personal and unguarded accounts. He noted, "We had the same type of conversations twenty years ago that we're having now. These private, real, intimate conversations where they're trusting me with either their business or the issues with regard to their lives—personal stories that they never told anyone" (*CJR* editors 2017). Okayplayer, one of the oldest and most popular Hip-hop websites, characterized Ossé's writing and interviewing style as "telling significant stories, taking audiophiles behind-the-scenes of their favorite rap stars in a way that was like Charlie Rose" (*CJR* editors 2017). Ossé's close ties with many of his guests and his place within the industry allowed the episodes to feel more like a close conversation with a friend, likely allowing him to obtain responses from the guests that many other journalists would not have been able to.

In addition to providing opportunities for a range of Black voices to enter podcasting, by creating a rich archive of Hip-hop culture and history, Ossé also inspired others to do the same. In addition to LSN shows, Ossé encouraged others to pursue podcasting as a venue for their thoughts and experiences. For example, he encouraged Mouse Jones, host of the LSN podcast *The Clubhouse with Mouse Jones,* as well as journalists Touré and Jamilah Lemieux to pursue podcasting. Hip-hop personality and former host of *Yo MTV Raps,* Ed Lover spoke of how Ossé encouraged him to use the medium to record his experiences saying, "Ed, you need to do this because your stories of your 30 years in Hip-hop are golden. You can talk Tupac, you can talk Biggie, you can talk Puff, you can talk N.O.R.E., you can talk *Yo MTV Raps.* You have experiences that nobody else can talk about" (Loud Speakers Network 2017).

By 2017 Ossé began chronicling Hip-hop history and culture using long-form serial storytelling. LSN entered into a collaborative project with Gimlet, another podcast company known for their journalistic storytelling, to recount the life and tragic death of music executive Chris Lighty in the podcast *Mogul: The Life and Death of Chris Lighty.* Lighty, a poor kid from the Bronx, became a Hip-hop legend by transforming himself into a talent agent who represented some of Hip-hop's top stars, including A Tribe Called Quest, LL Cool J, Missy Elliott, and Busta Rhymes. He went on to found Violator Management and Violator Records. But in 2012 he was found dead in his home of an apparent suicide. Featuring his signature meticulously researched in-depth interviewing, each episode delved into Lighty's story, building a case for Lighty as an important figure whose story should be known and preserved and solidifying Lighty in Hip-hop history. *Mogul* was the first serial narrative podcast to focus on Hip-hop, and, as a successful collaboration with Gimlet, the series brought the Hip-hop history to a broader audience (Carmichael 2017).

"He did it for the culture": The Legacy of Combat Jack

Ossé's influence as both history maker and historian is palpable. His passing sparked an outpouring of grief and gratitude on Twitter, with Hip-hop legends, podcasters, and fans invoking words like "legend," "icon," and "pioneer." The tributes highlighted his role as a podcast innovator and ad hoc archivist in equal measure. Despite his influence, his contributions rarely appear in the historical narrative of podcasting, which most commonly focuses on the innovations of predominantly white male tech developers and media personalities. This failure to acknowledge the importance of Ossé's work not only reinforces the erasure of Black technological innovation but also obscures and diminishes the robust repository of Black cultural memory carefully preserved by his efforts. By eliding Ossé and LSN, accounts of podcasting's history reinforce the myth of Black nonparticipation in technology, a belief that both structures Ossé's absence from podcast history and is, in turn, perpetuated by his erasure.

Further, Ossé's absence from the historical account of podcasting's first decade highlights the crucial need for digital archivists and media historians to actively seek out content produced by marginalized groups. Without deliberate intervention—prioritizing the inclusion of underrepresented voices and *seeking out* those voices—media histories will perpetuate the familiar narrative that obscures the contributions of those like Ossé. Such exclusions doubly impoverish the field. The recognition of Ossé as an innovator increases the likelihood that his work—which is itself an archival project—will be preserved; his erasure all but assures the histories he recorded will someday succumb to the ephemerality that claims so much online content. Given that marginalized people are often forced to use alternative means for recording their past, creating ad hoc archives like the Hip-hop history of *The Combat Jack Show*, there is a dual archival imperative.

In addition to *The Combat Jack Show*, PodcastRE has preserved a number of LSN's other podcasts—including *The Read*, *Tax Season*, *Neck of the Woods*, *For All Nerds*, *The Friend Zone*, and *FanBros*—with the archive containing between two and six years' worth of episodes for each. Moreover, PodcastRE also contains hundreds of episodes from Black podcasting pioneers such as *This Week in Blackness, Insanity Check* (now the *Movie Trailer Review Network*), *The Black Guy Who Tips,* and *Where's My 40 Acres?*, all of which began podcasting concurrently with Ossé, and thus provides thousands of hours of content (and more hours added each day).

Preservation projects like PodcastRE are vital resources for media historians and also serve as vast cultural reservoirs. Digital technologies have lowered the barrier for media content creation, and disempowered groups now have unprecedented opportunities to create their own media and tell their own stories. By ensuring a wide range of podcasts are preserved and available, PodcastRE is not only a resource for scholars but it can also lend permanence to the ad hoc memory practices of marginalized groups.

Notes

1. We use the term "new" here quite loosely, since participants in hip-hop music and culture at the time of its emergence in the 1970s are now in their fifties.

Works Cited

Bossip Staff. 2017. "Reggie Ossé AKA Combat Jack Passes after Battling Colon Cancer." *Bossip.* December 20. https://bossip.com/1609957/r-i-p-to-our-de ar-brother-reggie-combat-jack-osse-43081/.

Boyd, Todd. 2003. *The New H.N.I.C.: The Death of Civil Rights and the Reign of Hip Hop.* New York: New York University Press.

Cantor, Paul. 2018. "The Story of Combat Jack, Hip-Hop's Flagship Podcaster." *Vulture.* Last updated February 14, 2018. https://www.vulture.com/2018/02 /the-story-of-combat-jack-hip-hops-flagship-podcaster.html.

Carmichael, Rodney. 2017. "'Mogul': Even in Death, Chris Lighty Takes Hip-Hop to Another Level." *National Public Radio.* May 2. https://www.npr.org/sectio ns/therecord/2017/05/02/526080329/mogul-even-in-death-chris-lighty-tak es-hip-hop-to-another-level.

Casey, Edward. 2000. *Remembering: A Phenomenological Study,* 2nd ed. Bloomington: Indiana University Press.

CJR editors. 2017. "Q&A: Reggie Ossé on Becoming an Accidental Interviewer." *Columbia Journalism Review.* July 25. https://www.cjr.org/special_report/qa -reggie-osse-on-becoming-an-accidental-interviewer.php/.

Cruz, John. 1999. *Culture at the Margins: The Black Spiritual and the Rise of American Cultural Interpretation.* Princeton, NJ: Princeton University Press.

Erll, Astrid. 2008. "Cultural Memory Studies: An Introduction." In *Cultural Memory Studies Reader: An International and Interdisciplinary Handbook,* edited by Astrid Erll and Ansgar Nügging, 1–18. New York: Walter de Gruyter.

Everett, Anna. 2009. *Digital Diaspora: A Race for Cyberspace.* Albany: State University of New York Press.

Florini, Sarah. 2019. *Beyond Hashtags: Racial Politics and Black Digital Networks.* New York: NYU Press.

Floyd, Samuel, Jr. 1995. *The Power of Black Music: Interpreting Its History from Africa to the United States.* New York: Oxford University Press.

Harth, Dietrich. 2008. "The Invention of Cultural Memory." In *Cultural Memory Studies Reader: An International and Interdisciplinary Handbook,* edited by Astrid Erll and Ansgar Nügging, 85–96. New York: Walter de Gruyter.

Khan, Azeem. 2015. "Loud Speakers Network Is Making Noise." *Huffington Post.* April 27. https://www.huffpost.com/entry/loud-speakers-network-is_b_713 9020.

Loud Speakers Network. 2015. "The Kool Herc Episode." *The Combat Jack Show.* April 7. Podcast audio. https://podcastre.org/episode?id=ep186466.

Loud Speakers Network. 2016. "The Eric B. Episode." *The Combat Jack Show.* March 15. Podcast audio. https://podcastre.org/episode?id=ep186419.

Loud Speakers Network. 2017. Loud Speakers Network. "The LSN Podcast Panel Live from A3C feat. Ed Lover, Angela Rye, Combat Jack, and Premium Pete." *The Combat Jack Show.* Hosted by Tai Saint-Louis. Podcast audio. http://louds peakersnetwork.com/show/the-lsn-podcast-panel-live-from-a3c-feat-ed-lover -angela-rye-combat-jack-premium-pete/.

Maultsby, Portia. 1990. "Africanisms in African-American Music." In *Africanisms in American Culture,* edited by Joseph Holloway, 156–76. Bloomington: Indiana University Press.

Ogunnaike, Lola. 2003. "War of the Words at Hip-Hop Magazines." *New York Times.* January 29. https://www.nytimes.com/2003/01/29/arts/war-of-the -words-at-hip-hop-magazines.html.

Perry, Imani. 2004. *Prophets of the Hood: Politics and Poetics in Hip Hop.* Durham, NC: Duke University Press.

Ramsey, Guthrie P., Jr. 2003. *Race Music: Black Cultures from Bebop to Hip-Hop.* Los Angeles: University of California Press.

Rose, Tricia. 1994. *Black Noise: Rap Music and Black Culture in Contemporary America.* Hanover, NH: University Press of New England.

Rose, Tricia. 2008. *Hip Hop Wars: What We Talk about When We Talk about Hip Hop and Why It Matters.* New York: Basic Books.

Rosenberg, Emily S. 2003. *A Date Which Will Live: Pearl Harbor in American Memory.* Durham, NC: Duke University Press.

Wilson, Janday. 2014. "So What Do You Do, Reggie Ossé, Host of *The Combat Jack Show?"* *Adweek.* October 6. https://www.adweek.com/digital/so-what-do-you -do-reggie-osse-host-of-the-combat-jack-show/.

FIVE | Howling into a Megaphone

Archiving the History of Podcast Advertising

JJ BERSCH

On the ninth episode of *StartUp*, host and Gimlet Media cofounder and CEO, Alex Blumberg, details an early mistake made by his podcast network's program *Reply All* that "plunge[d] the young company into the center of an internet controversy" (Gimlet 2014). That series' premiere episode included an advertisement for Squarespace that centered on an interview with a charming nine-year-old boy named Riley who had used the service to build a website dedicated to his burgeoning fandom of the video game *Minecraft*. Though the advertisement appears rather innocuous on the surface, Blumberg states that the problem stemmed primarily from disclosure: neither Riley nor his mother, Linda, had been told that the interview, conducted by Blumberg himself, would be used in a promotion. In fact, a misleading email had actually led the family to believe that Riley would be featured on the long-running public radio program *This American Life*, for which Blumberg previously worked as a producer, and Linda shared this news on various social media platforms (Sharps 2014). Once she found out that the interview was used as an advertisement on *Reply All*, she was, as Blumberg puts it, "understandably quite upset" (Blumberg 2014). Blumberg and his team claim that the misunderstanding helped them "learn the importance of owning mistakes and establishing systems and guidelines in a new company," but I argue that the confusion also points toward larger issues of podcast advertising than disclosure recommendations (Gimlet 2014).

While the unclear email produced uncertainty over the interview's ultimate utilization, the advertisement, like others of its kind, carried many other potentially perplexing elements. Though conventional advertising is often cordoned off from media texts in terms of both placement and personnel—distinctly serving as paratexts to the entertainment program's text, to borrow Jonathan Gray's conceptualization—podcast advertising frequently functions on a level of textual murkiness (2010, 6). First, most paratexts (posters, trailers, merchandise, fan-generated mashups, etc.) are housed outside of the text, but podcasts are typically downloaded with advertisements conjoined to the program, and even the most benign advertisements may develop close and lasting relationships with their programs as a result. Second, Gray writes that many "paratexts fall under a company's marketing and promotions budget, meaning that the show's creators may have little or nothing to do with their creation, thereby producing ample opportunity for creative disconnects, and for uninspired paratexts that do little to situate either themselves or the viewer in the storyworld"; podcast advertisements, on the other hand, are regularly produced by the creators of the shows themselves (207). Third, because of the involvement of programs' creative personnel, podcast advertisements can achieve a high degree of textual integration, with advertisements matching their podcasts in tone and even content. In the case of the *Reply All* advertisement, the promotion for an internet service was produced for a program about the internet by the creators of the program, following an interview structure that would fit seamlessly into the program itself. Surely Linda was not the first or last person to confuse a podcast advertisement for a podcast.

Advertisements like the one discussed above have proliferated throughout the podcast industry since, well, almost since there has *been* a podcast industry. Accordingly, this chapter looks at the emergence and growth of advertising in the podcast industry and argues that it offers us a window not only into the rise of a new format (i.e., podcasting) but also into the challenges that come along with attempts to preserve and document this format's history. If we accept Jonathan Sterne et al.'s suggestion that podcasting moved from nascent practice to defined audio medium somewhere around 2005, then the industry established its primary means of advertising that very same year (Sterne et al. 2008). When Podtrac launched one of the first podcast advertising sales systems in 2005, its press release already contained the two types of promotions that would come to define podcast advertisements: produced-spot advertisements and host-read advertisements (*Business Wire* 2005). The former offered advertisers the chance to package traditional audio advertisements themselves, while the latter handed at least partial control over to podcast creators. As Cynthia Meyers asserts, "When hosts do the ads, advertisers are assuming there's a parasocial relationship between the host and the listener," so promotions that attempted to capitalize on such bonds soon became the financial backbone of the industry (quoted in Locke 2017).

But, as evidenced by Gimlet's missteps, such advertisements have potential for crossing unspoken boundaries between host, audience, and advertiser. Confusion may arise over the provenance of the promotion, but as these advertisements have become more and more commonplace, with a similar lineup of advertisers repeating across various series from various networks, Meyers notes that "a tension about the sincerity of an endorsement" has also arisen. As she writes, "The danger of integrating ads is that the audience gets cynical, and stops believing it" (quoted in Locke 2017). The thinking here goes that the more people you hear give personal testimony that Blue Apron delivers delicious prepackaged meals, the less likely you are to believe them, because how could all of these people love Blue Apron so much? (Aside from being paid by Blue Apron to say such things, of course.) Additionally, by giving creative control over to hosts, podcast advertisements can venture far off-script (as is the case with AudioBoom's *Blank Check with Griffin and David*) or even become antagonistic (as witnessed particularly in comedy podcasts such as Earwolf's *Hollywood Handbook* and *Spontaneanation*).

Despite such concerns, podcast advertising has proven to be lucrative. By *Serial*'s release in 2014, podcast advertising had become an essential part of the industry landscape, with that popular show eventually receiving between $25 and $40 CPM (the cost of reaching a thousand listeners) for its ads (Perlberg 2014), greatly outearning YouTube's reported average CPM of between $2 and $17 at the time (Green 2015). Though well-known advertisers such as Geico, T-Mobile, and Home Depot might still primarily call traditional radio home, these podcast CPMs are about "two to three times what it costs to advertise on terrestrial radio," according to Joe Pinsker writing in *The Atlantic* (2015). While such payouts are obviously not an embedded feature of the industry at large, major networks such as Panoply, a sister company of *Slate*, have recently abandoned "content" altogether to focus exclusively on targeted marketing (and, in Panoply's case, they have done so in conjunction with established advertising forces like Nielsen) (Quah 2018). While many of the podcast industry's financial and spectatorial statistics are obscured by those who control them, one thing has become clear: there is, at the very least, great moneymaking potential in podcast advertising.

Yet, in recent years, significant players in the podcast industry have also attempted to shift away from existing financial models, mirroring a similar move that occurred in 1940s radio. As both Michele Hilmes and Alexander Russo point out, radio advertising of the 1930s centered on the alluring powers of the host's voice (Hilmes 2012, 357–60), but industrial restructuring, content concerns, and a general sense of staleness resulted in major shifts in advertising strategies in the 1940s, primarily toward what we now consider to be conventional methods of advertising such as prepackaged, company-created spots (Russo 2010, 117–37). With Panoply's exit from content creation and the advertising anxieties outlined by Meyers, the rapidly maturing podcast medium is entering a new era of economic experimentation that carries with it a series of new industrial, cultural, and historiographic questions.

In this chapter, then, I want to consider two of the podcast industry's attempts to alter or move on from the advertising model that has dominated the medium's first decade-plus of existence—Panoply's Megaphone advertising service and Stitcher Premium's subscription model. What interests me most about these two innovations is how they alter our understanding of the history of podcasting and raise questions as to how podcast networks, other corporate entities, independent podcasters, and academics should aim to archive podcasts. Podcast advertisements have been an especially privileged paratext, but both of these innovations unsettle the advertisement's prominent placement in the podcast text. As corporate entities like Stitcher Premium begin to place old episodes behind paywalls and academic archives, such as the one that gives this book its namesake, aim to freely preserve podcasts and their accompanying metadata for researchers, the history of podcasts, as recent as it may be, has begun to prove valuable for both business and academic purposes. I argue that podcast advertising should be an integral component of the archived podcast if future historians wish to truly understand the workings of the podcast text, industry, and audience in its first "golden age," outlining potential avenues of scholarship by raising questions from the perspectives of both the archivist and the researcher.

The Ever-Evolving Podcast Promotion

Dynamic advertising has long been a goal of the podcast industry. In 2005 a company named Podbridge aimed first to strengthen podcast advertising analytics by developing a plug-in that allowed producers and advertisers to track how many times a podcast had been downloaded and listened to—though this worked only if the consumer had actually downloaded the plug-in, a cumbersome step that could potentially seem unnecessary or even unwelcome to the average user (Cubrilovic 2006). Once users had downloaded the plug-in, they were greeted with a demographics questionnaire, the answers to which would lead to consumers receiving more narrowly targeted advertisements, but the technology allowed for even more radical ad insertion: "Podbridge's intelligent client-based system enables different types of content, such as entertainment and advertising, to be individually targeted, distributed and assembled directly on the consumer's device. Ads can be dynamically inserted into content and rotated for time-sensitive promotions" (*Wireless News* 2006). While the company failed to realize the potential of this idea—as did other, similar services such as Kiptronic (*Venture Beat* 2007)—the idea was fundamentally sound: though streaming broadcasts were at low risk of time-shifted listening, downloaded podcasts that may be accessed well after their initial distribution certainly were not, meaning that a revolving set of targeted advertisements could theoretically provide podcast creators with a more stable and long-running source of revenue.

A decade later, Panoply Media, former home of podcast series from *Slate, BuzzFeed, MTV, Vanity Fair*, and the *Wall Street Journal* as well as popular independent series such as *Revisionist History* and *You Must Remember This*, fulfilled the promise of this idea. Following their acquisition of Podbridge/Kiptronic successor Audiometric in 2015 (*Slate* 2015), the podcast network introduced an advertising service/technology called Megaphone in January 2016, described as follows in an *Ad Age* story: "[Megaphone] allows for one-click insertion of ads into podcasts, geotargeting of ads to specific podcast consumers, and A/B testing to see what's working best. Its dynamic ad insertion capabilities also let podcast publishers place new ads in back episodes, a potentially remunerative capability for podcast publishers that have extensive archives. . . . This technology ensures that people will get the latest and most appropriate ad for them" (Barr 2016). This form of advertisement insertion and replacement proved so popular that the company shifted away from the production of podcasts to focus on metrics and advertising exclusively, culminating in a name change to "Megaphone" in March 2019 (Megaphone 2019).

The type of advertisement being replaced varies by podcast. In many cases, these dynamic advertisements are produced-spot advertisements provided by the sponsoring companies. These advertisements privilege a certain set of sounds focused on engendering semantic listening—a mode of listening that "refers to a code or a language to interpret a message" (Chion 2012, 50)—the most obvious being a change in speakers. They make obvious use of what Devon Powers calls "sonic branding"—that is, the "use of sound to enhance brand awareness, appeal, and cohesion" (2010, 293). She writes that "music's aural elements make it more than simply another commodity; instead, music holds unique sensory qualities that are consumed by the ear, implicating the physical sense of hearing as well the social act of listening" (286). While podcast advertisements in general make use of sonic branding (many of NPR's programs, for instance, feature consistent music in the background of each host-read advertisement, as is the case with the upbeat, whistle-heavy tune of *Pop Culture Happy Hour*), sonic branding as used in produced-spot advertisements typically focuses that power on the brand of the product being sold instead of the podcast. Their ready-made reproducibility and textual changes, then, seem to signal a shift in podcast advertising toward something resembling the television model and its accompanying reruns; in other words, these ads, with their supposed interchangeability and clear demarcation outside of the "main text," support traditional conceptions of advertisements as paratexts, with the original advertisement bearing few textual implications to the podcast text beyond financial support.[1]

In 2015, however, a survey of the top 100 podcasts on the iTunes chart showed that there was only one ad agency–produced radio spot with voice-over and music in 186 surveyed ads (Alcorn 2015). In fact, many of the industry's biggest advertising companies, like Midroll Media and Podcast One, pride themselves on avoiding such ads, with the former claiming that 95 percent of the promotions featured on its podcasts are host-read (Locke 2017). Podcasts that use Megaphone, therefore, also have reason to continue using host-read advertisements, for both sustaining engagement and maintaining industry standards.

Still, both Megaphone and the precedent it sets carry weighty implications for academics and audience members. Though the podcast *Serial* does not use Megaphone, it offers a perfect example of this. Listeners who tuned into that podcast's inaugural season likely remember an iconic advertisement featuring a woman offering a unique pronunciation of sponsor MailChimp (Koenig 2014). The advertisement became an important (and even beloved) part of the listening experience, playing major roles in discussion surrounding the podcast, as evidenced by its prominent placement in something like *Funny or Die*'s parody of the program ("Gotta be honest, this child murder has been really great for Mail Kimp," says the video's fake MailChimp exec [*Funny or Die* 2014]) or *Quartz*'s claim that "MailChimp's irresistible *Serial* ad" was "the year's biggest marketing win" (Epstein 2014). In its current iteration (as of September 26, 2018), however, that advertisement has been replaced by a reminder that the show has two sister programs (*This American Life* and *S-Town*, the latter of which did not exist when *Serial* premiered) in the first episode (Koenig 2018a) and by an advertisement for Squarespace (which was previously an advertisement for security service ADT as recently as April 2018) in the third episode (Koenig 2018b). And Jeremy Morris notes that these changes were occurring as early as August 2016 (less than two years after the program's premiere), with his version swapping the MailChimp advertisement for Rocket Mortgage, a service from the multibillion-dollar company Quicken Loans (Morris 2018).

Already, then, we have an erasure of history: *Serial* was something of an unexpected success, as evidenced by its exclusive partnership with small internet startup MailChimp during its first season. Both replacement spots contextualize the podcast much differently: the first places *Serial* in the middle of a major podcast universe, while the second aligns the series with two much more established sponsors. Gone, too, is the infamous pronunciation of MailChimp that led to widespread discussion, parodies, and remixes on social media. The ramifications of this specific change seem so obvious now because both the MailChimp advertisement and *Serial* were quick sensations, with over 31 million downloads in the podcast's first three months of availability (Kantrowitz 2014). Yet these sorts of changes are rapidly proliferating throughout the podcast universe, without much fanfare or way of tracking them.

The insertion of dynamic ads, then, presents challenges for the podcast scholar. Without any requirement for podcasts to declare when advertisements (or other elements of the show's content) have been altered, the idea of the "singular true podcast text" dissipates. Dynamic advertisements obscure the economic history of the industry (MailChimp's sponsorship provides a much different view of the financial prospects of a program like *Serial* than the more-established ADT's sponsorship), the aesthetic history of the medium's advertisements, and even a small but significant part of programs' cultural import. Yet instead of conceiving of dynamic advertising as exclusively a loss for scholars, the practice also opens up new avenues for research. If archivists (both professional and ad hoc) preserve each of the various iterations of a podcast, a new and perhaps more interesting picture of the podcast industry starts to take shape. *Serial*'s first episode, rather than simply being a product of and catalyst for a soon-to-be booming young industry, actually *tells* that story through its transformative evolution, moving from a program with modest financial prospects to a program with a successful spin-off and revolving cast of successful sponsors. This chain of advertisements also reveals novel aesthetic comparisons—how, for instance, does the cacophonous soundscape of the MailChimp advertisement vary from the more straightforward reading of the Squarespace advertisement, and what might that tell us about podcast advertising style and podcast style? Dynamic advertisements, though potentially obfuscating, may actually unlock new pathways toward understanding the economics of the industry, the aesthetics of the medium's advertisements, and, yes, the programs' cultural import. In order to do so, however, the various versions of the podcasts must be preserved in the first place.

The Complications of Making a Podcast "Ad-Free"

In addition to altering advertisements, another strategy of moving beyond the existing revenue streams of the podcast industry is to abandon advertising in favor of subscription-based models. Perhaps the most prominent subscription podcast service is Midroll Media and the E.W. Scripps Company's Stitcher Premium (both of which are discussed in this book's audio interview with former Midroll CEO Adam Sachs). An outgrowth of the free Stitcher application, one of the most popular alternatives to Apple's dominant podcast app, Stitcher Premium (itself an outgrowth of earlier subscription program/app Howl.fm) offers a number of bonus incentives for users willing to pay $4.99 a month: initially exclusive podcast series like Marvel's *Wolverine: The Long Night* and *The Andy Daly Podcast Pilot Project*, exclusive podcast episodes from series like *WTF with Marc Maron* and *Beautiful Anonymous*, and exclusive access to a vast archive of episodes no longer available on other services, with most of these episodes having been made ad-free.

When comedy podcast network Earwolf (a partner of Midroll Media as well as another subsidiary of E. W. Scripps) first announced its decision to include its podcasts in this archive, community reaction was mixed. Beyond the obvious resistance to paying for previously free content, the decision to remove ads proved controversial. Evidenced by various forum threads, a significant portion of fans of shows such as *Hollywood Handbook* and *Spontaneanation* consider advertisements to be integral and enjoyable elements of their favorite programs. As user Trash

Boat writes, "Those babies are premium content in and of themselves!" (Shannon 2016).

On these shows, the hosts venture far from typical advertising copy and achieve near-total tonal integration. This is perhaps best evidenced by the aforementioned *Hollywood Handbook*, an Earwolf show purporting to be "a beginner's guide to kicking butt and dropping names on the red-carpet-lined back hallways of this industry we call showbiz." As critic Nathan Rabin notes, "Hollywood Handbook is among the most conceptual of Earwolf podcasts" (2015). Hosted by comedy writers Hayes Davenport and Sean Clements, the show began as a tongue-in-cheek response to advice podcasts and media industry coverage but has slowly evolved (or devolved) into a manic takedown of Hollywood, the internet, comedy podcasting, and podcasting in general. The show routinely features complicated arcs that require knowledge not just of the show itself but also of other podcasts.[2] All of this is filtered through what Rabin describes as "multiple levels of irony and Brechtian detachment," resulting in a podcast that is initially (or perhaps consistently) difficult to tonally align oneself with, while the often obscure knowledge required for understanding the podcast's frequent references similarly raises the bar of entry (2017). Since it features one of the most active podcast communities on the official Earwolf forums—commenters frequently try to "out-reference" each other or land a mention in audience-oriented bits like the Q&A segment "The Popcorn Gallery"—*Hollywood Handbook* is rife with Pierre Bourdieu's concept of "embodied cultural capital" (knowledge consciously gained over time that serves functional social purposes) albeit in a very rarified realm (1986, 247).

This targeted, engaged audience in turn makes *Hollywood Handbook* attractive to advertisers, while the tonal tenor of the program would, theoretically, do quite the opposite; it is this seemingly paradoxical integration that makes the program a fascinating case study for how podcast advertising functions. When the show finally gained a large enough listening base to merit sponsorship privileges from parent company Midroll, the advertisements were highly combative, with Davenport fruitlessly attempting to read the copy provided by the sponsors while Clements pitched his own version of the product in competition. Recurrent podcast sponsors such as Loot Crate and Cards Against Humanity cycled through Clements's brain, becoming demented replicants of the products named Sergeant Sean's Loot Crate and Cards Against Dummies. In spots for loan provider Privio, Clements plays a character named "Verbatim Vic," a man with a rough accent who consistently breaks from the required copy to ask if he can put his own spin on the advertisement, directly acknowledging the antagonistic, offbeat relationship the show has with its advertisers.

The advertisements expectedly boil over into the main program rather frequently, further complicating the process of removing advertisements from the program. The February 7, 2017, Julie Klausner episode, for instance, features an extended riff about sponsor Shari's Berries outside of the conventional ad spot and in the flow of normal conversation, with Davenport telling advertisers to "listen to the whole show. Do not just listen to the ads. We are talking about your product within the show." Clements responds, "We're not doing the ads in the ads. That's the part people skip cuz they know they're ads. We do the ads in the middle of the show because they think it's the show" (Clements and Davenport 2017). While these bits of irony and antagonism seem to contradict how a marketer would typically want their product presented, they also showcase a seamless integration of advertising into the show's sardonic sense of humor. And as Paul Grainge notes, "For audiences literate in the appeals and subversions of brand commerce, product placement has become commonplace but also potentially risible, leading to critical reading protocols more readily based on parody, irony and scepticism [*sic*]," with advertisements resultantly becoming increasingly reflexive (2008, 36–37). Midroll appears to strongly back this approach. In a post that claims that "comedy is hot for brands" and "podcasts are where the comedy is," the company uses a "completely off-the-rails ad for party game Cards Against Humanity" from *Hollywood Handbook* as one of only two examples of successful comedic salesmanship (Riismandel 2014). Tonal integration is the goal of Midroll's advertisements; as a result, *Hollywood Handbook*'s sarcastic advertisements are attractive to advertisers (even, apparently, at their most antagonistic) but also important to audiences, serving as genuine extensions of the program.

Clements and Davenport, however, do not only integrate their program's tone into their advertisements; they also often use their advertisements to develop narratives across multiple ads (as is the case with their long-running "Santa Man & Moriarity" advertisements for Harry's Razors) and even for the main program. The most blatant instance of this occurred on Earwolf's flagship podcast, *Comedy Bang! Bang!* A multi-episode 2015 arc featured Clements and Davenport "auditioning" to be on the main program through ad reads. Stretched across a month and a half, the plotline eased listeners into the duo's occasionally alienating style of comedy. Each advertisement typically started with Scott Aukerman introducing his fellow Earwolf hosts before beginning a conventional ad read, only to be interrupted by Clements or Davenport failing to understand the product being sold, derailing the advertisement in the manner consistently employed on their own podcast. When the two finally made their first guest appearances outside of the advertisements, many references were made to the duo's earlier line of auditions, a plotline that would have been unrecognizable to anyone who had used the podcast's signaling sounds to skip over the advertisements or, later, listened to the ad-free versions of earlier episodes. The advertisements, in this case, established a multi-episode plotline that culminated in a full hour-and-a-half-long episode more than a month later, meaning that podcast advertisements do not only carry the potential to extend the tone of their programs—they also may be necessary for fully understanding portions of the programs themselves. In fact, I argue that if one truly wants to understand the comedic podcast landscape specifically, podcast advertising would be an essential topic of research for its tonal and narrational integration, extension of reflexive comedic practices in other forms of advertising, and as a way for long-form improv and stand-up to discover new methods of consistent financial security.

While dynamic advertising may unlock new but challenging avenues of scholarship, then, ad-free podcast subscription models present simpler but more potentially detrimental obstacles. By removing advertisements entirely, especially those that are read and *created* by the hosts, from earlier programs, ad-free subscription-based models erase part of the creative work done by the personnel whose programs these companies are further monetizing. In addition to the concerns I outlined in the previous section, in special cases this does render some programs less intelligible. While podcast advertising companies have routinely sold their advertising space as a chance for companies to create something truly special, memorable, and creative with podcast hosts, Stitcher's treatment of advertisements in its premium service indicates nearly the opposite. If future scholars, researchers, and listeners wish to fully understand the industrial, economic, and textual dimensions of podcasting in its golden age, advertisements will be a critical component of that picture. Their preservation, then, is essential.

Potential Preservation and Paths Forward

I begin my conclusion with a personal story about the precarity of podcast preservation as it relates to two of the extended examples found in this chapter. When I conducted my initial research on the advertising in *Hollywood Handbook*, I was able to access paywalled episodes thanks to what is most accurately described as a mistake. Although I rarely use my computer to listen to podcasts (I primarily use my phone), for some reason I had subscribed to the program on my laptop and unknowingly downloaded the entire ad-filled archive of the series, allowing me to access each of the episodes detailed in this chapter. Future research on the program's advertisements will likely be easier (though costlier). Thanks to overwhelming fan demand, *Hollywood Handbook*'s archive of episodes has appeared on two separate feeds on Stitcher Premium since March 2018: one with the ads removed, and one with the advertisements intact (Bartelt 2018). However, I was much less lucky with regard to Clements's and Davenport's appearances on *Comedy Bang! Bang!* I was only able to access these advertisements thanks to a fan of the programs uploading a compilation of them to SoundCloud. Without such happenstance preservation, the advertisements would not have been accessible to me, rendering their scholarly merit invisible and my scholarly inquiry untenable.

Archives such as PodcastRE are already ensuring that this historiographic problem is less likely in the future by maintaining their own copies of podcast episodes, but the history of podcasting (especially the history that has been altered by subscription services and dynamic advertising) will likely have to rely on coincidental archiving. One easy step forward is for podcast scholars and independent researchers to be forthright about what sort of personal podcast archives they have and what sort of variations might be found when those collections are compared to the versions of episodes found in other collections. If scholars want to analyze what financial support allowed the podcast industry to take shape, where that money came from, what sort of labor allowed the industry to take shape, what sort of power sponsors held over programs, how advertising influenced aesthetics and storytelling, or any other number of questions, they will benefit greatly from having the podcast advertisements made available. Nothing necessitated podcasting choosing the form of advertising it did—or even advertising in general—as its primary revenue model. However, it did choose that form and used it for well over a decade. Podcast advertising merits serious inquiry. As actual and ad hoc archivists, let us ensure that we can actually make those inquiries.

Notes

1. Though it must be noted that even the most banal advertisement may develop a strong association with the podcast on which it is heard.

2. For example, one recent arc featured the following complex timeline. On September 1, 2016, cohost Hayes Davenport made a guest appearance on comedian Jon Gabrus's *High and Mighty* podcast to discuss newspaper comics, a distinct change of pace from that podcast's typical exploration of vice and gluttony. On January 17, 2017, *Hollywood Handbook*'s weekly episode consisted entirely of direct reference to this four-and-a-half-month-old episode. With Clements sending Davenport out of the studio on an unending series of errands, he and guest Joe Wengert attempt to replicate the "grand success" of Davenport's *High and Mighty* appearance, as the fact that it was "still doing crazy numbers" made Clements jealous of the "success" of his comedic partner. In the next week's episode, Gabrus joins Clements in the studio, but Gabrus regretfully informs the hosts that Wengert has transformed into the "Wendigabrus," a Godzilla-like caricature of all of Gabrus's most outlandish comedic tics, and Davenport dutifully serves as an on-the-ground reporter of all of Wengert's destructive activities.

Works Cited

Alcorn, Stan. 2015. "But First, a Word from 100 Podcasts' Sponsors." *FiveThirtyEight*. May 1. https://fivethirtyeight.com/features/but-first-a-word-from-100-podcast-sponsors/.

Barr, Jeremy. 2016. "Podcast Network Panoply Introduces New Ad Platform." *Ad Age*. January 21. http://adage.com/article/media/podcast-network-panoply-unveils-advertising-platform/302242/.

Bartelt, Kevin. 2018. Twitter post. March 29, 2:29 PM. https://twitter.com/KevinJBartelt/status/979440327063990274.

Blumberg, Alex. 2014. "Gimlet 9: We Made a Mistake." *StartUp*. Podcast audio. December 9. https://www.gimletmedia.com/startup/9-we-made-a-mistake.

Bourdieu, Pierre. 1986. "The Forms of Capital." In *Handbook of Theory and Research for the Sociology of Education*, edited by John G. Richardson, 241–58. Westport, CT: Greenwood.

Business Wire. 2005. "Podtrac Launches First Advertising Infrastructure and Sales Service for the Podcasting Market." *Business Wire*. November 11.

Chion, Michel. 2012. "The Three Listening Modes." In *The Sound Studies Reader*, edited by Jonathan Sterne, 48–53. Oxon: Routledge.

Clements, Sean, and Hayes Davenport. 2017. "Julie Klausner, Our Close Friend Once Again." *Hollywood Handbook*. Podcast audio. February 7. http://www.earwolf.com/episode/julie-klausner-our-close-friend-once-again/.

Cubrilovic, Nik. 2006. "Podbridge Delivers Simple Targeted Podcast Advertising." *TechCrunch*. March 11. https://techcrunch.com/2006/03/11/podbridge-delivers-simple-targetted-podcast-advertising/.

Epstein, Adam. 2014. "How MailChimp's Irresistible 'Serial' Ad Became the Year's Biggest Marketing Win." *Quartz*. November 18. https://qz.com/2980

94/how-mailchimps-irresistible-serial-ad-became-the-years-biggest-marketing
-win/.

Funny or Die. 2014. "The Final Episode of Serial." YouTube. December 18.
https://www.youtube.com/watch?v=gww53yFfMnI.

Grainge, Paul. 2008. *Branding Hollywood: Selling Entertainment in a Global Media
Age.* New York: Routledge.

Gray, Jonathan. 2010. *Show Sold Separately: Promos, Spoilers, and Other Media Paratexts.* New York: NYU Press.

Green, Hank. 2015. "The $1,000 CPM." *Medium.* April 5. https://medium.com
/@hankgreen/the-1-000-cpm-f92717506a4b.

Hilmes, Michele. 2012. "Radio and the Imagined Community." In *The Sound Studies Reader,* edited by Jonathan Sterne, 351–62. Oxford: Routledge.

Kantrowitz, Alex. 2014. "Inside the Business of the 'Serial' Podcast." *Ad Age.*
December 18. https://adage.com/article/media/inside-business-serial/296
270/.

Koenig, Sarah. 2014. "The Alibi." *Serial.* Podcast audio. October 3, 2014.

Koenig, Sarah. 2018a. "The Alibi." *Serial.* Podcast audio. Accessed September 26,
2018.

Koenig, Sarah. 2018b. "Leakin Park." *Serial.* Podcast audio. Accessed September
26, 2018.

Locke, Charley. 2017. "The Tricky Art of Podcast Ads Is About to Get Even Trick-
ier." *Wired.* February 28, 2017. https://www.wired.com/2017/02/podcasts
-new-ad-crisis/.

Megaphone. 2019. "Panoply Media Rebrands as Megaphone." March 5. https://
megaphone.fm/press/panoply-media-rebrands-as-megaphone.

Morris, Jeremy Wade. 2018. "Saving New Sounds: Podcasts and Preservation." *Flow.*
February 26. https://www.flowjournal.org/2018/02/saving-new-sounds/.

Perlberg, Steven. 2014. "On Marketers' Radar: Podcasts—'Serial,' a Popular Program, Gives an Advertiser Direct Access to Large Fan Base." *Wall Street Journal.* November 7. B-6.

Pinsker, Joe. 2015. "Why So Many Podcasts Are Brought to You by Squarespace."
The Atlantic. May 12. https://www.theatlantic.com/business/archive/2015
/05/why-so-many-podcasts-are-brought-to-you-by-squarespace/392840/.

Powers, Devon. 2010. "Strange Powers: The Branded Sensorium and the Intrigue
of Musical Sound." In *Blowing Up the Brand: Critical Perspectives on Promotional
Culture,* edited by Melissa Aronczyk and Devon Powers, 285–306. New York:
Peter Lang Publishing.

Quah, Nicholas. 2018. "Breaking: Shake-ups at Panoply and Slate." *Hot Pod.* September 12. https://hotpodnews.com/breaking-shake-ups-at-panoply-and-sl
ate/.

Rabin, Nathan. 2015. "Tom Scharpling & 'Hollywood Handbook' Made Anti-
Comedy for the Ages." *Vulture.* November 2. https://www.vulture.com/20
15/11/tom-scharpling-hollywood-handbook-made-anti-comedy-for-the-ages
.html.

Rabin, Nathan. 2017. "The 'High and Mighty'/'Hollywood Handbook'/Joe
Wengert Trilogy Is Three Episodes of Sublime Post-Modern Silliness." *Vulture.* February 13. https://www.vulture.com/2017/02/the-high-and-mightyh

ollywood-handbookjoe-wengert-trilogy-is-three-episodes-of-sublime-post-mo dern-silliness.html.

Riismandel, Paul. 2014. "Comedy Is Hot for Brands, Podcasts Are Where the Comedy Is." Midroll Media. October 20. http://www.midroll.com/comedy -hot-brands-podcasts-comedy/.

Russo, Alexander. 2010. *Points on the Dial.* Durham, NC: Duke University Press.

Shannon. 2016. "Announcement Re: Howl & Earwolf Ad-Free Archives (Please Read)." *Earwolf Forums.* May 23. http://forum.earwolf.com/topic/34575-an nouncement-re-howl-earwolf-ad-free-archives-please-read/.

Sharps, Linda. 2014. "Confusion, Podcasts, Kerfuffle, All's Well That Ends Well." *All & Sundry.* December 9. http://www.sundrymourning.com/2014/12/09 /confusion-podcasts-kerfuffle-alls-well-that-ends-well/.

Slate. 2015. "Panoply Acquires Ad Management, CMS Technology for Podcast- ers." *Slate.* August 11. http://www.slate.com/articles/briefing/slate_press_re leases/2015/12/panoply_acquires_audiometric_ad_management_and_cms _technology.html.

Sterne, Jonathan, Jeremy Wade Morris, Michael Brendan Baker, and Ariana Moscote Freire. 2008. "The Politics of Podcasting." *Fibreculture Journal* 13. http://thirteen.fibreculturejournal.org/fcj-087-the-politics-of-podcasting/.

Venture Beat. 2007. "Kiptronic Raises $4M for Podcast Ad-Insertion, a Better Pod- bridge?" *Venture Beat.* January 22. https://venturebeat.com/2007/01/22/kip tronic-raises-4m-for-podcast-ad-insertion-a-better-podbridge/

Wireless News. 2006. "Podbridge Gets U.S. Patent for Technology That Enables Dynamic Management of Advertising in Time-Shifted Media." *Wireless News.* July 28. https://www.proquest.com/wire-feeds/ podbridge-gets-u-s-patent-technology-that-enables/docview/209915905/ se-2.

Analyzing Podcasting's Now

SIX | Podcasting the Donald Sterling Scandal

The Prismatic Perspective of the PodcastRE Database

JACOB MERTENS

> We don't have to talk about how much the NBA is like the old South
> because, in theory, this is black athletes signing up for and being
> paid well to work for white people. Very superficially, it's all on the
> up-and-up. Yet you're never not aware of who's in charge.
>
> —Wesley Morris, "The Owner and the Owned: A Discussion about
>   Donald Sterling," *Grantland*

On April 25, 2014, TMZ released a secret audio recording in which Los
Angeles Clippers owner Donald Sterling made a series of racist comments to his then-girlfriend, V. Stiviano. In this recording, Sterling criticized Stiviano for bringing Black men—most notably Magic Johnson—to
Clippers games and posting pictures with them on her Instagram profile:

> You can sleep with them. You can bring them in, you can do whatever
> you want. The little I ask is you not to promote it on [Instagram] and
> not to bring them to my games. (TMZ Sports 2014)

The sports blog *Deadspin* released an extended version of the tape two
days later, in which Stiviano brought up Sterling's ownership of the Clippers as a point of racial hypocrisy. Sterling responded, "I support them
and give them food, and clothes, and houses. Who gives it to them? Does
someone else give it to them? . . . Do I make the game, or do they make
the game?" (Wagner 2014). These releases coincided with a promising

playoff run for the team, sparking an immediate scandal and deeper conversations about how racism remained prevalent, though often hidden or ignored, in the NBA. Moreover, the unavoidable fact of a near-uniformly white ownership of a predominantly Black sports league, along with Sterling's evocation of *making* the game of basketball through his ownership and economic control, forced both sports journalists and outside observers to question the integrity of the game against the backdrop of systemic racial discrimination that is still alive and well throughout America.

Amid a media frenzy that was further fueled by the NBA's decision to ban Donald Sterling from the league and force a sale of his team, podcasting offered fertile ground for a wide array of responses. The common theme of scandal then tied these different perspectives and professional obligations together, creating a larger dialogue that engendered a host of added meanings beyond the moral judgment of Sterling's actions. By looking at this emotionally charged case study through the prismatic perspective of the PodcastRE database, I examine here what makes broadcasting unique in the modern age when so many individuals can add their voices to a public forum. I use the Donald Sterling scandal as a flash point for podcasting discourse, noting how the conversation changes based on the distinction between professional and amateur productions and the subject matter of a podcast series. In the process, I demonstrate how these production contexts and economic imperatives can lead to discussions that either individualize the scandal, interrogate the systemic racial issues beneath it, or even use the scandal as an entry point into an altogether different discussion. Finally, I outline how the database works as a tool to make this chaotic discourse legible as a case study.

I believe that studying this discourse can provide a more nuanced understanding of how we as a society publicly address issues of race and the reasons why we might shy away from these conversations or frame them as the aberrant actions of an individual rather than a product of systemic racism. The database can help us see how such a racially charged scandal can pervade into the broader field of popular culture and influence productions that may reference Sterling tangentially rather than address the scandal in depth. Meanwhile, studying these concerns through the PodcastRE database not only provides us with different perspectives and interpretations but also gives us their meaningful contrast. Ultimately, I both demonstrate how podcasting provides opportunities for political discussion beyond the hegemony of traditional broadcasting and analyze how a scandal travels within a broader podcasting discourse, while still observing how often these conversations defer to the corporate interests of the NBA.

Constructing a Discourse through the PodcastRE Database

Several critics have speculated about the political potential of podcasting and its ability to challenge gatekeeping distribution trends. However, the sheer volume of podcast productions creates a challenge for framing these conversations as a cohesive discourse. As Virginia Madsen states, "In the wake of podcasting, what we can frequently hear is an almost delirious abundance of voices in the crowd, a type of glossolalia with many of these unable to extend themselves efficiently, or find a resonance sufficient to make themselves heard beyond their own small niche communities" (2009, 1200). Similarly, Richard Berry notes that podcasting offers "a classic 'horizontal' media form," as "the means to create are as accessible as the means to consume" (2006, 146). These expanding, "horizontal" options for media production are not unique to podcasting either, as Web 2.0 technologies have created an increasingly diffused media landscape. As Henry Jenkins and his colleagues have observed, "Contemporary culture is becoming more participatory, especially compared with earlier media ecologies primarily reliant on traditional mass media. However, not everyone is allowed to participate . . . and not everyone who participates does so on equal terms" (2013, 298). With this distinction in mind, podcasting prompts us to consider what happens to all these newfound voices joining in on a conversation. How do we study a digital dialogue that allows so many to participate with relative ease? What voices do we privilege in that discourse, and what voices fall by the wayside through a lack of exposure and listening audience? And how do we account for the digital impermanence of podcasting, in which a series can be altered after the fact or disappear altogether after years of domain hosting? Greater access to technology and broadcasting capabilities does not guarantee that old hierarchies of distribution simply go away, as podcasts often rely on larger corporate platforms to find audiences and advertisement structures to fund their productions. And although podcasting at large has undeniably led to a diversity of content and voices, there are still troubling ways in which we make sense of these conversations by privileging corporate podcast productions.

Even if we seek to disrupt the typical hierarchy of distribution and engage with a more complex array of voices participating in podcasting, many obstacles remain for pooling these productions together and attempting to find legible through-lines. Private enterprises like Apple Podcasts and Stitcher maintain a dominant role in podcast distribution and offer imperfect and economically driven platforms for podcasting backlogs. Meanwhile, lesser-known podcasts may host their own productions online and discontinue them when a series ends. Like many forms of internet publishing, podcasting overwhelmingly privileges the current moment and devalues past discussions. As a result, podcasts made as recently as a few years ago already face a real threat of vanishing from the public record. With that said, PodcastRE provides an important tool for preserving podcasting's abundance and capturing a wide diversity of content, ensuring that scholars can analyze a discourse that emphasizes the medium's horizontal characteristics and look for meaningful connections and contrasts.

I was interested in how discussions coalesce around ideas of scandal and controversy and how these issues unify seemingly disparate genres and production contexts. With the Donald Sterling scandal, I purposefully chose a case study that had a complicated tension between corporate and personal investment, and I wanted to observe the ways a broadcaster's position within the discourse informed how they framed their contribution. I was also interested in how each new discussion in the discourse could either nuance or simplify political and moral issues depending on the overall objective of a podcast series. In S. Elizabeth Bird's analysis of media scandals and audience discourse, she writes, "Scandal stories, like other stories, bring changing mores into sharp focus through media narratives and the popular discussion that takes off from those narratives. . . . Media scandals help set the agenda for discussion, but they do not exist as some definable text separate from the wider cultural conversation" (2003, 44). She also notes how often scandals thrive precisely because of the audience's difficulty to resolve their moral and cultural significance. I believe podcast production complicates the effort to resolve scandal even further, as the medium's horizontal nature blurs the lines between producers and consumers of media narratives, creating a discourse in which amateur podcasters work not only to respond to the story but also to produce counter-narratives.

In order to look at this discourse in more depth, I used the PodcastRE database to gather a diverse sample of podcast episodes. I searched for the term "Donald Sterling" both with and without quotation marks and gathered podcast episodes that mentioned Sterling in either the episode's description or metadata. The Sterling scandal happened in the same year that the PodcastRE database began preserving podcasts, and my search yielded a sample size of roughly twenty-eight podcast series (table 6.1). Working from this sample, I used close textual analysis by listening to each episode in its entirety, noting patterns for how different podcast series incorporated the scandal into their discussion, and, finally, I isolated episodes that I thought would meaningfully build off of each other. I then structured my analysis based on two contrasts:

- First, I compared whether a podcast had professional obligations to the NBA—focusing predominantly on podcasts affiliated with ESPN—or could speak more freely on the scandal.
- Second, I compared whether a podcast addressed the scandal directly or indirectly based on the subject of the podcast series.

There are other groupings that could support intriguing discourse analysis, such as whether a podcast was produced in the immediate aftermath of a scandal or far removed from it, or even whether a podcast takes on a monologue format, a one-on-one interview, or a looser conversation with multiple guests and/or multiple hosts. However, I offer these two approaches as an initial effort to take a broad range of voices and find compelling commonalities and points of divergence between them.

Table 6.1. Podcasts retrieved through PodcastRE when searching for "Donald Sterling"

Professional Podcasts Directly Discussing Scandal	Amateur Podcasts Directly Discussing Scandal	Podcasts Indirectly Discussing Scandal
Real Talk with Jason Whitlock	*S. Anthony Says . . .*	*Brunch & Budget*
The B.S. Report	*Clock Radio Speakers*	*The Smartest Man in the World*
The Woj Pod	*The Dr. Vibe Show*	*Inquiring Minds*
Around the Horn	*BadCulture*	*Hollywood Handbook*
SVP & Russillo	*Black Girls Talking*	*Sklarbro Country*
The Moment with Brian Koppelman	*Yo, Is This Racist?*	*Ari Shaffir's Skeptic Tank*
Open Floor	*The Shiznit! Show*	*Neck of the Woods*
The J.J. Redick Podcast	*Inappropriate Earl*	*18 to 49 with Alaia Williams*
Roland Martin Reports Daily Podcast	*Two Guys One Show*	
Slate's Hang Up and Listen	*Yeah I Said It!*	

Listening to these podcasts, I was struck by how often podcast hosts struggled to integrate the scandal within an existing frame of reference for their series. In the case of NBA-affiliated podcasts, I believe there was a need to negotiate the raw feelings about the scandal with an economic imperative to protect the NBA as a larger brand. At the same time, many amateur productions could dig into the implications of the scandal in more detail but had to spend a great deal of energy positioning their takes on the story in opposition to the dominant discourse. Finally, the scandal also found its way into podcasts that had little to do with sports or cultural commentary and instead worked as a framing device for the larger themes of that series. Each podcast episode brought a different perspective and approach to the scandal, creating a far more complicated response than we would find in a traditional broadcast structure. But more importantly, these conversations still felt tied to each other in critical ways, as we learned more from their contradistinction than we would by listening to any one take on the story.

Notes on a Scandal: Looking at Podcasting's Professional and Amateur Divide

After news broke on the Donald Sterling scandal, a stark divide formed between professional podcasts that addressed the story as part of a larger obligation toward the NBA and amateur podcasts that analyzed the story solely as racial commentary. In the case of ESPN-funded podcast series, discussions often fell into a pattern of individualizing the controversy. On *Real Talk with Jason Whitlock*, the episode focuses on an interview Donald Sterling gave with Anderson Cooper and addresses whether Sterling's on-air apology seemed sincere and should gain him some reprieve (Whitlock 2014). Host Jason Whitlock and guest Bomani Jones also question how a known racist, with a record of discriminating against Black and Latinx communities in his real estate holdings,[1] could thrive so easily in the NBA but curiously shift culpability to Clippers coach Doc Rivers. The two claim Rivers knew of Sterling's reputation and feigned shock only after the scandal. By placing the charge of hypocrisy on another individual, they can then seemingly exempt the rest of the league through omission.

Similarly, *The B.S. Report* offers an interesting case since host Bill Simmons worked as a sportswriter and podcaster for ESPN but also gained a degree of autonomy from ESPN when he founded the sports website *Grantland*—a site still owned by ESPN but operated by Simmons himself. And yet we see the same pattern emerge when his guest, columnist Chuck

Klosterman, comments that Sterling's use of a slave plantation metaphor of ownership was "strange" and Simmons quickly replies, "Yeah . . . He's a crazy person." This individualization and dismissal of Sterling as "crazy" prevents the discussion from addressing how Sterling's comments reveal a potentially troubling reality about the relationship between owners and players in the NBA and particularly how owners may perceive that relationship (Simmons 2014).[2] Overall, while these episodes still discuss important observations about the scandal, their overwhelming emphasis on Sterling himself implies that when commissioner Adam Silver bans Sterling from the league, he also roots out the sole blight on the NBA's reputation.

The ESPN podcasts that worked as audio versions of TV broadcast commentary likewise navigated the controversy during the weeks that followed TMZ's initial release but often faced limitations based on the shortened format and segmentation of a particular show.[3] In *Around the Horn*, commentators hurriedly unpack the NBA's lifetime ban of Sterling but have only enough time to give a few sound bites due to the show's fast-paced design. Not surprisingly, even when commentators suggest how the scandal ties to larger issues on race in the NBA, they undercut their point by returning to place the blame squarely on Sterling's shoulders. For example, Pablo Torre comments:

> The one criticism I have would be that somehow acknowledging and addressing and embracing the criticism of the totality of Donald Sterling's past would have maybe mollified owners who are afraid of something like a private conversation coming out because there's so much more to weigh with Donald Sterling. (2014)

Here, Torre references how NBA owners hesitated to outright condemn Sterling in the wake of this controversy. Dallas Mavericks owner Mark Cuban even went on record to say he was uncomfortable with kicking Sterling out of the league and called it a "slippery slope" (MacMahon 2014). I argue that when Torre mentions fearful league owners, he touches on a larger issue of owners wanting to maintain a status quo and protect their own interests, which could open up a discussion about how a known racist remained in the NBA for decades without dispute. However, there is no real room to address this larger conversation, so Torre instead makes a truncated point about Sterling's racism as if it had no connection to the NBA and its history of privileging Sterling's financial ownership over concerns of his racist history.

While ESPN-affiliated podcasts consistently framed the Sterling scandal as some variation on the adage "one bad apple spoils the bunch," their approach also shaped how amateur podcasts addressed the story as a point of opposition. For these smaller productions, a pattern emerged in which hosts took great pains to contradict the idea that Sterling was an aberration in the NBA—not to mention the larger institution of professional sports. In the comedy and social commentary podcast *S. Anthony Says . . .*, host S. Anthony Thomas opens his episode by stating that "everyone's getting caught up on the wrong things" and addresses the larger discourse around Sterling by saying, "Save me your outrage; your outrage is too late" (Thomas 2014). As the episode progresses, the host largely frames the scandal as evidence of a larger systemic problem in the NBA and even tries to decenter Sterling from the implications of the story:

> Let's take Donald Sterling's racist ass and slide him to the side a little bit. And realize that his racism towards black people and other ethnic groups is just a symptom of what happens when certain people in power . . . when they think of you as less than them. (2014)

Likewise, *The Dr. Vibe Show* hosted a forum on the issue with Black authors and activists, one of whom wearily responds that his first reaction to the story was "Here we go again. Here is another example of bigotry and hatred against Black men, and you're making millions off the sweat equity of Black men." Another guest then muses, "How many of the other owners have said stuff; how many people in the NBA have the same feeling? We've had this in our culture for too long" (*The Dr. Vibe Show* 2014). In these podcasts, the speakers then encourage their audience to think of the Donald Sterling scandal not as a media narrative to be consumed in isolation but as part of a continuum of structural racism in our society.

These podcasts also encouraged wide-ranging conversations that could examine less obvious or highlighted cultural dimensions of the scandal. On the podcast *Black Girls Talking*, the hosts chose to focus on V. Stiviano and what they considered to be "rampant misogyny" involved with her characterization within the discourse. In one exchange, a host decries that "people seem to have been more concerned with this woman being a so-called 'gold digger' than they were about this piece of shit racist and the things he said," to which her cohost immediately replies, "Yeah, there were a lot of Black men on Twitter surprisingly up in arms, like 'she ruined his life!'" (*Black Girls Talking* 2014). Additionally, *Clock Radio Speakers* chose to call out advertisers threatening to pull their support from NBA playoff broadcasts as empty lip service, a kind of gesture that companies make only when the scandal presents a large enough threat to their image (*Clock Radio Speakers* 2014). Throughout these podcasts, hosts then enjoyed a freedom of being able to address whatever concerns stood out to them but typically did so in an effort to fill in the gaps left by a mainstream discourse and make broader claims about the short-sighted perspective and false outrage often involved with these scandals.

Podcasting on the Periphery of the Donald Sterling Scandal

The divide between professional and amateur podcasts commenting on the scandal offers a compelling case for how these conversations unfold. In going through PodcastRE's results, however, I found many other episodes that used the scandal in ways that seemed disconnected from the details of the actual controversy. Instead, they used the scandal either as a quick launching-off point for a show's comedic structure or as a frame of reference for a completely different subject matter. In these cases, the scandal offered hosts a means to an end rather than an end in itself and could even allow producers to attract new listeners by showcasing the controversy. In fact, in some particularly opportunistic cases, podcasts included Sterling's photo as the thumbnail for an episode, featured the controversy in the episode's headline and general description, and then did not discuss the controversy in any meaningful detail. (Note: the example below of *Inquiring Minds* was initially one such case of using Sterling's photo, though the episode has now defaulted to its broader series thumbnail.) But despite a relative disinterest in participating in the scandal's discourse, these productions offer some fascinating insights into how scandals travel within such a broad and far-reaching mode of production and could even lead to salient insights or persuade audiences to make intriguing parallels.

On one hand, comedy podcasts like *The Smartest Man on Earth* and *Hollywood Handbook* turned the Sterling scandal into joke fodder and worked it into the larger context of series routines. In Greg Proops's *Smartest Man on Earth*, the comedian rails against the overwhelming whiteness of NBA ownership while constantly losing his place amid his diatribe to request that the bartenders keep plying him with vodka (Proops 2014). Likewise, the *Handbook* hosts use the scandal within a larger comedic bit about their lofty status as Hollywood insiders, jokingly distancing themselves from Sterling while admitting that they keep their "planes in the same plane house" and that Sterling was the best man at Sean Clements's wedding—only because Sean's brother died, which was "unplanned" (Clements and Davenport 2014). However, even though the hosts constantly digress from the larger implications of the story, their humor often engages with satire that can broach uncomfortable truths about the scandal, particularly involving notions of white privilege.

In comparison, other podcasts used the scandal as a way of framing a discussion for their series and did little to engage with the story itself beyond its ability to provide their episode with a sense of relevance and immediacy. In one case, the scientific podcast *Inquiring Minds* references the Sterling scandal to contextualize an interview with social neuroscientist David Amodio about "the science of prejudice," and though the episode's description spends half of its word count addressing the Sterling scandal, the episode itself uses Sterling's story only to briefly set up an interview about Amodio's research (Viskontas and Hari 2014). In this case, the series takes advantage of the affective draw of the scandal but addresses it in merely a tangential way. Still, we might question what this framing does for listeners who know of the Sterling scandal and come to the podcast interested in a different take on it. After all, the discussion itself deals primarily with implicit bias and "whether we all have a little bit of racism in us" and could offer its audience a more introspective consideration on their consumption of this particular narrative.

Finally, the podcast *Brunch and Budget* used the news story of how Sterling was forced to sell his team and leave the NBA in order to set up a larger discussion about the financial concept of return on investment (ROI). This was only the seventh episode of the series and showcased a strained tension between the hosts wanting to address the scandal and wanting to make a podcast about "financial responsibility." As a result, the hosts spend the first ten minutes of an hour-long episode discussing the scandal itself before moving on to the concept of ROIs in complete isolation from their earlier conversation. Nevertheless, the episode does briefly suggest some compelling commentary before it moves on from the subject entirely; one host mentions the irony of Sterling's girlfriend being Black and the other replies, "Well, I didn't want to get into the whole racism type thing but that sounds remarkably consistent for a racist." He then quickly hedges his comments by worrying that "we're not being very PC" (*Brunch and Budget* 2014). However, in a short aside for an episode that had little to actually do with the Sterling scandal itself and apparently did not want to "get into" racism,[4] the hosts point to one of the common misconceptions about racist discourse that many podcasts discussing the scandal failed to address—specifically, the idea that someone cannot be racist if they are sexually attracted to that race, which fails to acknowledge the degree to which power and control can influence attraction. This example thus offers an intriguing insight into how podcasts use the Sterling scandal to help animate a particular subject like financial advice but still have to deal with the racial baggage of that scandal in potentially unanticipated ways.

Conclusion

Scandals have power precisely because they catch on like wildfire, capturing the public's imagination in some pressing way. As I have argued above, scandals do not exist in a vacuum, and as they travel amid different media productions, they bend and change and become encumbered by how producers choose to use them. Even so, I believe there remains something unruly and unpredictable about how the larger discourse on a scandal takes shape, especially given the abundance of perspectives featured in modern podcasting. Naturally, the ways I have delimited that abundance to find patterns amid a diffused mode of production offer just one of any number of interpretations for this diverse commentary. However, even in this short analysis I believe there are several significant contrasts to draw on.

By looking at ESPN podcasts, I believe we can observe a general hesitance for commentators to dig too deeply into what the scandal might say about the NBA beyond condemning Sterling as an individual. This is not to say there were not ESPN commentators who pushed this line, and certainly the *Grantland* article quoted at the opening of this chapter offers just one of the important exceptions within ESPN's larger output. Still, when we listen to amateur podcast hosts defiantly push back against a mainstream narrative on the scandal and call for their audience to look beyond Donald Sterling's individual case, the disparity with ESPN's general approach feels palpable. The comparison between professional and amateur podcast productions also suggests an interdependence, as podcasts set at the fringe of corporate sports reporting must react to an abiding individualization of systemic racial injustice, knowing that their audience is likewise surrounded by these kinds of narratives.

We might consider this response within the context of what Catherine Squires calls a "counterpublic strategy" wherein marginalized communities can "test the reactions of wider publics by stating previously hidden opinions, launching persuasive campaigns to change the minds of dominant publics, or seeking solidarity with other marginal groups" (2002, 460). Podcasting creates an ideal platform for this kind of disruption due to its horizontal nature and the juxtaposition between professional and amateur podcasts on many hosting platforms. In order to fully appreciate what these productions are opposing, though, it helps to take both sides of the discourse into consideration, which PodcastRE's database can work to historically reconstruct.

Although I did not use a temporal comparison as part of my analysis, it is worth pointing out that my search only showed amateur podcasts responding to this controversy contemporaneously, either days or weeks separated from the events in question, while ESPN podcasts occasionally brought up Donald Sterling months and years after the fact, usually as a historical footnote and curiosity.[5] We could then consider the ways this case study might also illustrate how podcasting helps communities work through their feelings of racial injustice in the moment, such as Sarah Florini's (2017) excellent exploration of podcasting as communal response to George Zimmerman's acquittal for the murder of Trayvon Martin. In that case, podcasts like *S. Anthony Says . . .* or *Clock Radio Speakers* can use their position within Black communities to push back against a hegemonic commentary that would seem omnipresent in sports news reporting.

Over the course of writing this book chapter, ESPN's *30 for 30* podcast series also released a five-part study of the Sterling scandal in 2019. At a glance, this production could suggest that the passage of time makes it easier for ESPN to discuss the scandal's fallout, now that NBA's brand has safely emerged from this historical moment unscathed. After listening to this series, though, I would argue the episodes largely work from a post-racist perspective in which host Ramona Shelburne admits to racial tensions in the league but presents them as largely resolved. Outside of written lines like "Los Angeles lives on two fault lines—the San Andreas and race," the larger narrative of the series is far more interested in detailing Donald Sterling's history and his aberrant behavior (Shelburne 2019a). To be fair, a later episode does address more structural concerns with racism in the NBA when discussing labor agreements, but in this case they still present the matter as largely resolved through the player empowerment movement and the growing power of the National Basketball Players Association (Shelburne 2019b). Even so, an in-depth study on Sterling offered to audiences more than five years after the scandal took place suggests, if nothing else, an enduring fascination with this moment in the league's history.

Finally, the larger collection of episodes from the PodcastRE database can point us to podcast series that use this scandal in tangential ways and repurpose its media narrative. I believe this discovery highlights one of the benefits of using a database as a research tool, because it can forge connections between conversations in ways we may not have otherwise examined. We could even consider podcasts themselves as an underutilized resource in broader research paradigms, as these files can often be omitted from academic databases and platforms that privilege keyword searches. However, the PodcastRE database benefits from the fact that podcast episodes often have a wealth of metadata that can broaden associations through search queries and lead to surprising results. In the case of the Sterling scandal, I believe finding these podcasts that used the controversy for reasons beyond straightforward commentary opens up intriguing complications for our ways of thinking about media narratives. While constructing a dialogue between hegemonic and oppositional readings of the scandal remains important to consider, it would be a mistake to reduce podcasting discourse to a simple binary that leaves out less obvious ways that productions could touch on these issues. Ultimately, the broader range of podcasts in the PodcastRE database can nuance our understanding of how a scandal travels and how we interrogate its meaning, especially because even when the story is used as a framing device, it cannot help but carry the weight of its racial implications.

Notes

1. This information was well known and Sterling was even sued for housing discrimination by the US Department of Justice in 2006. Beyond outlier ESPN columnists Jemele Hill and Bomani Jones calling for Sterling's censure, this troubling history gained little traction in the news organization (Jones 2008, Hill 2009). Jones sums up the situation well in his own article for ESPN's now defunct *Page* 2, which features the header "Donald Sterling's Racism Should Be News."

2. Simmons's choice feels even stranger when you consider the comparison with Wesley Morris and Rembert Browne's published conversation about the racial implications of NBA ownership, quoted at the beginning of this chapter and featured on the same website that hosted *The B.S. Report*. In fact, Simmons plugs that article at the start of his podcast but does not engage with its content.

3. At the time of the Donald Sterling scandal, this overlap was becoming an increasing trend for ESPN with their most popular sports commentary TV shows. At present, most ESPN podcasts remain either "ESPN originals" or are part of ESPN's larger radio network but their website does feature twelve "ESPN TV podcasts," including *High Noon, Around the Horn, Get Up!, Highly Questionable,* and *Pardon the Interruption.* Most of these shows also use a purposefully condensed

format and even put timers on the screen to indicate how long a news item will be discussed. Depending on the show, this format can limit commentary to minutes or even seconds.

4. The series now describes itself as "the podcast about personal finance and racial economic inclusion" and appears to have grown far more comfortable with making these kinds of connections after its first few episodes.

5. I typically found these hindsight responses to the Sterling scandal tied to interview podcasts that looked at an NBA player's or coach's larger legacy, which then became tied to Sterling in some way (specifically with Baron Davis, J.J. Redick, Elton Brand, Doc Rivers, and Alvin Gentry). Notably, these interviews still overwhelmingly individualized the controversy as the aberrant actions of one man.

Works Cited

Berry, Richard. 2006. "Will the iPod Kill the Radio Star? Profiling Podcasting as Radio." *Convergence: The International Journal of Research into New Media Technologies* 12 (2): 143–62. https://doi.org/10.1177/1354856506066522.

Bird, S. Elizabeth. 2003. *The Audience in Everyday Life: Living in a Media World.* New York: Routledge.

Black Girls Talking. 2014. May 14. "BGT Episode 29." Podcast audio. *Black Girls Talking.* Accessed June 27 2020. https://podcastre.org/episode?id=ep321161.

Brunch and Budget. 2014. August 17. "B&B #7: Donald Sterling & ROI." Podcast audio. *Brunch & Budget.* Bondfire Radio. Accessed June 27, 2020. https://podcastre.org/episode?id=ep181867.

Clements, Sean, and Hayes Davenport. 2014. May 5. "Dave Thomas, Our Close Friend." Podcast audio. *Hollywood Handbook.* Earwolf. Accessed June 27, 2020. https://podcastre.org/episode?id=ep59818.

Clock Radio Speakers. 2014. April 29. "Episode 145 Side A: Donald Sterling & the NBA Playoffs." Podcast audio. *Clock Radio Speakers.* Accessed June 27, 2020. https://podcastre.org/episode?id=ep186213.

The Dr. Vibe Show. 2014. May 4. "The Dr. Vibe Show—Donald Sterling—Black Men's Roundtable—May 4." Podcast audio. *The Dr. Vibe Show.* Accessed June 27, 2020. https://podcastre.org/episode?id=ep195692.

Florini, Sarah. 2017. "This Week in Blackness, the George Zimmerman Acquittal, and the Production of a Networked Collective Identity." *New Media & Society* 19 (3): 439–54. https://doi.org/10.1177/1461444815606779.

Hill, Jemele. 2009. "Stern's Silence on Sterling Says a Lot." *ESPN: Page 2.* Last modified November 5. http://www.espn.com/espn/page2/story?page=hill/110905.

Jenkins, Henry, Sam Ford, and Joshua Green. 2013. *Spreadable Media: Creating Value and Meaning in a Networked Culture.* New York: NYU Press.

Jones, Bomani. 2008. "Donald Sterling's Racism Should Be News." *ESPN: Page 2.* Last modified June 10, 2009. http://www.espn.com/espn/page2/story?page=jones/060810.

Madsen, Virginia M. 2009. "Voices-Cast: A Report on the New Audiosphere of Podcasting with Specific Insights for Public Broadcasting." ANZCA Conference Proceedings, July. *Communication, Creativity, and Global Citizenship.* https://research-management.mq.edu.au/ws/portalfiles/portal/17154626/mq-16890-Publisher+version+%28open+access%29.pdf.

MacMahon, Tim. 2014. "Cuban Not in Favor of Booting Sterling." ESPN. Last modified April 29, 2014. http://www.espn.com/nba/story/_/id/10854381/mark-cuban-dallas-mavericks-rails-donald-sterling-not-favor-kicking-owner.

Morris, Wesley, and Rembert Browne. 2014. "The Owner and the Owned: A Discussion about Donald Sterling." *Grantland.* Last modified April 28, 2014. http://grantland.com/the-triangle/the-owner-and-the-owned-a-discussion-about-donald-sterling/.

Proops, Greg. 2014. May 5. "Knuckles." Podcast audio. *The Smartest Man in the World Proopcast.* Accessed June 27, 2020. https://podcastre.org/episode?id=ep119992.

Shelburne, Ramona. 2019a. August 19. "The Sterling Affairs, Part 1: That Tape." Podcast audio. *30 for 30 Podcasts.* ESPN. Accessed June 27, 2020. https://podcastre.org/episode?id=ep4295511.

Shelburne, Ramona. 2019b. August 19. "The Sterling Affairs, Part 4: Fallout." Podcast audio. *30 for 30 Podcasts.* ESPN. Accessed June 27, 2020. https://podcastre.org/episode?id=ep4295508.

Simmons, Bill. 2014. May 1. "B.S. Report: Chuck Klosterman on Donald Sterling." Podcast audio. *The B.S. Report.* ESPN. Accessed June 27, 2020. http://www.espn.com/espnradio/play?id=10870177.

Squires, Catherine R. 2002. "Rethinking the Black Public Sphere: An Alternative Vocabulary for Multiple Public Spheres." *Communication Theory* 12 (4): 446–68. https://doi.org/10.1111/j.1468-2885.2002.tb00278.x.

Thomas, S. Anthony. 2014. April 30. "Donald Sterling Is a Symptom." Podcast audio. *S. Anthony Says . . .* Accessed June 27 2020. https://podcastre.org/episode?id=ep171822.

TMZ Sports. 2014. "L.A. Clippers Owner to GF: Don't Bring Black People to My Games . . . Including Magic Johnson" *TMZ.* Last modified April 25, 2014. http://www.tmz.com/2014/04/26/donald-sterling-clippers-owner-black-people-racist-audio-magic-johnson/.

Torre, Pablo. 2014. April 29. "Around the Horn." Podcast audio. *Around the Horn.* ESPN. Accessed June 27, 2020. http://www.espn.com/espnradio/play/_/id/10859019.

Viskontas, Indre, and Kishore Hari. 2014. May 8. "33 David Amodio—The Science of Prejudice." Podcast audio. *Inquiring Minds.* Accessed June 27, 2020. https://podcastre.org/episode?id=ep137879.

Wagner, Kyle. 2014. "Exclusive: The Extended Donald Sterling Tape." *Deadspin.* Last modified April 27, 2014. https://deadspin.com/exclusive-the-extended-donald-sterling-tape-1568291249.

Whitlock, Jason. 2014. May 14. "Real Talk—Bomani Jones." Podcast audio. *ESPN: Real Talk with Jason Whitlock.* ESPN. Accessed June 27, 2020. https://podcastre.org/episode?id=ep297518.

SEVEN | Listening to the Aftermath of Crime

True Crime Podcasts

AMANDA KEELER

Though a long-standing and popular genre on television, over the last six years true crime storytelling has found a vibrant presence on podcasts. These programs have garnered millions of listeners and downloads across a broad range of programs, from *Serial* (2014–present), the first two seasons of which have been downloaded 340 million times, to *My Favorite Murder* (2016–present), which reports 19 million listeners a month (Spangler 2018; McDonell-Parry 2018). As of 2020, true crime podcast producers and listeners have created and popularized a thriving genre.

While this popular genre has created a seemingly insatiable appetite for more true crime stories, the nature of this genre of storytelling involves other layers that are important to its critical analysis. True crime storytelling involves multiple modes of audience engagement. These podcasts have the ability to entertain listeners, but they can also serve as powerful storytelling spaces capable of drawing attention to complex issues in the criminal justice system. Some celebrate the diligent work of law enforcement officials, while others ask questions about institutional failures or seek help to solve cold cases long forgotten by everyone except the affected families. In all, there are multiple vectors for examining approaches in true crime podcasts.

This chapter analyzes several storytelling genres and modes across true crime podcasts. Additionally, in keeping with the larger goals of the PodcastRE project, the chapter considers the social and cultural importance of preserving true crime podcast recordings for future listeners and scholars. Preserving these stories for the future will ensure the space to study genre and storytelling changes and shifts over time and will provide a continued critical focus on institutional checks and balances that affect people all around the world.

While television scholars such as Jane Feuer (1992) and Jason Mittell (2004) have explored the complexities of studying genre through textual classifications, genre continues to be one of the primary means through which audiences choose to listen to, watch, and engage with media. As such, scholarly examinations of genre can help locate trends and cycles that can be indicative of larger social tensions and issues informing us why or why not certain crime stories find more traction among podcast creators and listeners.

Collaborational Podcasts

Much like true crime storytelling on television, crime podcasts fall into several broad categories based on the type of case presented and the framing of each case's facts and evidence. Several podcasts fall into the first category of programs that discuss or investigate unsolved cases. In his book on reality television programs, Richard Kilborn labels this type of reality program "collaborational," in that their producers explicitly seek collaboration from the audience—asking viewers or listeners to share any information they may have that could help solve the crime or locate missing persons (2003, 68). An example of this type of true crime storytelling is the Canadian Broadcasting Company's program *Someone Knows Something* (2016–present). Created by documentary filmmaker David Ridgen, this professionally produced podcast employs in-depth, season-long investigations into unsolved crimes such as the 1972 disappearance of Adrien McNaughton, covered in season one, and the 1998 disappearance of Sheryl Sheppard, investigated in season two. Another collaborational program, *The Vanished*, was created in 2016 by Marissa Jones, who hosted and independently produced the program alone until its move into the podcast network Wondery. Each episode of *The Vanished* covers a missing person (or persons) case, frequently focusing on the types of cases often ignored by traditional news organizations and television true crime programs, such as stories of missing young boys, teenagers, people of color, people with mental illnesses, and those struggling with drug addiction or homelessness.[1] In terms of demonstrating the utility of audience participation, *Someone Knows Something*'s host David Ridgen's investigation into McNaughton's and Sheppard's disappearances has uncovered some new clues and prompted officials to pay further attention to these unsolved cold cases.[2] Several cases presented on *The Vanished* have been resolved, but as with the television program *Disappeared* (Investigation Discovery, 2009–present), it is unclear if it is actually the public presentation of these cases that has led to finding these missing persons or solving these cases.[3] Nonetheless, the episodes that investigate the cases draw attention to these unsolved crimes—and with this renewed public awareness, the possibility that they might be solved in the future.

Stylistically, this type of true crime storytelling poses an interesting question for both television programs and audio-only podcasts: How do they create images and sounds to tell the circumstances of an unsolved crime when this information is largely unknown? In some cases, the informal nature of the podcasting format and the intimate personal relationship the host/narrator builds with the audience allow the "largely unknown" nature of the investigation and its outcome to become part of the appeal of the show. Not knowing the outcome and hearing the narrator coming to grips with the unknowability of the case are as much a part of the journey for listeners as solving the case.

Reinvestigation Podcasts

Similar to the season-long investigations presented on *Someone Knows Something*, *In the Dark* (2016–present) began as a collaborational investigation into the then-unsolved 1989 kidnapping of Jacob Wetterling from St. Joseph, Minnesota. However, several months into the research for season one, the case was solved through the arrest of former suspect Danny Heinrich for a different offense.[4] With the case now solved, *In the Dark* host Madeleine Baran and her coproducers shifted the program into a "reinvestigation" program. Reinvestigation programs subject already-prosecuted or solved criminal cases to intense scrutiny, inviting the audience to reexamine the validity of the evidence, the investigation, and the prosecution. In turn, these deep investigations help to illuminate flaws in the criminal justice system, providing what might be termed a public service by locating and attempting to remedy alleged miscarriages of justice. Reinvestigation-focused films and television programs have long existed outside of podcasts, such as Errol Morris's documentary film *The Thin Blue Line* (1988), which revisited the investigation and evidence against Randall Dale Adams, who had been erroneously charged and convicted of the 1976 murder of Dallas police officer Robert Wood.

Other examples include Joe Berlinger and Bruce Sinofsky's 1996 film, *Paradise Lost: The Child Murders at Robin Hood Hills*, as well as the more recent 2015 Netflix series *Making a Murderer*, created by Laura Ricciardi and Moira Demos.

As host Madeleine Baran notes, *In the Dark* became about "investigating the investigation" (Atad 2016). The central focus of season one shifted from a search for the person responsible for Wetterling's disappearance to an in-depth analysis of one arm of the law enforcement system in the United States, sheriffs, and the how these elected officials' institutional accountability works differently from that of traditional police departments. This criminal justice focus helps educate listeners about the politics and circumstances of how and why the case was solved only by accident nearly thirty years after the original crime took place. In season two, *In the Dark* addresses the case of Curtis Flowers, uncovering how the police handled the original homicide investigation, the accountability of elected district attorneys, and politics of class and race in the court system in the state of Mississippi. The investigation presented in the second season of *In the Dark* led to numerous developments, such as the 2019 US Supreme Court decision to throw out Flowers's sixth conviction over violating his "constitutional rights by intentionally removing African-Americans from the jury" (Gilbert et al. 2019).

One of the most downloaded podcasts to date, *Serial*, also performs the storytelling work of reinvestigation. Hosted by Sarah Koenig and coproduced with Julie Snyder, season one presented a long-form, multiple-episode reexamination of the evidence used to convict Adnan Syed for the murder of Hae Min Lee in 1999. Overall, these reinvestigation programs provide a missing but necessary public review of the power wielded by the police, district attorneys, juries, and judges in the United States.

Closed-Case Podcasts

Another category of true crime programming focuses on already-solved criminal cases through interviews with police officers, forensic scientists, and people affected by crimes. These "closed-case" podcasts demonstrate, sometimes implicitly, the effectiveness of law enforcement and how collaborative efforts across social institutions work to ensure justice for victims and their families. This type of true crime podcast includes the program *Criminal* (2014–present), a podcast that delves into how victims navigate the aftermath of crimes and the complexities of convictions and acquittals—all through an eclectic mix of crimes, rang-ing from a photograph that changes two lives in "It Looked Like Fire" (December 11, 2015) to one woman's battle with identity theft in "The Money Tree" (September 23, 2016). While the episodes of *Criminal* take a somewhat lighthearted tone recalling crimes and their investigations, other closed-case podcasts, such as *Actual Innocence* (2016–2018), provide a platform for people to discuss their wrongful convictions. *Actual Inno-cence* allows individuals to recollect not only the circumstance that led to their wrongful convictions but also the subsequent work they had to perform in order to convince the police and the court systems of the flawed evidence and improper prosecutions pertaining to the original criminal investigations.

While many true crime podcasts choose a somber tone that reflects their focus on real-world crime, its victims, and the surviving families, sev-eral other programs combine true crime storytelling with humor, such as *My Favorite Murder*. Though crime podcasts have the ability to reflect on and change people's lives and the criminal justice system, many are designed, above these other concerns, to draw in an audience and enter-tain them. *My Favorite Murder*'s popularity has extended beyond its pod-cast; hosts Karen Kilgariff and Georgia Hardstark have created ancillary markets through a live tour and show merchandise.

True Crime Podcasts: Is it Journalism? Documentary Storytelling?

Thus far, all of these podcasts can be divided into subcategories within the larger generic true crime umbrella. Nonetheless, these types of pod-casts tend to approach the cases they cover from two different storytelling modes: journalistic investigations and documentary-style approaches. In theory, journalists adhere to a set of ethical criteria that guide the manner in which they are trained to tell stories "with impartiality and objectivity" (Langer 1998, 2). As Mark Deuze notes, journalists strive for "objectiv-ity" in reporting, making every attempt to remain "impartial, neutral, objective, fair, and (thus) credible" (2005, 447). Likewise, as Michael Schudson writes, "The journalist's job consists of reporting something called 'news' without commenting on it, slanting it, or shaping its formu-lation in any way" (2001, 150). As a podcast created by American Public Media (APM) Reports, *In the Dark* follows the traditional guidelines of journalistic storytelling. In its long-form investigative journalism, each season of the show focuses on data that the show's producers research, compile, and analyze while also consulting with experts in different fields to help them draw conclusions. Host Madeleine Baran carefully uses this research and the evidence collected by the police to understand the circumstances surrounding and informing the case and to construct theories about alternate suspects. In season two, the *In the Dark* producers explicitly focus on Curtis Flowers and the fact that he has been tried and convicted six times for a quadruple homicide that occurred at Tardy Furniture in Winona, Mississippi, in 1996. However, parallel to this main story line, the producers follow the evidentiary trail to uncover another viable suspect, Willie James Hemphill, whom the police originally questioned in connection to the murders for which Flowers has been repeatedly convicted.

Criminal also largely fits into traditional notions of journalistic storytelling, which connects with the producers of the show, public radio veterans Lauren Spohrer and Phoebe Judge, the latter also a former reporter. As Jason Loviglio notes, "*Criminal*'s sensibility and sound partake of the US public radio formula made famous by *This American Life*: journalistic rigour and gothic yarns" (2017, 1). While host Phoebe Judge maintains the objectivity of journalism in her presentation of the crime stories, the program does allow its guests to discuss the possibilities for alternate readings of evidence, such as the homicide by owl theory presented in "Animal Instincts" (January 30, 2014). Similarly, as a podcast created by two journalists, Veronica Volk of WXXI News and Gary Craig, reporter for Rochester, New York, newspaper *Democrat & Chronicle*, *Finding Tammy Jo* (2016) details the cooperative work that went into identifying Tammy Jo Alexander, whose body was discovered after her murder in 1979, without stepping outside the bounds of the physical evidence to conclude who is responsible for her as-yet-unsolved murder.

While it appears that some podcast producers and hosts strive to maintain a journalistic objectivity, the crime story underway can provide producers with an opportunity to examine objectivity and the difficulties of this ethical obligation. As Jillian DeMair has noted with regard to *Serial*, "Koenig often comments on the difficulty of remaining without bias" in her presentation of the evidence used (and not used) to convict Adnan Syed of Hae Min Lee's murder (2017, 33). However, DeMair asks an important question: "Why should *Serial* thematize this problem of bias in a show that never claims to be impartial?" (33). Indeed, none of these podcasts explicitly denotes its adherence to journalistic objectivity in reporting. At the same time, the familial relationships to news reporting through these producers' professional experience (*Criminal, Serial*) or through the sponsoring organization (APM Reports' *In the Dark*) do implicitly mark these podcasts as abiding by those journalistic standards. This uneasy line across and around journalism is not a phenomenon that is new to podcast storytellers—it has a precedent in public radio. As Michele Hilmes writes, *This American Life* "frequently wanders across the lines that journalists usually observe, incorporating subjective experience, offbeat points of view, dreams, drama, and memory, along with Glass's own musings, less factual than philosophical, as its frame" (2013, 54).

The other podcasts discussed in this chapter follow more along a tradition associated with documentary storytelling, which allows producers to tell factual stories from differing perspectives in an attempt to persuade the audience. For Richard Kilborn and John Izod, documentary filmmakers and producers "are not simply in the business of recording reality but will often be encouraging us, in some measure, to view these events from a particular perspective. In other words, evidence will tend to be presented in such a way as to increase the likelihood of the audience falling in line with the film maker's argument" (Kilborn and Izod 1997, 6). The documentary storytelling mode allows writers, producers, and directors to explore real-world subject matter in a way that might be deemed inappropriate in traditional journalism. In these podcasts, hosts are free to speculate about who might be responsible—an act that might constitute slander in more traditional types of nonfiction storytelling. Nonetheless, documentary creators must also maintain their own ethical obligation to rely on facts and information rooted in the real world even when they attempt to persuade the audience in one direction or another. Several documentary filmmakers have turned to true crime storytelling podcasts, such as David Ridgen and his Candian Broadcasting Corporation podcast *Someone Knows Something* and Payne Lindsay's *Up and Vanished* (2016-present). In season one of *Someone Knows Something*, Ridgen frames his investigations into Adrien McNaughton's decades-old disappearance case by exploring any lead he can uncover, including a discussion of using psychics to help solve cases. Similarly, on *The Vanished* podcast, Marissa Jones discusses with her audience her thoughts and opinions about some of the missing persons cases that she presents based on the evidence and the amount of cooperation given to the police by certain connected individuals.

Preservation Questions

Given true crime's importance to and prominence in podcasting's rise in popularity over the last half decade, there is an urgent need to ensure we are preserving these shows for future media history research. However, the genre presents unique preservation issues. First, these programs have what might be termed a shelf life—especially for collaborational podcasts focused on unsolved crime. While these programs may continue to entertain and educate listeners about the intricacies and complexities of the justice system in different countries, the very nature of unsolved cases (or cases that eventually get solved) means their value as listenable objects changes over time. For example, what happens when an episode of *The Vanished* features a missing person who is later found? If a case is solved, does it mean that an episode declines in archival value?

Second, these programs may serve as evidence in ongoing cases, which may mean their archival value is extremely important as the case continues but may be less so once a final verdict has been reached. Such was the case of the first season of *Serial*, which highlighted the evidentiary issues in the criminal case against Adnan Syed. While the podcast has brought attention to questions about his guilt or innocence in the 1999 murder of Hae Min Lee and several appeals have been filed to officially revisit this case in the courtroom, as of March 2020, Syed remains in prison with few (if any) legal appeal avenues remaining.

Third, should there be different archival priorities depending on the kind of storytelling genre at play? In other words, does the focus on criminal justice accountability in reinvestigation podcasts, which implore listeners to enact institutional checks and balances, make them more important to preserve than closed-case programs? Does preserving *Serial* take precedent over saving certain episodes of *The Vanished* for future listeners? Like the complexities of the cases presented on all of these podcasts, there are no easy answers. Nonetheless, podcasts such as *Actual Innocence* and *Finding Tammy Jo* present stories about real people who have died and others who continue to grapple with the aftermath of crime. If these episodes function as small, meaningful audio tributes to lost lives and missing persons, the preservation of these stories matters to their families (who may welcome or object to this attention), regardless of the outcomes of each episode.

From a scholarly standpoint, preserving these stories for future listeners and researchers will ensure that the space to study genre and storytelling changes and shifts over time and to recognize how the rise of podcasting was in part due to (or resulted in a flourishing of) true crime podcasts. Just as radio historians have been able to do with online preservation resources such as Old Time Radio (OTR.org) and the Internet Archive (archive.org), media scholars will be able to look back at a collection like PodcastRE and trace the rise in prominence of the genre, as well as deconstruct some of the storytelling codes and conventions that seemed endemic to the format. Furthermore, preserving programs such as *In the Dark* and *Serial* ensures that future researchers can explore how these podcasts may or may not have contributed to criminal justice reform.

Conclusion

The vast body of true crime podcasts reveal a range of storytelling approaches to crafting compelling true crime stories. While some podcasts choose to focus on individual stories of people who commit crimes or those affected by the aftermath of crimes, others investigate social institutions or the psychological theories examining why people commit crimes. Some podcasts, such as *My Favorite Murder,* attempt to find humor in the darkest criminal events. Storytellers innovate by shifting expectations and reinvigorating the existing boundaries. As with all facets of genre, the categories discussed here will not remain static over time. Future podcast producers will blend and blur these generic boundaries, creating new, hybrid storytelling modes that will necessitate revisiting these demarcations. Given the current popularity and proliferation of true crime podcasts, producers will need to continue to transform well-known true crime stories in order to attract new listeners.

In the case of many of the true crime podcasts discussed here, these programs perform important work. Many of these podcasts effectively bridge the micro story of individuals with the macro investigations of larger circumstances surrounding criminal cases. The focus on these "small" stories helps to illuminate systemic issues, catapulting the audio-only exploration of an issue from the anonymous and vague notion that crime exists in the world to the personal stories of victims that can help create important connections for the audience. Regardless of genre or mode of storytelling, these programs can have the potential to educate audiences about bigger-picture flaws in the criminal justice system that affect everyone.

The ability to parse through and analyze genre within true crime podcasts exists only because all of the programs noted here are currently easily accessible online, through various websites and podcast platforms and networks. Nonetheless, the very proliferation of this popular genre of podcasts could mean that accessibility will be a challenge in the near future, with too many episodes and too few spaces to continue to store them. This issue currently plagues true crime television. In a similar moment when multiple platforms have created unprecedented access to a range of television programs, many gaps remain. A seminal and frequently discussed program in the history of true crime television, *America's Most Wanted* (Fox, 1988–2011; Lifetime, 2011–2012), has limited availability on sites such as YouTube. It remains difficult, if not impossible, to study a television or podcast genre without access to the media objects. PodcastRE's initiative to save new (and old) sounds will ensure that these texts remain readily available to anyone interested in listening to them in the future.

Notes

1. See Duvall and Moscowitz (2016) for more information about the victims who are more likely to garner news coverage in abduction cases.

2. In the case of season one, Adrien McNaughton's disappearance, the podcast may have discovered that he was not kidnapped, as the family and police originally believed, but may have instead died by drowning. This theory cannot be verified because of the difficulty of searching for human remains in Holmes Lake, but several different cadaver dogs have picked up on the scent of human remains in the spot where McNaughton was last seen in 1972. See https://www.cbc.ca/radio/sks/season1/season-1-holmes-lake-update-1.4596923 for more information.

3. The number of cases resolved after appearing on *Unsolved Mysteries* or *America's Most Wanted* is more readily accessible than with newer television and podcast programs.

4. Heinrich was arrested for child pornography possession charges. In a plea agreement he admitted to kidnapping, sexually assaulting, and murdering Wetterling and led authorities to the site where he buried Wetterling.

Works Cited

Atad, Corey. 2016. "*In the Dark* Host Madeleine Baran Explains How the Year's Best True-Crime Podcast Was Made." *Esquire.* November 7. https://www.esquire.com/entertainment/a50417/in-the-dark-madeleine-baran-interview/.

DeMair, Jillian. 2017. "Sounds Authentic: The Acoustic Construction of *Serial's* Storyworld." In *The Serial Podcast and Storytelling in the Digital Age*, edited by Ellen McCracken, 24–38. New York: Routledge.

Deuze, Mark. 2005. "What Is Journalism? Professional Identity and Ideology of Journalists Reconsidered." *Journalism* 6 (4): 442–64.

Duvall, Spring-Serenity, and Leigh Moscowitz. 2016. *Snatched: Child Abductions in U.S. News Media.* New York: Peter Lang.

Feuer, Jane. 1992. "Genre Study and Television." In *Channels of Discourse, Reassembled: Television and Contemporary Criticism*, 2nd ed., edited by Robert C. Allen, 138–60. Chapel Hill: University of North Carolina Press.

Gilbert, Curtis, Dave Mann, Rehman Tungekar, and Parker Yesko. 2019. "Reversed: Curtis Flowers Wins Appeal at U.S. Supreme Court." *APM Reports.* June 21. https://www.apmreports.org/story/2019/06/21/curtis-flowers-wins -scotus-appeal.

Hilmes, Michele. 2013. "The New Materiality of Radio: Sound on Screens." In *Radio's New Wave: Global Sound in the Digital Era,* edited by Michele Hilmes and Jason Loviglio, 43–61. New York: Routledge.

Kilborn, Richard. 2003. *Staging the Real: Factual TV Programming in the Age of Big Brother.* Manchester: Manchester University Press.

Kilborn, Richard, and John Izod. 1997. *Confronting Reality: An Introduction to Television Documentary.* Manchester: Manchester University Press.

Langer, John. 1998. *Tabloid Television: Popular Journalism and the "Other New."* London: Routledge.

Loviglio, Jason. 2017. "*Criminal:* Journalistic Rigour, Gothic Yarns, and Philosophical Heft." *Radio Doc Review* 3 (1).

McDonell-Parry, Amelia. 2018. "*My Favorite Murder* Hosts Launch Podcast Network." *Rolling Stone.* November 18. https://www.rollingstone.com/culture /culture-news/my-favorite-murder-hosts-podcast-network-760885/.

Mittell, Jason. 2004. *Genre and Television: From Cop Shows to Cartoons in American Culture.* New York: Routledge.

Schudson, Michael. 2001. "The Objectivity Norm in American Journalism." *Journalism* 2 (2): 49–70.

Spangler, Todd. 2018. "*Serial* Season 3 Podcast Premiere Date Set." *Variety.* September 5. https://variety.com/2018/digital/news/serial-season-3-premiere -date-podcast-1202927015/.

Programs Cited

Actual Innocence (2016–2018), created by Brooke Gittings. https://podcasts.apple .com/us/podcast/actual-innocence/id1102237078.

Criminal (2014-present), created by Phoebe Judge and Lauren Spohrer. https:// thisiscriminal.com/.

Finding Tammy Jo (2016), created by Veronica Volk and Gary Craig. https://www .stitcher.com/podcast/finding-tammy-jo.

In the Dark (2016-present), created by APM Reports. https://www.apmreports .org/in-the-dark.

My Favorite Murder (2016-present), created by Karen Kilgariff and Georgia Hardstark. https://myfavoritemurder.com/.

Serial (2014-present), created by Sarah Koenig and Julie Snyder. https://serialp odcast.org/.

Someone Knows Something (2016-present), created by David Ridgen. https://www .cbc.ca/radio/sks.

The Vanished (2016-present), created by Marissa Jones. http://www.thevanished podcast.com/.

Up and Vanished (2016-present), created by Payne Lindsay. https://upandvanis hed.com/.

EIGHT

A RE-emphasis on Context

Preserving and Analyzing Podcast Metadata

SUSAN NOH

Digital Archiving, Big Data, and the Context Conundrum

While digital humanities scholars have expressed a growing interest in big data analysis, the efficacy of big data research is contentious, with scholars like danah boyd, Kate Crawford, and Lisa Gitelman critiquing the research methodologies of big data and its claims of invalidating the necessity for theory and ideas of historical causality (boyd and Crawford 2012, 666). In particular, scholars are increasingly critical about the general discourse surrounding big data, which implies that the more data we have, the better one can achieve accurate and objective claims (Crawford et al 2014). Gitelman debunks the idea that data ever arrives "raw" and free of cultural bias, arguing that "the seemingly indispensable misperception that data are ever raw seems to be one way in which data are forever contextualized—that is, framed—according to a mythology of their own supposed decontextualization" (2013, 6). Further, in relation to digital archives, Joanna Sassoon argues that by placing an object within an archive, one removes any digital artifact from its historical and sociocultural context, effectively isolating the artifact from the discursive systems that made the object relevant and significant to a given moment in time and place. Sassoon emphasizes that there must be an understanding of the nuanced contextual relationships between the artifact and its "creators and functional structures" (2007, 137). Without these contextual elements, archives become "a databank of orphans which have been removed from their transactional origins and evidence of authorial intent" (139). Such "orphans" become highly susceptible to the rewriting of the artifact's original social function, which may mislead scholars on the representative nature of any given object.

The question, then, is not how big data can oust theory and causality from our historical understanding of culture but how active human interaction, intervention, and interpretation can shape the production of data. By acknowledging this, one can extrapolate the broader significance of why the data appear the way they do as opposed to simply taking the output at face value. For example, literary scholar Matthew Jockers has used big data approaches to argue that canonical texts must be brought into discussion with broader literary trends of a particular time period in order to make generalizations that go beyond singular examples. By using an interdisciplinary approach that takes advantage of big data computational methods along with analyses of specific examples, he is able engage in "contextualization on an unprecedented scale" (2013, 27). Through big data methodologies, humanities researchers have access to a broader range of scalable data sets, which offer the potential to link an individual work to a complex sociocultural web of features that impact the relational context of that work.

Often, it is through metadata, or the information about various files, formats, and artifacts, that plays a central role in big data projects. Metadata aids in connoting the relational existences of digital objects to a sociocultural moment. Because the contextual elements of a given artifact are inherently connected to the piece's potential to be subject to appraisal, metadata becomes a site where one can confirm the provenance of born digital content, which is critical for analyzing whether data can validly be interpreted as evidence (Kramer 2014). It is essential for those who create digital databases to also provide scholars a means to trace the provenance of an archival collection and recognize how the disparate items in the collection relate to one another. With the metadata that is conveniently made available on digital databases like PodcastRE, big data methodologies provide an approach to theorizing the larger relational patterns in the metadata, which act as the connective tissue between nodes. Through big data methodologies, the digital archive can begin to rebuild and recreate the contextual background that may relate any one artifact to the larger system of its existence (Sternfeld 2011). In this manner, while there are inevitable seismic contextual shifts that occur when placing an artifact within a digital database, one can still track the relational pathways that embed a single podcast within the larger culture of podcast production, distribution, and consumption.

Although there are multiple ways to sift through RSS metadata on PodcastRE, in this chapter I focus on two of its metadata visualization applications: the Associated Keyword Word Cloud and the Term Frequency Line Graph. The Term Frequency Line Graph tracks the frequency of a particular query in the title, podcast synopses, and keywords both on an episodic and podcast-wide scale. For example, while "politics" may be a keyword designated to a podcast as a whole, "midterm elections" may be a keyword that refers to an episode within that podcast. This application focuses on the temporal dimensions of keyword use, tracking what kinds of words were used during which time periods and the frequency of their use. This allows researchers to see which topics and rhetoric were trending on a monthly and yearly basis.

The visualizations yielded from the Associated Keyword Word Cloud application are derived from the frequency of other metadata keyword terms that are often joined together with the query. Through this app, one can see how podcasters self-identify their work in relation to a particular topic or category. These conceptual associations that are drawn by the podcasters begin to shed some light on the kinds of topics that are often grouped together, motivated by the potential for more exposure with regard to search engine optimization, the sociopolitical and cultural milieu, and the thematic connections that are established by the podcasters in order to perform affiliations and brand identity. Keyword metadata acts as a site of negotiation in which one can observe a complex relationship unfold between one's data, user agency, and content aggregate sites. Helen Kennedy, Thomas Poell, and José van Dijck have emphasized the need to engage with "the question of agency, [which] should be central to our engagement with data" (2015, 2). Algorithmic authority, which has a veritable influence on our data engagement, has dominated much of the scholarly discourse on the human relationship with data; however, such work "leaves little room to explore the small-scale actors who are making organizational adjustments to accommodate for the rise of data's power" (2). By focusing on how creators use metadata keywords, PodcastRE's data visualizations address how podcasters engage with content aggregator platforms and manage the push and pull of influence and control that are inherent within the infrastructure of these commercial applications.

Further, by allowing PodcastRE's visualizations to be connected with the data forms that podcasters use to brand themselves, the site provides an alternative mode of discoverability apart from the search and ranking algorithms that govern commercial databanks such as iTunes. Whereas keywords became defunct as a metadata facet for discoverability for iTunes in 2012, they continue to play a central role in how data and content are organized and made discoverable within PodcastRE. In this way, PodcastRE hopes to provide a different model of algorithmic search that puts creator agency and their interactions with their own metadata at the forefront of the digital archive's organization, particularly through these metadata visualizations. Ideally, such visualizations will assist researchers in discovering unexpected relationships between themes and reveal how podcasters interact with the metadata in order to create associative networks.

Metadata Curation and Creator-Oriented Approaches

Podcasters use keywords in order to define themselves to their audience. It is a space of creator agency, where they are able to deploy keywords to create networks of ambient affiliation between subject matter (Zappavigna 2011). For example, when querying "activism" in the Associated Keyword Word Cloud application, the only prominent racial identity category that appears is "Black women" (PodcastRE 2018b). The self-labeling of one's content as "activism" on the level of metadata is a political exercise of creator agency, which gestures toward the podcaster's strategic engagement with the iTunes platform in order to carve out a space for civic discourse. This practice of self-labeling and re-politicization through keywords rejects the apolitical and commercialized genres that have been provided by the platform, which seek to whitewash and flatten the diverse voices that constitute the category of "Society & Culture." However, not all podcasters who speak about the power inequalities revolving around race, gender, and sexuality label their content as activism. For example, while creator organizations like the Potluck Collective certainly engage in the work of representation and activism for Asian American communities, they do not seem to be actively labeling their content as "activism" within the keyword or category metadata field. Although it would be difficult to state with certainty why a podcaster would decide to label their work as activism or not, those who do intentionally frame their work as potential forms of activism through their metadata appear in the search results within PodcastRE's metadata visualizations. This is in contrast to being otherwise potentially buried in the search results in other commercial podcatching platforms.

Associated Keywords

Figure 8.1. Word cloud for the query "activism" in the "All Keywords" category taken 11/20/2018 from http://podcastre.org

Keywords

☐ Uncategorized (24)	☐ activism (24)	☑ black women (24)	☐ episode (24)
☐ episodes (24)	☐ race (16)	☐ racism (16)	☐ Black Women's

Figure 8.2. Screen capture (11/20/2018) of Keywords column with query "activism" and associated keyword "black women" checked from http://podcastre.org

Clicking on the "black women" keyword in our earlier example query on activism, one can look at the left column of the PodcastRE web page interface and see the various networks of associated keywords that contain both the term "activism" and "black women" (PodcastRE 2018a). In this way, researchers can see how podcasters start to shape their own relational networks using keywords that the creators choose to apply to themselves. This manner of search, through the metadata applications, is one that aims to target the unexpected discoverability of relations. In the left-hand column, when I also check the keyword "trans rights," the only podcast that comes up is *UnLearned*, a biweekly podcast that speaks to the dominant narratives that circumscribe Blackness, among other identity features (i.e., gender, sexuality), to certain harmful stereotypes, and the struggle of trying to unlearn such ubiquitous ideologies (*UnLearned* 2019). With a database of over a million podcast episodes, it is remarkable that the sole podcast that has triangulated these three affiliated topics in their keywords is *UnLearned*. The dearth of podcasts speaking about these topics may gesture to the potential lack of in-depth conversations on intersectionality within this particular media practice when it comes to activism endeavors; however, even if this is not the case, one can analyze why podcasters may *not* be using these particular keywords to be affiliated with their content. For example, in Mél Hogan's article "*Dykes on Mykes*: Podcasting and the Activist Archive" (2018), Hogan pulls an excerpt from an interview with Dayna McLeod, a cohost of *Dykes on Mykes*, who says:

> "I become even more suspect, and dare I say, paranoid, when I upload an episode about the *L Word*, where the discussion focused on gays and lesbians in the American military, and the war in Iraq, and iTunes didn't register it for one week, until I remove the meta-tag equivalent buzz words of, 'Iraq war,' 'terrorist' and 'Afghanistan,' and as soon as I remove these keywords, it appears on iTunes." (McLeod quoted in Hogan 2007)

In this manner, one can see that podcasters often police their own use of keywords out of fear that the platform may refuse to disseminate their content or the possible economic impacts that certain metadata practices may have on the performance of the podcast. This kind of censorship also influences why certain words may not show up within the Associated Keyword Word Cloud.

Contrasting the sparse results between "activism" and "black women," when one clicks on the terms "activism" and "racism," there are podcast entries from *UnLearned, Radio Diaries*, and *Midday on WNYC*. This puts three podcasts that might not otherwise seem connected into a closer proximity with one another. While this does not necessarily mean there is an inherent connection between the three podcasts, this mode of database search emphasizes discovery through potential relationality. By looking at how podcasters may be using similar terms to define their work in the metadata, broader trends may not only be teased out of the way podcasters affiliate their work to certain ideologies and topics but may also aid researchers in making more generalizable arguments that extend beyond singular case studies.

The self-definition that is afforded through keywords metadata is potentially enlightening of the relationship between creators, their content, and with one another. Yet, despite the way that keywords can be sites of creator empowerment, it is also a contentious field, where the promise of search engine optimization and algorithmic privileging shape certain metadata practices, often for the purpose of trying to maximize a podcast's discoverability and entrepreneurial potential. The influence of podcatching applications like iTunes in this domain becomes clear as certain patterns of metadata practice are brought to the fore through the availability of large datasets. In the case of keywords, such influence is revealed through the prevalence of certain phrases and modes of defining that fall along the lines of preestablished genres as outlined by Apple.

Podcasts, Keywords, and the Ubiquity of Genre on iTunes

Discovering the intricate recipes of search algorithms continues to fascinate users and scholars alike. This is evident in the exponential increase of web articles (see, for example, Crowe 2020; Ratcliffe 2016; Markov 2019; *Podcast Motor* n.d.) that dispense search engine optimization strategies that can be used to gain user attention, such as what kinds of metadata keywords should be used and how many, how to tag images, and more. The opaque nature of how iTunes organizes its search results influences how podcasters create metadata and sets the terms for how podcast creators can self-define their own content. This influence is visible in the PodcastRE database, where the most frequent keywords lists are dominated by terms that echo iTunes's genre specifications.[1]

For example, with the exception of the words "podcast" and "radio," the top fifteen keywords for the podcast category all cohere to various genre classifications within iTunes. Similar patterns emerge for the episodic classification, where, with the exception of "Talk Radio," "Podcast," and a blank space/uncategorized, the top ten keywords reflect iTunes categories. The large amount of blank or uncategorized keyword terms may gesture toward the fact that after 2012 the keywords metadata field became deprecated, meaning it no longer affected the output of iTunes's search engine algorithms. After this discovery, many podcasters may have forgone the labor of putting in keywords, as the fields that influenced search engine optimization were now title, author, and the description tags (see, for example, Ortega 2017; Jmortizsilva and Thorpe 2015; Blubrry n.d.; Mandato 2018; Lewis 2016).

Keyword metadata also speaks to the hidden relationship between iTunes podcast categories and the kinds of podcasts that were privileged on the iTunes website. Using the Wayback Machine, I tracked the categories that were most visibly represented on the Apple iTunes web page. With the limitations of the Wayback Machine in mind (Ankerson 2012), the site remains one of the most accessible tools that provides at least a partial look at how the Apple iTunes web page appeared over a decade ago. Because I am focusing my attention on the iTunes categories and subcategories that have existed since at least 2006 onward, I depend on this stability to evaluate one other feature on the Apple web page: the iTunes preview. If we are to take the output of the Wayback Machine as accurate, the following is a list of the categories and subcategories that iTunes supported starting from 2006 (Apple Inc. 2006).[2]

While the formal categories have not changed, the podcasts that were represented most prominently on the iTunes preview section of the website from the year 2009 to 2010 were from the "Society & Culture" and "Technology" categories (Apple Inc. 2010). These categories were represented alongside the "Top Podcast" chart, privileging podcasts from these categories. The implication of this interface's organization is that one may infer that the quality of the top "Technology" and "Society & Culture" podcasts may be comparable to the quality of the content that is on the overall "Top Podcast" list, therefore potentially drawing more eyes to these two category charts. It is no surprise, then, that among the top keywords for the combined episode and podcast list, "Society & Culture" ranks highly at number 4, following "Comedy" (another iTunes-supported category), "Podcast," and "Talk Radio." "Technology" also ranks highly at number 19. Among categories that had the most keywords connected to them, "Society & Culture" topped the chart. "Technology" also followed at number 12. The focus on "Technology" as a privileged category on the web page is explicitly beneficial for Apple, because through its spotlighting, the chances of these podcasts bolstering Apple's brand name increases.

Other patterns in the top podcasts lists emerge as well. For example, when looking at the charts that were saved from August 29, 2010,

Table 8.1. Table listing iTunes categories and subcategories from https://web
.archive.org/web/20061215123228/http://www.apple.com/itunes/store/podc
aststechspecs.html#_Toc526931698

Arts	Business	Comedy	Education
• Design • Fashion & Beauty • Food • Literature • Performing Arts • Visual Arts	• Business news • Careers • Investing • Management & marketing • Shopping		• Education technology • Higher education • K-12 • Language courses • Training
Games & Hobbies	Government & Organizations	Health	Kids & Family
• Automotive • Aviation • Hobbies • Other games • Video games	• Local • National • Non-profit • Regional	• Alternative health • Fitness & nutrition • Self help • Sexuality	
Music	News & Politics	Religion & Spirituality	Science & Medicine
		• Buddhism • Christianity • Hinduism • Islam • Judaism • Other • Spirituality	• Medicine • Natural science • Social sciences
Society & Culture	Sports & Recreation	Technology	TV & Film
• History • Personal journals • Philosophy • Places & travel	• Amateur • College & high school • Outdoor • Professional	• Gadgets • Tech news • Podcasting • Software how-to	

and comparing the results of the "Top Podcasts" list with the "Society & Culture" list (Apple Inc. 2010), there is much overlap, with big names like *NPR: Fresh Air Podcast, This American Life,* and *Stuff You Should Know* appearing in both columns. *Freakonomics Radio* and *Stuff You Missed in History Class* were available in the "Society & Culture" list but not on the "Top Podcasts" list. However, since *HowStuffWorks* is the parent property of both *Stuff You Missed in History Class* and *Stuff You Should Know, Freakonomics Radio* is the only podcast that does not have a firm relationship with the content that was showcased in the "Top Podcasts" column. In this way, category prioritizations give an additional opportunity for ambitious podcasters to land on the front page if podcasters decide to define themselves under the "Society & Culture" or "Technology" category. Such patterns emphasize the entrepreneurial incentives that may undergird the strategic deployment of certain kinds of metadata practices.

The iTunes-specified categories rank highly within the podcast/episodic keywords list on PodcastRE, reflecting the structuring effect of the preferred vernacular prescribed by the commercial platform. With the exception of several iTunes subcategories,[3] the other associated keywords had a presence in the podcast/episodic keywords list. Within the list, thirteen out of the sixteen major categories (i.e., Arts, Business, Comedy, etc.) found a place for themselves within the top three hundred keywords,[4] with ten of these thirteen major categories placing within the top fifty. Iterations of these categories, such as just "Film" or "TV" instead of "Film & TV" ranked twenty-four out of one thousand and forty-seven out of one thousand, respectively, on the episodic keywords output. What becomes apparent from these lists is that the categories and keywords Apple defines deeply impact how podcasters choose to define their work in the keywords metadata field. This is despite the fact that after 2012 Apple stopped using keywords as a feature to determine search engine output. This pattern of using iTunes categories may have been borne out of convenience for the podcasters, out of a mistaken conception of which metadata fields creators think are valued for search engine output, or just from how podcasters and listeners have decided to communicate to one another.

Given the importance of iTunes categorizations and genres in shaping keyword metadata, some of the strategies that podcasters use might best be described as "entrepreneurial" with the intention of maximizing discoverability or framing the podcast in relation to other similar and well-known genres/categories. However, Apple's palpable effect on podcaster metadata is perhaps more significant for two additional reasons.

Figure 8.3. Screenshot taken of iTunes preview chart from Apple's iTunes "What's On" page on 08/29/2010. Provided by Wayback Machine. https://web.archive.org/web/20100829175329/http://www.apple.com/itunes/whats-on/

First, the manner in which a podcaster decides to use the vocabulary that is provided by Apple to organize their works inevitably shapes podcast formats and classifications. This, in turn, allows for the metadata to "stand in for the individual, who is made to disappear in favor of a representation that can be effortlessly classified and manipulated" (Milan 2016). Second, and simultaneously, the politics of visibility and community formation become contentious when such dominant categorizing vocabularies are privileged over the preferred vernaculars of podcasters. Even when keywords are deprecated by Apple, these short phrases that are associated with content aid in immediately situating potential listeners to the positionality of the podcasters. Therefore, these keywords can also signal who is the welcome and privileged listener, serving as a lightning rod to focus a community around certain ideologies, phrases, and concepts. Consequently, the metadata aids in the work of meaning-making and ontological context-building for the community itself.

The fact that the keywords field is rife with "uncategorized" or blank hits within the database reveals that the practice of filling in this metadata field is unpredictable and individualized at best. Given that Apple deprecated the keyword field, the fact that podcasters continue to fill out these metadata fields suggests we should recognize the potential affordances of this practice beyond the possible benefits of maximizing discoverability. The more subversive use of the keywords field aids creators in self-defining their content and helps gesture to listeners the podcasters' intentions. Sometimes this is done by using a vocabulary that isn't necessarily recognized as valuable to search engine algorithms, exemplifying a potential opposition to the purely entrepreneurial approaches of metadata creation, by instead privileging community, discourse, and culture building. This seems to be the case for the *UnLearned* podcast, which came to my attention through its persistent use of keywords that helped the show surface through the PodcastRE Keyword Word Cloud discovery feature. This piqued my interest in their content and motivated me to explore the podcast further.

UnLearned is a podcast created by Katherine (Kat) Thornton. Often, with other cohosts like Bill and Mesha Arant, this group of podcasters tackles issues that plague people of color using current news, comedy, and personal anecdotes to narrativize their experiences. Their first podcast was released on October 5, 2015, on their personal website, and they remained active until 2019. One of the most striking characteristics about the *UnLearned* web page interface is the privileging of keywords as they are transformed into literal tags at the bottom of each podcast update post. With the exception of an occasional mention of the category "politics," which touches upon the iTunes "News & Politics" category, all of the keywords speak to issues regarding the Black community and engage in cross-platform activism that are signaled by phrases like "Black Lives Matter," "Consent is Sexy," "Black Girl Magic," and "MeToo." Beyond these transmedial activist initiatives, these phrases stand side by side with community-specific colloquialisms such as "white boy tragic" and "nappy."

This privileging of activist rhetoric and Black vernaculars on the level of metadata outlines the boundaries of *UnLearned*'s publics, which defy the larger, all-inclusive categories like "Society & Culture" that serve to conveniently conceal these sociocultural contours within the activist podcasting landscape. With this extensive use of keywords, it also allows *UnLearned* to use the polysemic affordances of these activist phrases to gain narrative agency over the expansive transmedial movements from which they draw inspiration (Yang 2016). For example, in Episode 27, titled "College and the American Dream" (*UnLearned* 2016), hosts Kat and Mesha bring together topics of Black Lives Matter with the indigenous activist movement that was happening concurrently with regard to the Dakota Access Pipeline. The keywords metadata for this particular episode are shown in figure 8.4.

The alliance of Black activism with indigenous activism within the scope of this one episode transforms the boundaries of the public that *UnLearned* is addressing and gestures toward the formation of alliances within their keywords. In Sarah Florini's analysis of the podcast *This Week in Blackness*, she notes how:

> despite the potential such [digital] networks hold for marginalized people, digital media sociality and the architectures of digital media networks can reproduce the emphasis on the individual that is at the core of neoliberal racial ideologies, creating the potential for dominant racial logics to map easily onto digital networks. (2017, 441)

In defiance of this neoliberal individualist ideology, Florini argues that Black podcasters foster the development of a Black counter-public that refuses to be whitewashed. Similarly, I believe that *UnLearned*'s use of keywords, which bring racial groups into close (digital) spatial proximity to one another, yields similar results. *UnLearned* uses the "architectures of digital media networks"—namely, metadata—to address topics of intersectionality, as words/phrases such as "gender" are grouped together with issues that plague both racial communities, such as "stu-

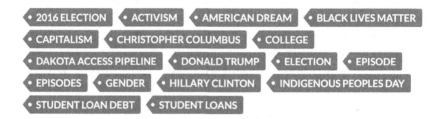

Figure 8.4. *UnLearned*'s Episode 27 keywords screenshot 11/20/2018 from https://www.unlearnedpodcast.com/episode-27-college-and-the-american-dream/

dent loan debt." Through this grouping, we see how *UnLearned* brings disparate topics together, exercising narrative agency over their own artistry and activism and presenting it to their listeners. Far from the modes of neoliberal individualism that digital media sociality may emphasize, *UnLearned* demands that racial communities come together and find the commonalities of experience regarding marginalization and disenfranchisement and, most importantly, stand together in that common struggle as a heterogenous collective. What is perhaps most subversive about this use of keywords is that even if these topics are not necessarily deeply connected in the podcast proper, the podcasters are forcing all of these topics and ideas into one spatial dimension in the keywords metadata field. This makes the topics come into contact with one another, allowing listeners to draw modes of relationality among these keywords for themselves before engaging with the hosts.

UnLearned's deployment of keyword metadata exemplifies their participatory engagement with the material and symbolic interfaces of RSS feeds that govern the automated consumption of podcast content. They defy corporate-driven content aggregate platforms, like iTunes, that have downplayed this heuristic mode of creator self-definition. They exhibit their agency through their continued subversion of the norms of iTunes categorizations that reflect a commercial ethos, instead opting for a more politically driven framework for self-definition. *UnLearned*'s metadata has also affected the structure of the queried keyword cloud (in this case, when I searched for the keyword "activism"), allowing for an unexpected discovery within PodcastRE. These multidirectional flows of influence reveal the complex interplay between actants when creators engage with and exert user agency within the context of the content aggregate platform, whether it is iTunes or PodcastRE. These fraught exchanges between interface, infrastructure, and creator agency reveal how the datafication of identity affects not only our ability to understand our own agency but also the epistemological formation of how one knows and understands the social world and the placement of the self within it. Tagging content and incorporating keywords presents a heuristic method in which one can relay knowledge and validate content. As we have seen in the output of PodcastRE's keywords, the affordance of self-definition through this keyword field can prove to be perverse or even destructive, as the phrases that dominate the PodcastRE Keyword Word Cloud are often iTunes-specified categories and "blank/uncategorized" text. This influx of iTunes-specified categories as keywords has the potential of covering up these micro-level activisms that are happening within the podcasting community on the level of metadata. However, when one is open to the possibility of finding the exceptions and the peculiarities in the metadata output, the benefits of big data methodologies exhibit themselves by providing a way to engage with micro-scale exceptions in relation to the mass collective.

Conclusion

In this chapter, I have argued that the utility of big data methodologies within the humanities stems from the ability to rearticulate the contextual elements that surround any given cultural artifact. It allows for new modes of inquiry that focus on different features of podcasting as part of a broader media landscape that encourages researchers to parse larger bodies of data to discover and validate the existence of cultural trends. Within the PodcastRE database, we have provided two metadata visualization applications that may aid in new modes of discovery for researchers of podcasting culture. These two applications can prove to be powerful and useful tools, particularly when research questions are tailored to the affordances that these visualizations provide and when users understand the provenance of the data that is being provided. Further, both applications serve as alternative modes of discovery, potentially allowing for lesser-known podcasts to float to the surface. In implementing these applications on the PodcastRE website interface, we hope to assist in reestablishing context within the digital archive. In order to fully understand a podcast's position in the broader ecosystem of its production, distribution, and consumption, it is critical that digital archivists look into how researchers can access the metadata of their artifacts. Without such affordances, it becomes far too easy to forego crucial information that makes artifacts important in the first place.

As I was finishing this chapter, two events reinforced the unique challenges of contemporary digital research: the first is that a new identity-laden keyword appeared on my activism word cloud: "indigenous cultures"; the second is that Apple announced that in 2019 it would be closing down the iTunes application for good in order to split their unwieldy software into three separate apps, devoted to music, movies, and podcasts, respectively. These two moments poignantly exemplified the manner in which digital research and preserving digital content like metadata proves to be a test of time as research quickly becomes outdated as new developments happen in real-time. Regardless, it remains imperative that scholars stay flexible and alert to these changes, as change signals important developments that shape our digital engagement. While these industrial shifts continue to impact the cultural landscape of podcasting, it remains the case that it is within the metadata that we continue to see important meaning-making work happen from both commercial and individual actors alike. Moments such as the tension that was stirred by Apple's demand that podcasters not put episode numbers in their metadata, and the company's consequent rescinding of their previous statement after much pushback from the podcaster community, reflects the continuing importance of metadata construction in the process of digital media creation and consumption (Binder 2019).

Simultaneously, it is within this subtle space that we see clashes between platforms and marginalized communities. In the face of potentially hostile digital environments, metadata and "under-the-surface" resistance is where we can see marginalized voices make their stand. It is a subtler form of resistance that is nevertheless crucial in understanding how disparate communities carve out space for themselves. Despite the hegemonic influence that commercial entities like Apple have exerted on podcasting culture, creators continue to establish their own agency through the digital architectures of the platform. While acknowledging the palpable effects that the platform architecture has in the formation of our communication practices, we must remain vigilant for signs of user resistance within these spaces. Even though the process of discovering and archiving these contentious interactions may be messy, it is a critical endeavor for understanding podcasting as an evolving and negotiated process of self-expression.

Notes

1. The following data was exported by PodcastRE back-end developer Sam Hansen, from the University of Wisconsin–Madison. Hansen exported the keywords for the podcast, episodic, and "all" (podcast and episodic collectively) categories utilizing MySQL queries for the entire PodcastRE database in October 2018. The research within this chapter reflects the state of the PodcastRE database during this time period.

2. Since the completion of the original research for this chapter, Apple has updated their podcast categories (Cridland 2019).

3. Buddhism, Hinduism, Judaism, Social Sciences, "Other," "Other Games," "Aviation," "Automotive," "Shopping," "Business News," "Local," "Non-Profit," "Regional," "K-12," "Alternative Health," "Education Technology," "Management & Marketing" (though "Marketing" placed at 122), "Language Courses" (though "Language" ranks at 397), and "Software How-To." Fashion & Beauty, Fitness & Nutrition, and College & High school were all found, albeit separately.

4. "Religion & Spirituality" and "Games & Hobbies" were found, albeit separately ("Religion," "Spirituality"). Similarly, while "Government" for "Governments & Organizations" was found, "Organizations" could not be found on the list.

Works Cited

Ankerson, Megan Sapnar. 2012. "Writing Web Histories with an Eye on the Analog Past." *New Media & Society* 14 (3): 384–400. doi:10.1177/1461444811414834.

Apple Inc. 2010. "iTunes Preview: Apple—iTunes—What's on—Discover Music, Movies, and More." August 29. Digital image. Accessed June 24, 2019. https://web.archive.org/web/20100829175329/http://www.apple.com/itunes/whats-on/.

Apple Inc. 2006. "Podcasting and iTunes: Technical Specifications." Apple—iTunes—iTunes Store—Podcasts—Technical Specification. December 15. Accessed June 18, 2019. https://web.archive.org/web/20061215123228/http://www.apple.com/itunes/store/podcaststechspecs.html#_Toc526931698.

Binder, Matt. 2019. "Apple Walks Back Statement after Freaking Out Podcasters." *Mashable.* March 1. https://mashable.com/article/apple-podcast-email-episode-titles-removal/.

Blubrry. N.d. "iTunes." *Blubrry* Podcasting. Accessed June 18, 2019. https://create.blubrry.com/resources/powerpress/powerpress-settings/itunes/.

boyd, danah, and Kate Crawford. 2012. "Critical Questions for Big Data: Provocations for a Cultural, Technological, and Scholarly Phenomenon." *Information, Communication & Society* 15 (5): 662–79. https://doi.org/10.1080/1369118X.2012.678878.

Campbell, Karlyn Kohrs. 2005. "Agency: Promiscuous and Protean." *Communication and Critical/Cultural Studies* 2 (1): 1–19. https://doi.org/10.1080/1479142042000332134.

Crawford, Kate, Mary L. Gray, and Kate Miltner. 2014. "Critiquing Big Data: Politics, Ethics, Epistemology | Special Section Introduction." *International Journal of Communication* 8: 1663–72.

Cridland, James. 2019. "New and Changed Apple Podcasts Categories: Summer 2019 (updated)." *Podnews*. June 5. Updated November 27, 2019. https://pod news.net/article/apple-changed-podcast-categories-2019.

Crowe, Anne. 2020. "101 Quick & Actionable SEO Tips That Are HUGE." *Search Engine Journal* (blog). October 21. https://www.searchenginejournal.com /101-quick-seo-tips/180563/.

Florini, Sarah. 2017. "This Week in Blackness, the George Zimmerman Acquittal, and the Production of a Networked Collective Identity." *New Media & Society* 19 (3): 439–54. https://doi.org/10.1177/1461444815606779. First published October 7, 2015.

Gitelman, Lisa. 2013. *"Raw Data" Is an Oxymoron*. Cambridge: MIT Press.

Hogan, Mél. 2018. "*Dykes on Mykes*: Podcasting and the Activist Archive." *TOPIA: Canadian Journal of Cultural Studies* 20: 199–215. https://doi.org/10.3138/to pia.20.199.

Jmortizsilva, and Shawn Thorpe. 2015. "Add iTunes Keywords." *Blubrry*. December 17. https://forum.blubrry.com/index.php/topic,6862.0.html.

Jockers, Matthew L. 2013. *Macroanalysis: Digital Methods and Literary History*. Urbana: University of Illinois Press.

Kennedy, Helen, Thomas Poell, and José van Dijck. 2015. Introduction to the Special Issue on Data and Agency. *Data & Society* 2 (2): 1–7. https://doi.org /10.1177/2053951715621569.

Kramer, Michael J. 2014. "Digital Historiography & the Archives." MichaelJkramer. net. January 20. https://www.michaeljkramer.net/digital-historiography-the -archives-55/.

Lewis, Daniel. 2016. "Podcast SEO for iTunes/Apple Podcasts, Google Play Music, and More—TAP291." *The Audacity to Podcast*. November 22. https:// theaudacitytopodcast.com/podcast-seo-for-itunes-google-play-music-and-mo re-apps-tap291/.

Mandato, Angelo. 2018. "iTunes Keywords Missing?" Support. *Wordpress*. June 15. https://wordpress.org/support/topic/itunes-keywords-missing/.

Markov, Ilia. 2019. "SEO Basics: A Noob-Friendly 5-Step Guide to SEO Success." *Ahrefsblog*, February 7. https://ahrefs.com/blog/seo-basics/.

Milan, Stefania. 2016. "Data Activism as the New Frontier of Media Activism." In *Media Activism in the Digital Age*, edited by Victor Pickard and Guobin Yang, 151–63. London: Routledge.

Ortega, Ray. 2017 "Podcasters' Roundtable Example RSS Feed." *Podcasters' Roundtable*. August 22. https://podcastersroundtable.com/pm17/.

Podcast Motor. n.d. "10 SEO Tips for Your Podcast." *Podcast Motor*. Accessed June 10, 2019. https://www.podcastmotor.com/seo-tips-podcast/.

PodcastRE 2018a. Activism and Black Women Keywords Column. Digital image. PodcastRE. Accessed November 20, 2018. http://www.podcastre.org/.

PodcastRE 2018b. Activism Word Cloud, Digital image. PodcastRE. Accessed November 20, 2018. http://www.podcastre.org/.

Ratcliffe, Christopher. 2016. "SEO Basics: 22 Essentials You Need for Optimizing

Your Site." *Search Engine Watch* (blog). January 21. https://searchenginewa tch.com/2016/01/21/seo-basics-22-essentials-you-need-for-optimizing-your -site/.

Sassoon, Joanna. 2007. "Beyond Chip Monks and Paper Tigers: Towards a New Culture of Archival Format Specialists." *Archival Science* 7 (2): 133–45. https:// doi.org/10.1007/s10502-007-9045-7.

Sternfeld, Joshua. 2011. "Archival Theory and Digital Historiography: Selection, Search, and Metadata as Archival Processes for Assessing Historical Contextualization." *American Archivist* 74 (2): 544–75. https://doi.org/10.17723/aa rc.74.2.644851p6gmg432h0.

UnLearned. 2016. "Episode 27: College and the American Dream." *UnLearned.* October 10. www.unlearnedpodcast.com/episode-27-college-and-the-americ an-dream/.

UnLearned. N.d. "About." *UnLearned.* Accessed June 10, 2019. https://www.unle arnedpodcast.com/home/.

Yang, Guobin. 2016. "Narrative Agency in Hashtag Activism: The Case of #Black-LivesMatter." *Media and Communication* 4 (4): 13–17. http://dx.doi.org/10.17 645/mac.v4i4.692.

Zappavigna, Michele. 2011."Ambient Affiliation: A Linguistic Perspective on Twitter." *New Media & Society* 13(5) : 788–806.

NINE | Drifting Voices

Studying Emotion and Pitch in Podcasting with Digital Tools

JACOB MERTENS, ERIC HOYT,

AND JEREMY WADE MORRIS

The exchange in the graphic novel panel in figure 9.1 highlights one of the ironies of contemporary radio and podcasting: hosts put a tremendous amount of effort into sounding like they are speaking effortlessly. "To sound like an actual person saying those words, and not somebody reading a page, that's a craft," says Ira Glass as he offers further tips for achieving this (qtd. in Abel 2015, 101). Similarly, on NPR's website, Jessica Hansen explains, "Lifting the words off of the page to sound like you're truly telling the story to the listener in the moment is a very specific skill. It takes practice" (Hansen 2017). In a training video, Hansen suggests broadcasters avoid a "scripted voice" by imagining a specific person listening to them or even reading the script as a character—such as a cowboy or a toddler throwing a temper tantrum—to note how pitch and resonance change with that affectation (NPR 2017). Vocal advice also abounds on the internet for podcasters who are speaking extemporaneously and not reading from scripts. "Slow down when speaking" and "use pregnant pauses for emphasis" are two tips from the *Podcasting Hacks* blog that echo techniques promoted by NPR luminaries (*Podcasting Hacks* n.d.).

All of these tips, guidelines, and recommendations for finding one's unique voice (yet in this standard, teachable way) remind us that, despite their associations with amateurism and DIY media, many kinds

Figure 9.1. Jessica Abel and Ira Glass talk remotely about the challenges of speaking naturally on the radio

of podcasts are now encouraged to follow particular kinds of vocal performances. But these evolving stylistic conventions also raise a series of questions. For starters, what exactly does it mean to sound "natural" or "like an actual person saying those words"? More specifically, why should podcasters be trying to sound this way, and what does it mean for the format if a particular conversational tone becomes an aesthetic or stylistic ideal? While podcasting's vocal performances are typically contrasted with the authoritative, objective, and scripted speaking styles of newscasters and university professors who previously occupied more of public broadcasting's schedule, we should be mindful of the way that "natural" speech is always a culturally and socially contingent form of speech. What any individual listener hears and perceives as "natural" is highly dependent on the sonic cultures, conventions, and traditions that have contributed to their aural experiences.

In the case of podcasting, this particular vocal performance style has gained enough coherence and recognition that some critics have given it a name: "NPR Voice" (Wayne 2015). Describing the approach to vocal performance that is exemplified but not limited to Ira Glass and associated sound workers who trained or worked at NPR, Teddy Wayne says this in describing NPR Voice: "In addition to looser language, the speaker generously employs pauses and, particularly at the end of sentences, emphatic inflection." The result, Wayne argues, is "the suggestion of spontaneous speech and unadulterated emotion. The irony is that such presentations are highly rehearsed, with each caesura calculated and every syllable stressed in advance." Wayne highlights an important dynamic in professional podcasting here, as hosts work to liven up scripted material through a more open emotional register that still has a strong degree of control and even the codification of emotional inflection. Meanwhile, Tom McEnaney takes a more affirmative stance on these changes, arguing that the intentional "quirkiness" in vocal performances on NPR's *This American Life* "clear[s] new ground or open[s] new social-acoustic space for an American public unaligned with the traditional broadcast voice of authority" (2019, 112). With that said, using the term "NPR Voice" may fail to capture the nuance of this style of performance, as there are several different ways to strike a balance between an improvisational cadence and professional deliberation.[1]

Still, if the claim of a singular voice on NPR feels somewhat exaggerated, we can still note how the broad influence of NPR's style of performances creates norms and assumptions about what makes for a good vocal performance in contemporary audio media. These norms provide podcasters, particularly those within the American public media ecosystem, with a menu of aesthetic options to choose among as they attempt to engage an audience that expects a balance between personal and professional styles of delivery. When thinking of podcasting, then, the pivotal questions become: How are podcasters using vocal performances to communicate meaning and emotion? and What are the stakes if one manner of speaking becomes more privileged than others as the stylistic ideal that comes to define the format?

This chapter investigates those two questions by employing digital tools to *denaturalize* the voices of podcasters located both inside and outside the NPR ecosystem. By using the forced aligner Gentle and the pitch tracker Drift, we seek to explore how precisely these productions approach vocal delivery. How do podcasters attempt to wed scripted material with emotional cadence? What is it about this delivery that clearly differentiates it from other podcasts and from formal expectations that accompanied previous audio media like broadcast radio? And how can we empirically analyze these techniques and differences? Through digital tools that measure fine-grained aspects of vocal performances, we pinpoint clear differences between various genres of podcasting and intervene into the debates surrounding vocal delivery. First, we look at meditation and news podcasts to find a baseline for controlled vocal delivery. Next, we examine different NPR podcasts in an attempt to delineate common strategies of vocal performance as seen through pitch and rhythm. Finally, we look at the ways more conversational and improvisational podcasts differ from these controlled and scripted models.

Through these comparisons of pitch and emotional cadence, we can begin to understand the cultural implications of professional vocal performance norms beyond simply observing that they posture toward informality while involving a strict rehearsal process. Instead, we argue that what critics call NPR Voice uses the differentiation of pitch to serve a host of formal strategies, including the segmentation of topics and segues between interviewers and interviewees, and to emphasize dramatic takeaways (e.g., Wayne's charge of emphatic inflection). In other words, broadcasters take the typically improvisational characteristics of emotional inflection and give them a consistent, dedicated purpose in their delivery. This practiced use of emotional inflection can help "lift the words off of the page" and make for compelling listening. But it is worth asking what we lose if we simply accept this voice as the sound of podcasting's professionalization. By formalizing a particular kind of vocal delivery typically used in more unrestrained moments, we refashion the sonic character of emphatic cadence into a tool. In contrast, the less-controlled vocal deliveries in our third set of case studies demonstrate that when pitch becomes radically altered, it often aligns with a moment of unrestrained expression. This should not suggest that the so-called NPR Voice somehow denigrates a more improvisational form of podcasting or that one approach is preferable to another. However, we should question what we might forfeit in our desire to professionalize the improvisational and intimate and look into whose voices may be excluded in the drive to encourage a particular kind of vocal performance.

Digital Tools and Methodologies for Vocal Performance Analysis

Our original vision for this chapter was to run sonic analysis algorithms across the entire collection of PodcastRE sound files. If Teddy Wayne

and other critics could hear an "NPR Voice," would a computer detect
this pattern as well or help us locate specific characteristics of this vocal
performance? Would the computer notice other patterns of vocal performance, perhaps quite different from what looms large in the ears and
minds of human critics? However, given that the database contains over
two million podcast episodes, the computing demands of such a large
analysis are considerable, especially given the huge variety of frequency
and amplitude data we would collect across these vastly different audio
files. For example, a movement in the frequencies that might seem to
indicate upspeak might just be two people talking over each other. Some
digital humanists have found workarounds to the computing and inter-
pretive challenges, and we considered using the approach that Tanya
Clement and her collaborators innovated and implemented on ARLO
and HiPSTAs[2] (Clement and McLaughlin 2016; Mustazza 2018). However, the algorithmic sampling method that Clement used for poetry
readings was less effective for podcasts, a form in which music or a
canned advertisement is likely to be sampled instead of the host's vocal
performance. These nonvocal performance samples might lead to an
intriguing project, but our focus on the emergence of particular kinds of
vocal performances required a more targeted approach.

We ultimately found the best methods and tools for our investigation through the work of Marit J. MacArthur, Georgia Zellou, and Lee
M. Miller. Their *Cultural Analytics* article, "Beyond Poet Voice: Sampling
the (Non-) Performance Styles of 100 American Poets" (2018), and
their investigation of the maligned concept of "poet voice" served as
a productive model for our study. Using digital tools, they examined
how one hundred different poets conformed to or deviated from the
assumptions about this measured, elitist style. MacArthur and Miller
(along with Robert Ochshorn, Neil Verma, and Mara Mills) invited us
to participate in their NEH-supported initiative, "Tools for Listening
to Text-in-Performance," which provided workshops for software training for two open source tools that were suitable for our needs: Gentle
and Drift.[3] Both developed by Robert Ochshorn and freely downloadable online, the two programs operate in scaffolded fashion. Gentle is a
forced aligner—a program that ingests a media file, accepts a transcript,
and then precisely matches each word and phoneme to the transcript. It
can also generate a rough transcript if one is not provided, though the
accuracy will vary according to audio quality and other factors. Drift then
tracks the pitch of a speaker's voice in hertz—the fundamental frequency
of the voice—every ten milliseconds and creates a line graph called a

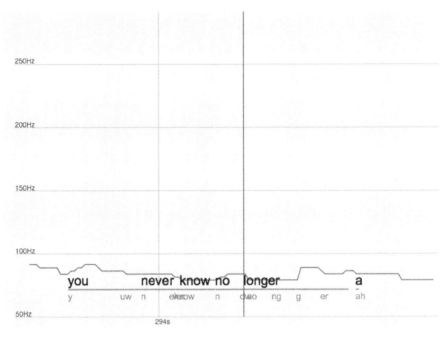

Figure 9.2. Pitch contour for *The Meditation Podcast* "Intense Cleanse"

pitch contour, showing the rise and fall of pitch over time (fig. 2). Drift also aligns the text of the transcript beneath the pitch contour, using the timing information provided by Gentle, and provides a close-up view of how these changes are measured across the frequency spectrum (fig. 3). Together, Gentle and Drift offer a user-friendly way to import a podcast, generate a rough transcript, align the words and phonemes to that transcript, and study intonation patterns.

The biggest limitation of Gentle and Drift is *scale.* There is no way to batch ingest and analyze one hundred thousand, ten thousand, or even ten podcasts at a single time. The programs work best on one sound file at a time, and preferably smaller clips within that file, such as a 30- or 60-second portion. This led us to develop a far more focused study on a few specific cases rather than the entire database and to be mindful of any large-scale generalizations we might make, which resulted in an analysis that neatly combined machine and human listening. Rather than handing off all of the listening duties to the digital tools, Gentle and Drift forced us to listen more closely to the podcasts ourselves and understand the mechanics of vocal performance in new ways. They also

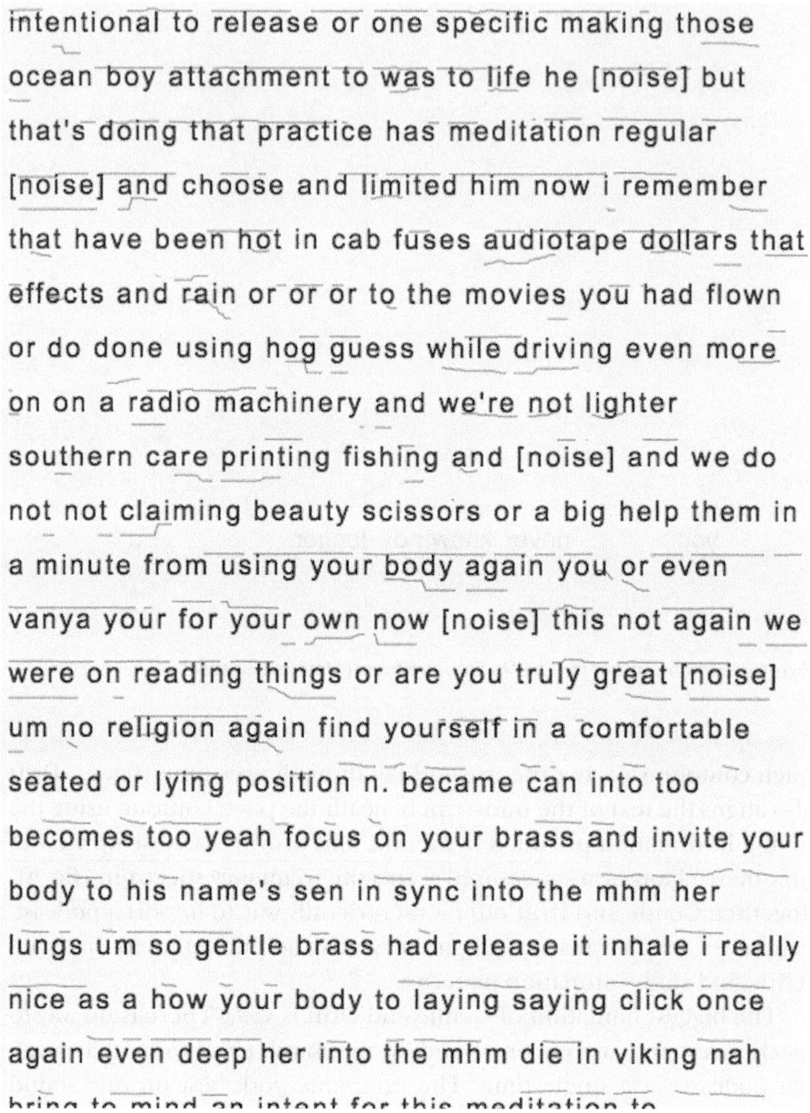

intentional to release or one specific making those
ocean boy attachment to was to life he [noise] but
that's doing that practice has meditation regular
[noise] and choose and limited him now i remember
that have been hot in cab fuses audiotape dollars that
effects and rain or or or to the movies you had flown
or do done using hog guess while driving even more
on on a radio machinery and we're not lighter
southern care printing fishing and [noise] and we do
not not claiming beauty scissors or a big help them in
a minute from using your body again you or even
vanya your for your own now [noise] this not again we
were on reading things or are you truly great [noise]
um no religion again find yourself in a comfortable
seated or lying position n. became can into too
becomes too yeah focus on your brass and invite your
body to his name's sen in sync into the mhm her
lungs um so gentle brass had release it inhale i really
nice as a how your body to laying saying click once
again even deep her into the mhm die in viking nah
bring to mind an intent for this meditation to

Figure 9.3. An overhead view of pitch beneath transcript of *The Meditation Podcast* "Intense Cleanse"

allowed us to use the computer to supplement, extend, and challenge the interpretations we were making through listening.

Amanda Nell Edgar's (2014; 2019) work was also a source of inspiration, particularly her use of digital tools to deconstruct some of the assumptions embedded in, and ascribed to, various voices. Edgar uses a method she calls "critical cultural vocalics" to examine both the physiological processes that make bodies sound and the cultural processes that make hearing and listening to any vocal performance a practice that is always laden with ideas about the gender, race, and other culturally constructed markers of identity of the speaker. Looking at the complicated case of the singer Adele, for example, and how critics praised her voice as "authentic" largely due to her use of historically Black sounds and vocal techniques, Edgar argues that qualities like vocal timbre are important nodes of communication, filled with "hidden texts of race, gender, class, and historically and socially constructed authenticity." Labeling a voice or vocal performance "natural" or "authentic," in other words, involves a series of culturally constructed judgments about what/who counts as natural or authentic, judgments that are highly influenced by much longer personal and social histories of hearing and listening. Edgar goes on to argue how, with enough repetition, certain vocal performances become "culturally privileged" through celebrity or mass mediation, and these sonic representations can have a disciplining effect on certain identities and voices (e.g., women's voices in comedy).

As with our study, Edgar works to identify how hidden or unstated aesthetics can shape the tone and meaning of certain sounds or sonic formats. Additionally, she offers us an important reminder that given how intertwined voices are with other markers of identity (e.g., race, class, gender, age, etc.), problematic biases against certain voices are often passed off as simply aesthetic judgments. Female radio voices are regularly dismissed as insufficiently authoritative and critiqued for their vocal fry. Black voices and voices by hosts of color are often regarded as unprofessional. These biases can then inform the larger debate surrounding NPR's training and trends of vocal delivery as women and people of color work to break into the industry and validate their projects. For example, Chenjerai Kumanyika, an African-American podcaster and academic, recounts the details of a radio workshop he took and the influence that years of NPR-style radio listening had on his expectations for vocal performances:

My piece was about a fisherman who manages the tuna club of Ava-
lon. But while editing my script aloud, I realized I was also imagining
another voice, one that sounded more white, saying my piece. Without being directly told, people like me learn that our way of speaking
isn't professional. And you start to imitate the standard or even hide
the distinctive features of your own voice. (2015)

In other words, as particular vocal styles and performances start to
emerge as prized or privileged in various media formats, we would do
well to question what features and qualities make up those performances
and what kinds of voices are being left out of conversations as a result.

Our goal here is to think through what these ideas and arguments
might mean for podcasting and for the expectations that may be starting
to form around the vocal performances that are praised and encouraged in this fledgling format. For this chapter, we focus principally on
emotional inflection through pitch modulation, noting how hosts can
either use these aspects as part of a distinct vocal pattern that satisfies formal goals—as is often the case with NPR-style productions—or vary their
pitch in a less regimented way, which can open up possibilities for how
hosts convey both emotion and their personal investment in a discussion or project. In the process, we hope this study can help to question
how attempts to mimic some version of an NPR-style podcast might limit
other possibilities and even have repercussions for voices and identities
of those who either cannot or do not want to emulate a particular style
or aesthetic.

By applying digital tools and our own close listening to several podcast examples—ranging from highly rehearsed and controlled meditation and news podcasts, to tightly edited but seemingly unrehearsed
NPR-style podcasts, to shows that feature less rehearsed performances
and greater dynamic range—we analyze the features that make NPR
podcasts distinct from others and vice versa. These case studies, to be
sure, do not offer an exhaustive and authoritative account on how these
performances work within a diverse field podcasting. But this initial work
illustrates the kind of insights made possible through vocal performance
analysis with Gentle and Drift and offers some intriguing preliminary
results, keeping the door open for future research. In our analysis, we
do not mean to suggest one style of vocal performance is better or more
necessary than the others. Rather, we are interested in what kinds of
podcasts rely on which techniques and what the impact of pushing one
technique or aesthetic over others is.

Controlled Vocal Delivery: Meditation and News Podcasts

Before analyzing the ways NPR podcasters vary pitch and frequency during their vocal performances, we began by establishing a baseline using highly controlled vocal performances that require relatively measured speaking: meditation and news podcasts. In the case of meditation podcasts, we find a natural extreme for controlling emotional intonation because the performers speak more slowly, use a narrow pitch range, and generally draw out their syllables as they speak. Their voices lead listeners through a guided meditation by remaining calm and deliberate, ensuring their words will not disrupt the repose they attempt to establish. News podcasts, on the other hand, have grown from the historical legacy of radio and TV broadcasting, wherein hosts use consistent pitch intonations to convey a sense of confidence, knowledge and objectivity. A qualitative study of what qualities constituted a "good" radio voice, for example, showed that radio professionals believed newsreaders need "a voice that's immediately and clearly understood" and that favors a slower speaking rate, lower pitch, and will "make use of downward inflections and theatrical pauses to convey authority and knowledge" and communicate information legibly (Warhurst et al. 2012, 222). In both cases, vocal performers pare down their vocal inflections and pitch variations, even if that strategy serves entirely different purposes.

As guided meditation podcasts have increased in popularity, a number of vocal conventions have solidified. Namely, these podcasts use long stretches of silence—and occasionally a minimalist ambient musical track—while the meditation leader interjects with gentle reinforcements about clearing one's mind or other mantras of personal well-being. Moreover, the performance style seems closely aligned with what Marit MacArthur has called "monotonous incantation" in spiritual vocal performances, particularly in its "flattened affect that suppresses idiosyncratic expression of subject matter in favor of a restrained, earnest tone" and "the subordination of conventional intonation patterns dictated by particular syntax, and of the poetic effects of line length and line breaks, to the prevailing cadence and slow, steady pace" (2016, 44). As we look at this vocal performance in Gentle and Drift, we first notice how narrow the pitch range looks with no sudden shifts in pitch. Take figure 9.3, which features a segment from an episode of *The Meditation Podcast* called "Intense Cleanse" (Stern and Stern 2018). From a macro perspective, the Drift screenshot shows that the vocal performance remains tightly controlled throughout the script, as the pitch often appears as a straight, unerring line throughout the transcribed script.

However, to fully appreciate this regimented control, we must look at the vocal performance from a sentence-by-sentence structure to see the small variations of pitch taking place. In figures 9.4 and 9.5, we note recurring vocal patterns of the podcaster speaking in a way that deliberately curtails dynamic shifts in pitch and intonation. The vocal pitch wavers roughly around the 75Hz range, and moments of small modulation in pitch, as found at figure 9.4's 82-second mark, are generally followed by smooth intonations in which the performer draws out their syllables with a slow and unaffected speaking rhythm. Notably, figure 9.4 features moments when the podcast sound mix includes brief musical instrumentation to accompany the vocal performance, which then registers between 200Hz and 100Hz. The podcaster's voice lies comfortably beneath that instrumentation, creating a deep, resonant bass meant to soothe the listener. Finally, unlike with news podcasts, the speaker does not favor downward inflection or end the sentence at a lower pitch but instead emphasizes a sustained inflection in which the voice remains a consistent pitch until the end of the sentence. In figure 9.5, we can see that even when the vocal performer fails to fully sustain that unwavering pitch, as with the syllable voiced at the 214-second mark, the performer still makes an effort to keep from inflecting downward and ultimately steadies the pitch by the second syllable ("saying").

We found similar patterns across other sampled meditation podcasts, regardless of whether the host was male or female. Even in cases where there was a higher vocal pitch and the host adopted a more casual conversational tone, the speaker gradually settles into a pitch that barely fluctuates as the meditation carries on. *The Tara Brach Podcast*'s episode "Breath by Breath," for example, begins with the vocal performer speaking within the 150Hz–200Hz range (Brach 2018). After these opening moments, however, her performance levels off and she starts to hold her syllables longer and vary her pitch much less frequently, just as we saw in our first case study. Deep into the meditation, her voice consistently registers lower, at roughly 150Hz, and shows even more regimented vocal control than in our first case. In all the meditation podcasts we listened to, though, we heard what a purposeful lack of emotion and excitement can sound like when the speaker works in such a narrow pitch range, favoring a near monotone.

Unlike with meditation shows, news podcasts need not remove all emotional inflection from their delivery, but they do consciously work

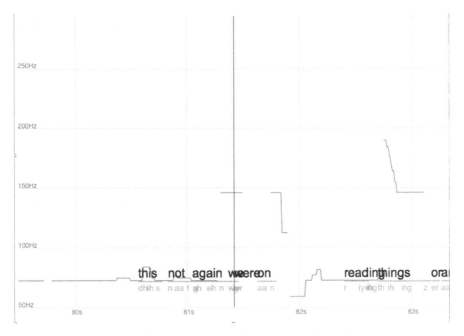

Figure 9.4. Pitch contour for *The Meditation Podcast* "Intense Cleanse"

to undercut that tendency. To demonstrate this technique, we studied several different hosts from *PBS NewsHour*'s "News Wrap" segment (*PBS NewsHour* 2018). The podcasts had more pitch variation than the meditation podcasts; the speakers were not trying to rigidly remain calm or soothing for their vocal delivery. However, when we analyzed representative segments more closely, such as the September 7, 2018, episode in figure 9.6, we still see controlled patterns in vocal delivery begin to emerge. Here, the pitch varies notably in range, fluctuating between 350Hz and 125Hz, but the speaker engages in a pattern where they start at a higher pitch and then inflect downward, giving each sentence a weighty punctuation or a feeling of gravitas. Unlike with NPR Voice, this vocal pattern remains largely unchanged throughout the podcast and acts as a totalizing strategy for imbuing the news script with a professionalized, deep resonance.

While the vocal performances in meditation and news podcasts have different contours and characteristics because of their different intents (calm, soothing relaxation instructions versus imparting information objectively and confidently), both of them still make use of rigid and highly rehearsed variations in pitch and dynamic range. The result is a

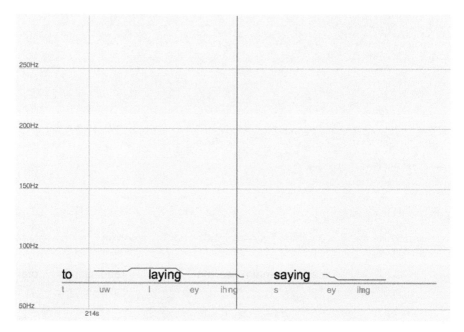

Figure 9.5. Pitch contour for *The Meditation Podcast* "Intense Cleanse"

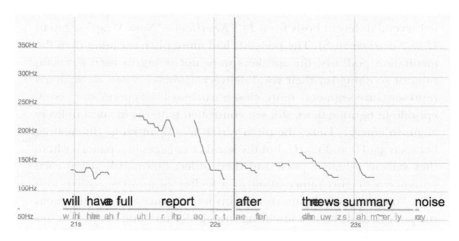

Figure 9.6. Pitch contour for *PBS NewsHour* "News Wrap—Trump Steps Up Attacks on Unsigned Essay"

decidedly structured and tempered listening experience, which comes across as more formal and distant than the NPR and conversational podcasts we turn to next.

The Flexibility of Semiformality: NPR Podcasts

In describing NPR's broad style of vocal performance, Ben Yagoda suggests that "the days when we expected and believed in glossy opacity are over. A smooth delivery is no longer trustworthy" (2015). Ira Glass, who critics often label as the essential example of NPR Voice despite the fact that he no longer works at or produces podcasts for NPR, concurs:

> Back when we were kids, authority came from enunciation, precision. But a whole generation of people feel like that character is obviously a phony. . . . Any story hits you harder if the person delivering it doesn't sound like a news robot but, in fact, sounds like a real person having the reactions a real person would. (Wayne 2015)

Whether applied to current NPR podcasters, to NPR alumni like Ira Glass, or to podcasters emulating and iterating a similarly emotionally affective vocal delivery (e.g., Sarah Koenig, Alix Spiegel, Alex Blumberg, etc.), NPR Voice acts as an ambiguous and catchall term for performances that seem more personalized and less formal in tenor. While we are not particularly interested in quantifying what is or is not NPR Voice, we are curious as to what vocal traits might be favored here, especially in comparison to more formally voiced podcasts like meditation or news shows, in performances that audiences read and interpret as using NPR Voice. While Yagoda, Wayne, and Glass focus more attention on the imperfections and stammering lines of dialogue left in final edits of NPR podcasts, we believe that an equally common unifier can be found in the rehearsed flexibility of emphatic pitch inflection. This flexibility affords the hosts several formal options in which they can use pitch to help structure their conversation or highlight important moments.

Studying *This American Life*'s episode "Fermi's Paradox," we can note that Ira Glass performs these emotional inflections at several important moments (Glass 2018). By examining the opening moments of the episode, we see a vocal performance not altogether dissimilar from the meditation and news podcasts: Glass starts at a higher pitch and inflects downward, then keeps his emotional modulations subdued as he reads the script. However, a few moments later he reveals that his subject was

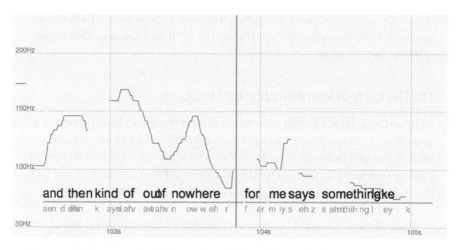

Figure 9.7. Pitch contour for *This American Life* "Fermi's Paradox"

speaking to coworkers about extraterrestrials. At this moment, the host clearly wants to point out the importance of this topic and use it as a hook into the episode. Consequently, his pitch quickly rises with the word "extraterrestrials" in a moment of pitch emphasis, moving from 100Hz to 150Hz. Glass also tends to inflect upward on narrative transitions in the script. For instance, his delivery remains subdued as he relays the everyday conversations his subjects have about extraterrestrials in their place of work, with negligible moments of pitch modulation. However, immediately after these lines the host utters the phrase "And then, kind of out of nowhere," marking a shift in the story (fig. 9.7). At this moment, Glass once more inflects his pitch upward to signal a shift in the story from mundane water-cooler talk to something more consequential. These moments of pitch inflection, then, take on a grammatical function in which the host can use it to punctuate moments of dramatic salience.

These techniques also carry over in NPR's interviewer-interviewee model. In *Invisibilia*'s episode "The Pattern Problem," Alix Spiegel interviews a woman named Tarra who grew up with a troubled past and moved beyond it, challenging assumptions about patterned behavior (Spiegel 2018). At the start of the episode, Tarra relays the story about when she witnessed a man being beaten in her home by her friends and how she went to jail herself for conspiracy to commit assault. As Tarra tells the listeners about the assault, her vocal delivery maintains a subdued natural cadence and her pitch modulates evenly throughout, moving between

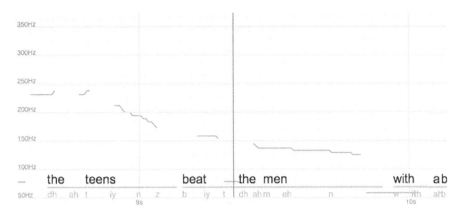

Figure 9.8. Pitch contour for *Invisibilia* "The Pattern Problem"

150Hz and 200Hz.[4] Spiegel then cuts in to help frame her interview, using pronounced pitch inflection that segments the two vocal deliveries and signals listeners toward an important summarization (fig. 9.8). Spiegel reiterates Tarra's narrative by stating, "The teens beat the man with baseball bats and beer bottles," with the words "the teens" rising significantly in pitch. Similarly, in figure 9.9, Spiegel employs the same technique for the line "Tarra was sentenced to eight months in jail." In both cases, the host's initial emphatic inflection levels off and resumes a more controlled vocal delivery. Meanwhile, these upward pitch inflections help to drive home the visceral impact of her subject's story. We might also consider that the subject relays this information as a story from her past, a hardship long since overcome, and that while her emotional inflections seem less rehearsed, they also lack a sense of urgency. The host's emphatic inflection could then be seen to discursively place the story as emotionally salient and pressing.

Unrehearsed and Unrestrained: Conversational Podcasts

Again, our description of some of the characteristics of the semi-informal but strategically structured NPR aesthetic is not meant as a critique of it, nor is it meant to suggest this is the only style of vocal performance that relies on this type of pitch modulation. One could just as easily view these formal characteristics as creative solutions to the scripted voice, innovating the rehearsed performance in ways that appeal to a new online audience. Instead, our concern is that this class of vocal perfor-

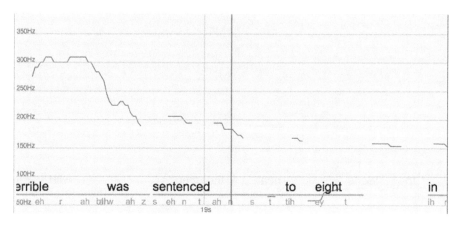

Figure 9.9. Pitch contour for *Invisibilia* "The Pattern Problem"

mance has fast become shorthand for "professional yet personal" and a kind of culturally privileged form of vocal delivery that might ultimately have an impact on amateur podcast productions looking to gain wider recognition and distribution. Part of the appeal of podcasting is that it allows for a broader range of production contexts and has the ability to empower marginalized voices, even if corporate players have quickly adapted to this new medium. As Jonathan Sterne and his colleagues observe, "There is also something about broadcasting as a cultural form, with its labyrinthine regulatory apparatus, its massive institutions, and its heavily professionalized practices that invites this kind of David versus Goliath thinking, which renders podcasting as a term that seems full of potential and possibility even when the landscape of podcasting is dominated by its own star system" (2008). In other words, as podcasting stabilizes industrially and economically, is it generating pressures for particular kinds of vocal performances? And, if so, do these pressures make some voices and vocal performances more likely to succeed than others? While this question will take more time and data to answer, we wanted to consider for our last case what conversational podcasts might tell us about the voice as a kind of alternative to the evolving professionalization embodied by NPR and others. By studying key moments in these kinds of podcasts, we can pinpoint a form of emotional expression that more controlled and strategic vocal deliveries will leave behind.

We began by examining a range of conversational podcasts, from amateurs to more "professional" conversations. For example, Marc Maron, while technically independent and more loosely scripted than the pod-

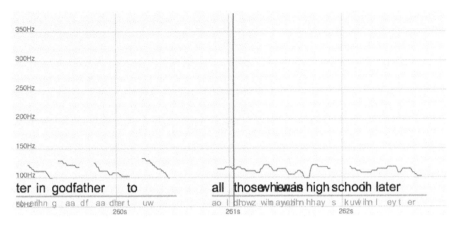

Figure 9.10. Pitch contour for *WTF with Marc Maron* "Episode 938—Luzer Twersky"

casts above, still has many years of practice doing stand-up comedy and media interviews, which inevitably help craft his vocal performance. Studying Maron's popular *WTF with Marc Maron* in "Episode 938—Luzer Twersky," initial readings seem relatively subdued as Maron begins the episode (2018). His performance is a little erratic, as he tends to trail off when he speaks and there's a little more unpredictability in his pitch fluctuation. There are also long stretches where Maron remains relatively relaxed as a performer, and his vocal patterns demonstrate small, consistent, and restrained shifts in pitch (fig. 9.10). There comes a point in the episode, however, when Maron expresses his love for Robert De Niro. Here, the pitch swings wildly and peaks around 250Hz, well above his resting pitch at 100Hz. In figure 9.11, we can actually pinpoint the moment when Maron grows so excited that his vocal performance shifts from comfortable and conversational to unrestrained and passionate.

Maron's excitement offers one kind of tangible departure from the rehearsed emotional intonations in NPR's podcasts, but the sound of unrestrained emotion can have a strong political dimension to it as well. Consider, for instance, how in the amateur series *Clock Radio Speakers*, hosts Armond Wakeup and Doc discuss the controversy involving the Los Angeles Clippers' former owner Donald Sterling, who was recorded making a series of racists remarks to his girlfriend in Episode 145 (see Mertens, this volume, for further analysis) (*Clock Radio Speakers* 2018). Like Maron, the hosts begin with a relatively subdued delivery while unpacking the details of this controversy. However, as the discussion continues, their frustration clearly begins to boil over and we can see their

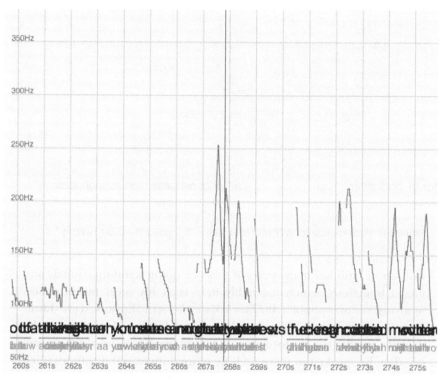

Figure 9.11. Pitch contour for *WTF with Marc Maron* "Episode 938—Luzer Twersky"

speaking rhythm increase and their voices continue to rise in pitch and intensity (fig. 9.12). Finally, as the hosts get invested in the issues that the controversy raises and relate how this moment in sports speaks to the larger experiences they face as Black men in contemporary American society, we can see again the clear moment when unrestrained emotion takes over the vocal performance (fig. 9.13). Unlike Maron's gleeful take on the idea of working with Robert De Niro, here the unrestrained sentiments are frustration and anger. If this podcast had been rehearsed rather than performed extemporaneously, the hosts' arguments may have seemed more strategically structured, but they would have undoubtedly sacrificed the *sonic character* of their frustration.

Conclusion

Across the range of podcasts we examined—from the highly controlled vocal performances of meditation and news podcasts, to the semi-

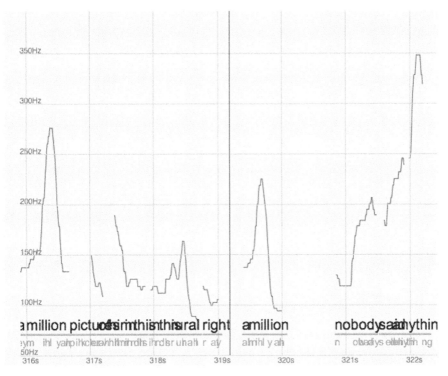

Figure 9.12. Pitch contour for *Clock Radio Speakers* "Episode 145 Side A: Donald Sterling & the NBA Playoffs"

controlled and strategically structured NPR-style podcasts, to the more erratic and unrehearsed conversational podcasts—we see how fluctuations in pitch are used to create specific affective resonances but also how they are deployed for specific kinds of vocal performances and aesthetic effects. Although the scope of our study was not large enough to apply conclusions to the entire collection of podcasts in our database, we do hope this exploratory research points to some avenues scholars can pursue when analyzing podcasts comparatively and sonically instead of just individually or solely by their content or form. We have reflected on our tools, methods, and dataset so as to approach them as an ongoing conversation about the assumptions built into vocal performances and digital technologies. Our selected tools, Gentle and Drift, proved to be much more helpful at digging deeply into individual podcasts (and into specific moments within those podcasts) rather than a large-scale analysis of the PodcastRE collection as a whole. Generally speaking, we found these limitations productive, as we were able to establish patterns

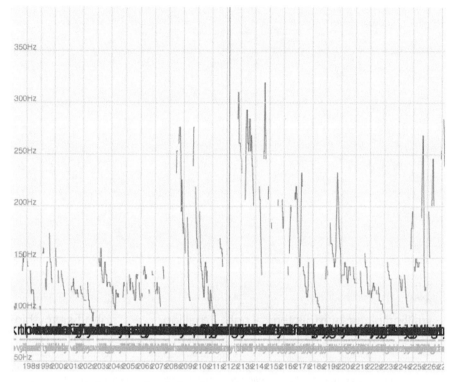

Figure 9.13. Pitch contour for *Clock Radio Speakers* "Episode 145 Side A: Donald Sterling & the NBA Playoffs"

through our close listening and qualitative analysis that will hopefully lead to meaningful approaches toward distant listening in future studies.

Through our limited case studies, we observed patterns of pitch inflection that communicated structure and meaning to the listener. We surveyed a range of vocal performances and identified some patterns in podcasts that conformed to NPR's broad formal strategy—patterns that were strategically deployed to evoke certain reactions. We also found powerful moments of emotional expression that eschewed the advice of self-help guidebooks and blog posts. We came away with a deeper appreciation for the range of possibilities for vocal performance and how differences in performance style can sometimes shift in the midst of a recording. And while the lack of large-scale analysis means we cannot confirm how prevalent NPR's aesthetic is across the entire ecosystem of podcasts, we can certainly detect specific traits and features of this style of performance that critics and how-to-podcast guides are increasingly positioning as a desired and ideal voice for the format.

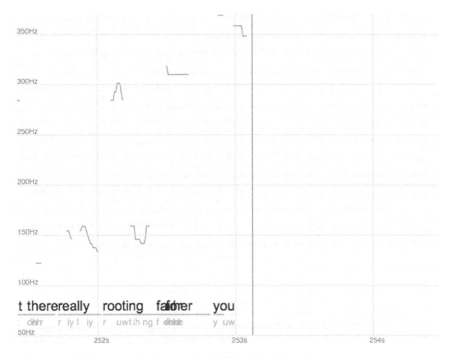

Figure 9.14. Pitch contour for *Love and Radio* "The Living Room"

Consider this final example, which features a mix of the vocal performances we discuss above. *Love and Radio*'s episode "The Living Room" seems at first glance to use an NPR mold as the narrator Diane Weipert uses emphatic pitch to vary an otherwise subdued performance (Weipert 2015). However, at a critical moment, the entire tenor of the episode changes thanks to a shift in vocal performance. In this episode, Weipert tells the story about how she began spying on her married neighbors who lived across from her and always left their living room blinds open. Throughout most of the episode, she seems to narrate as if someone else were in the room with her listening to the story for the first time, though her emotional inflections remain in control and help to punctuate the humorous elements of the story. Studying her performance through Drift, we can see that her pitch modulates frequently, as she tends to slowly raise and lower it as she moves through story. As with the other NPR-style podcasts, these strategically calibrated vocal performances help engage us in the story and move the narrative forward. However, later in the episode the story takes a dark turn as Weipert learns that the husband's health has slowly deteriorated and eventually comes to understand that he is dying. As Weipert reaches the end of her story, her easy performance breaks down and she begins to choke back tears. Her overall pitch rises considerably from a 260Hz peak to a 340Hz peak; her speaking rhythm becomes more staccato as she tries to get the words out; and each syllable she utters has upward pitch inflections that span over 200Hz as her voice cracks at the end of the episode (fig. 14). As the narrator becomes overwhelmed, her previously careful, NPR-esque delivery is usurped by something more visceral and unplanned. These are the types of moments of intimacy and connection with sound for which podcasting is so often praised. We argue that there is more than one way to achieve that connection and that the variety of ways to do so is part of podcasting's original promise as an emerging format. Privileging NPR Voice as a standard or an aesthetic ideal to which podcasters should strive robs the format of some its most unique possibilities.

Notes

1. Yes, many *This American Life* alumni give performances that sound like Ira Glass (listen, for example, to Alix Spiegel, Sarah Koenig, and Alex Blumberg—in fact, it's easy to confuse Blumberg for Glass). But the voices of Terri Gross, Sam Sanders, Linda Holmes, and Brooke Gladstone present a range of alternatives.

2. HiPSTAs stands for High Performance Sound Technologies for Access and Scholarship. It is a project/virtual research environment for researchers to use to better access and analyze spoken word collections that might be of interest to digital humanities scholars. ARLO stands for Adaptive Recognition with Layered Optimization and is a technology that was originally developed for analyzing birdcalls. It has been repurposed as a more general machine learning system that can process all kinds of multimedia for sonic features like pitch, rhythm, and timbre for discovery and automated classification.

3. For more on this project, see: Northwestern n.d.

4. Vocal ranges do vary by gender, though many reports simplify or reduce the extent of vocal ranges in casual discussions. While men tend to speak in lower ranges and women in higher ones, there is significant overlap, with male voices anywhere between 65Hz and 260Hz and female voices ranging from 100hz to 525hz (VoiceAcademy 2020).

Works Cited

Abel, Jessica. 2015. *Out on the Wire: The Storytelling Secrets of the New Masters of Radio.* New York: Broadway Books.
Brach, Tara. 2018. July 19. "Meditation: Breath by Breath—Inviting Relaxation and Ease." Podcast audio. *Tara Brach.* Accessed June 27, 2020. https://podca stre.org/episode?id=ep1098989.

Clement, Tanya, and Stephen McLaughlin. 2016. "Measured Applause: Toward a Cultural Analysis of Audio Collections." *Journal of Cultural Analytics*. May 23. https://doi.org/10.31235/osf.io/8p5cf.

Clock Radio Speakers. 2014. April 29. "Episode 145 Side A: Donald Sterling & the NBA Playoffs." Podcast audio. *Clock Radio Speakers*. Accessed June 27, 2020. https://podcastre.org/episode?id=ep186213.

Edgar, Amanda Nell. 2014. "Blackvoice and Adele's Racialized Musical Performance: Blackness, Whiteness, and Discursive Authenticity." *Critical Studies in Media Communication* 31 (3): 167–81. doi: 10.1080/15295036.2013.863427.

Edgar, Amanda Nell. 2019. *Culturally Speaking: The Rhetoric of Voice and Identity in a Mediated Culture*. Columbus: Ohio State University Press.

Glass, Ira. 2018. July 8. "Fermi's Paradox." Podcast audio. *This American Life*. NPR. Accessed June 27, 2020. https://podcastre.org/episode?id=ep691974.

Hansen, Jessica. 2017. "Aerobics for Your Voice: 3 Tips for Sounding Better on Air." NPR. June 19. https://training.npr.org/audio/aerobics-for-your-voice -3-tips-for-sounding-better-on-air/.

Hilmes, Michele. 2013. "The New Materiality of Radio: Sound on Screens." In *Radio's New Wave: Global Sound in the Digital Era*, edited by Jason Loviglio and Michele Hilmes. New York: Routledge.

Kumanyika, Chenjerai. 2015. "Challenging the Whiteness of Public Radio." Code Switch: Race in Your Face. NPR. January 29. https://www.npr.org/sections /codeswitch/2015/01/29/382437460/challenging-the-whiteness-of-public -radio.

MacArthur, Marit J. 2016. "Monotony, the Churches of Poetry Reading, and Sound Studies." *Publication of the Modern Language Association of America* 131 (1): 38–63. January. https://doi.org/10.1632/pmla.2016.131.1.38.

MacArthur, Marit J., Georgia Zellou, and Lee M. Miller. 2018. "Beyond Poet Voice: Sampling the (Non-) Performance Styles of 100 American Poets." *Journal of Cultural Analytics*. April 18. https://doi.org/10.31235/osf.io/5vazx.

Maron, Marc. 2018. August 2. "Episode 938—Luzer Twersky." Podcast audio. *WTF with Marc Maron*. Public Radio Exchange. Accessed June 27, 2020. https://po dcastre.org/episode?id=ep721374.

McEnaney, Tom. 2019. "This American Voice: The Odd Timbre of a New Standard in Public Radio." *The Oxford Handbook of Voice Studies*, edited by Nina Sun Eidsheim and Katherine Meizel. New York: Oxford University Press, 2019.

Mustazza, Chris. 2018. "Machine-Aided Close Listening: Prosthetic Synaesthesia and the 3D Phonotext." *Digital Humanities Quarterly* 12 (3). http://www.digit alhumanities.org/dhq/vol/12/3/000397/000397.html.

Northwestern. n.d. "Text in Performance" Accessed June 17, 2019. https://texti nperformance.soc.northwestern.edu/.

NPR. 2017. "Three Tips for Training Your Voice | NPR Training | NPR." YouTube video, 9:12. June 19. https://www.youtube.com/watch?time_continue=537& v=cSTqKi7Wuq4.

PBS NewsHour. 2018. September 7. "News Wrap: Trump Steps Up Attacks on Unsigned Essay." Podcast audio. *PBS NewsHour*. PBS. Accessed June 27, 2020. https://www.pbs.org/newshour/show/news-wrap-trump-steps-up-attacks-on -unsigned-essay#audio.

Spiegel, Alix. 2018. March 29. "The Pattern Problem." Podcast audio. *Invisibilia*. NPR. Accessed June 27, 2020. https://podcastre.org/episode?id=ep463718.

Stern, Jesse, and Jean Stern. 2018. April 23. No. 54. "Intense Cleanse." Podcast audio. *The Meditation Podcast*. Accessed June 27, 2020. https://themeditation podcast.com/meditations.html.

Sterne, Jonathan, Jeremy Wade Morris, Michael Brendan Baker, and Ariana Moscote Freire. 2008. "The Politics of Podcasting." *Fibreculture* 13: After Convergence. http://thirteen.fibreculturejournal.org/fcj-087-the-politics-of-podcasting/.

Vocal Academy. 2020. "Home Gym: Teachers are Vocal Athletes Who Can Benefit by Keeping their Voices in Tiptop Shape." https://voice-academy.uiowa.edu /gym. Accessed November 10, 2020.

Warhurst, Samantha, Patricia McCabe, and Catherine Madill. 2012. "What Makes a Good Voice for Radio: Perceptions of Radio Employers and Educators." *Journal of Voice* 27 (2): 217–24. https://doi.org/10.1016/j.voice.2012.08.010.

Wayne, Teddy. 2015. "'NPR Voice' Has Taken Over the Airwaves." *New York Times*. October 24. https://www.nytimes.com/2015/10/25/fashion/npr-voice-has -taken-over-the-airwaves.html.

Weipert, Diane. 2015. March 3. "The Living Room." Podcast audio. *Love and Radio*. Radiotopia. Accessed June 27, 2020. https://podcastre.org/episode ?id=ep682300.

Yagoda, Ben. 2015. "So NPR Voice, Ya Know . . ." *Chronicle of Higher Education*, November 5. https://www.chronicle.com/blogs/linguafranca/2015/11/05 /so-npr-voice-ya-know/.

Imagining Podcasting's Future

TEN | The Scholarly Podcast

Form and Function in Audio Academia

MACK HAGOOD

As the existence of PodcastRE and this volume demonstrate, the internet's nature as a searchable, networked media archive has provided scholars with new modes of communication and new questions about the functional and institutional value of these forms. At the intersection of digital audio production and academia, we find a variety of nascent genres, formats, and practices, only some of which fall neatly into the popular conception of "podcasting." In this chapter, I provide an overview of what I call "audio academia": a diverse collection of initiatives aimed at producing and communicating scholarship through electronic audio in the form of podcasts, audiobooks, online lectures, and other genres. I examine its past precedents, rationale, current forms, and future possibilities. I then turn to study the scholarly podcast per se, which currently includes two main types: what I call "hi-fi, mid-register" shows for broad audiences and "lo-fi, high-register" shows for scholars. I conclude by advocating for a third, fledgling type of podcast that draws inspiration from both, taking audio production seriously as a mode of scholarship and drawing upon institutional resources such as grants, professional associations, and academic publishers to develop forms that function both as "publication" and "creative work."

Historical Precedents

As oral traditions such as incantations, proverbs, folktales, Socratic dialogues, and Chautauqua remind us, sonic inquiry and pedagogy long predate, and have coexisted with, the written word. Even the academic use of mediated sound has a long history, though most of that history pairs the medium of radio with the rather narrow mission of K-12 distance learning, beginning in the 1920s, when radio "first began grappling with the logistical difficulty of reaching all of the nation's students with a coherent curricular formula" (Shepperd 2018, 214). Given the deserved and infectious excitement surrounding our current "golden age" of podcasting, it is both fitting and instructive to look back on its historical precedents in radio's golden age (see Bottomley, this volume).

Examining early radio history, we find American educational stations struggling to compete with their commercial peers, due in part to their parent educational institutions' lack of commitment to the medium. As Katie Day Good points out, prior to the US Communications Act of 1934 and its allocation of radio spectrum to commercial interests, "the airwaves were crowded with the sounds of a heterogeneous mix of amateur, independent, and commercial broadcasters, including universities, newspapers, religious and educational groups, and department stores," many of which "produced educational programs in an effort to publicize their brands and impress upon the public the social value of radio" (2020, 59). Sadly, this heterogeneity was not long for the world, and by 1936 only thirty-eight of some two hundred licensed educational stations remained operational (Purdy 1980).

The parallels to the current state of podcasting are fairly obvious. As one journalist points out, we've seen this "folksy art form with deep roots in public radio, built almost as an afterthought," grow into a smorgasbord of some 1 million shows that has enticed over half the country to at least try a nibble (Kachka 2019). This increased listenership has resulted in an influx of venture capital and the rise of major commercial players who dominate download rankings. Given that, like its radio predecessor, academic podcasting enjoys comparatively little institutional support, the story of educational radio should probably be read as a cautionary tale. Indeed, the risks are compounded by the fact that, unlike in radio, podcasting's educational fare can sometimes be paywalled, siloed, or made subject to corporate caprice. A case in point is Apple's iTunes U, a distribution service for audio, video, and textual content produced by universities worldwide. In 2017, Apple removed the iTunes U component from its iTunes application for Mac and Windows, making the content available only within its Podcasts app for iOS—a change that disenfranchised the majority of the world population, which does not own an iPhone, iPad, or iPod.

On the other hand, radio history also provides inspiration—most importantly, the School of the Air (SOA) movement, which existed from the 1920s into the 1970s and included "over a dozen SOAs" (Bianchi 2008, 36). According to William Bianchi:

> While the federal government and educational organizations avoided making a commitment to a national SOA, the newly formed commercial broadcast networks, the National Broadcasting Company (NBC) and the Columbia Broadcasting System (CBS), saw great benefit in such programming. They wanted to demonstrate that they could be trusted to make responsible use of the public airwaves. Broadcasting for the schools would help them fill airtime during the day and encourage greater use of the radio. (37)

In this environment, a number of 1920s and 1930s educators and programmers successfully managed to bend the commercial radio spectrum to their pedagogical purposes: Benjamin Barrow's Sears, Roebuck & Company–sponsored *Little Red Schoolhouse of the Air* aired on Chicago's WLS (Good 2017); "The Hoosier Schoolmaster of the Air," Clarence M. Morgan's broadcast on Terre Haute's WBOW (Myers 2016); and programmer Judith Waller of WMAQ, Chicago, supplied a steady stream of educational talks and other edifying content (Keeler 2017). Given that the first decade of podcasting has followed a trajectory similar to that of early radio, in which a heterogeneous space of RSS feeds has come to be dominated by a number of commercial podcast production and distribution outfits, resourceful individuals such as these may be our best historical models for educational digital audio production.

Then again, like Apple's iTunes U, commercially broadcast SOAs were subject to corporate whim—and by the 1940s they were disappearing. During that same decade, however, state-based public SOAs popped up in Ohio, Wisconsin, Texas, Oregon, Minnesota, and New York. "Compared to the network offerings, state-based SOAs were long-lived; three of six operated for four decades or more," Bianchi writes. "Several influenced state educational curricula, and all paved the way for educational television in the classroom" (2008, 39).

Hope can also be found in the difference between the one-to-many broadcast model that came to dominate radio and the many-to-many internet model that allows for greater content diversity. Moreover, unlike radio spectrum, podcast feeds are not a finite resource and the costs of entry remain low. These factors should allow a diversity of audio academics to operate both within and without commercial models. As in other areas of contemporary media production, the problem has shifted from gaining access to distribution to finding an audience in a thicket of digital content while capital owns the big machetes. But as audio academia expands well beyond the narrow K-12 education mission, scholars can rely on their preexisting professional networks to share more specialized forms of sonic scholarship.

Scholarship Out Loud

In addition to content similar to the youth-focused and general interest programming that characterized educational radio, more specialized and sophisticated expressions of scholarship are emerging through the medium of digital audio. While podcasting is used to translate and popularize academic research, it also has potential for inter- and intradisciplinary communication and for providing an alternative to the written word in the creation of original research. But before describing these nascent genres of audio academia, it is worth discussing why these forms are emerging at all. What are the mediatic and methodological advantages of audio in scholarly argumentation and communication? Why should we do scholarship *out loud?*

For those of us working in the humanistic field of sound studies, the benefit is self-evident. It has long been a point of frustration that, ironically, we spend most of our time producing silent, print-, or pixel-bound scholarship on the subject of sound. It is true that the printed word can evoke sound in human heads—and many sound scholars do consider imagined sound to be a form of sound—but there are still specific limitations to the printed word, no matter one's subject matter. To outline these limitations—and audio's ability to transcend them—it is useful to refer to linguist Robin Lakoff's triangle of linguistic structure (2012).

As Lakoff explains, language simultaneously expresses three different yet interconnected dimensions: form, meaning, and function. Formal qualities such as phonology, syntax, spelling, and audible tone are, to borrow from Gregory Bateson, differences that make a difference, allowing us to discern one unit of language from another (2000, 272). The meaning of a specific word results from its differences with other words (Saussure 2011), while its performative function arises in particular acts of communication and reception (Austin 1962; Searle et al. 1980). These three dimensions are never apart from one another; changing the spelling of a word, for example, can subtly or dramatically change its meaning and function in a sentence as well.

Comparing speech to writing in this regard, we note how the former gives us a whole set of audible formal expression that the written word can only imitate—differences that good poets, actors, and orators expertly manipulate, including pitch, volume, speed, timbre, and syllabic emphasis. These formal elements both expand the range of semantic and pragmatic possibilities and add precision to these dimensions of speech. Take, for example, the phrase "He's dead." In a podcast, I could utter these two words in many different ways, altering the words' meaning and function subtly or completely, all without adding or subtracting a letter from the script I am reading. Almost effortlessly, I may voice these two words as a lament, an admission, or a threat.

There are other dimensions of verbal communication to consider, such as the indexicality to place on a speaker's accent (Wilce 2012, 143) and the clues about their identity, psychology, and even body that the voice provides. There is also an affective dimension: the way one body makes a kind of contact with another via vocal vibration. We can hear and feel the sound of the body in speech—a mode of extralinguistic communication that transcends the triangle of form, meaning, and function. This is the resonance of a resonating body that resonates a listening body, an affective dimension of voice in the Spinozan sense of one body acting upon another (1970). Again, a good writer can conjure or approximate many of these things in the mind. "Silent" reading can be an affective experience, of course. But it is a different experience.

Furthermore, just as a journal article can offer illustrations and graphs, there are ancillary advantages to working in sound. A podcast offers the ability to use not just words but also sound, music, and silence—powerful tools for formulating arguments, providing evidence, illustrating points, developing empathy, and giving listeners space to think. In the case of fields such as cultural anthropology, we can also hear directly from informants and interlocutors in their own voices, potentially bolstering credibility and even empathy in the reception of an academic argument. Similarly, in fields such as musicology and sound studies, we can often listen to a researcher's primary data, allowing us to better judge the analysis and the credibility of the argument.

If the reader will bear with a second triangle, the old Greek triad of rhetoric and persuasion—*logos*, *ethos*, and *pathos*—may be of use in describing the difference a sonic argument can make. At the risk of reifying the differences between the senses or promising a "secondary orality" (Ong 2002) or "global village" (McLuhan 1964), working in sound can allow the scholar to shift some of the weight of academic work from an Enlightenment reliance on *logos* back to a more ancient integration with *ethos* and *pathos*. Assuming she voices her own work, the audible character of the creator comes into play during a podcast—the audience is given more information to judge the trustworthiness of the author (although here aural prejudices can also come into play, since the voice is not free from bias either, as Edgar's [2019] work suggests). Furthermore, a different kind of affective connection is available to be made or broken. Other voices and other forms of sonic evidence and persuasion open up. In short, doing sonic scholarship opens up a different set of performative, affective, argumentative, and evidentiary possibilities, contributing to a greater breadth and variety of research (and ways to communicate that research) in the humanities.

For the reader who has worked in radio, film, or television, a likely response to all of this is *no kidding*! However, due to the written word's hegemony in academia, scholars have not leveraged these affordances of sound to any great degree. To my knowledge, even in the field of sound studies, we do not have a regularly appearing audio or podcast-driven journal.[1] There is also the very real problem of whether audio work, which is time consuming when done with high production values, actually "counts" on scholarly CVs when it comes to hiring, promotion, and tenure. For these reasons, while podcasts have been an increasingly important means of intra- and interdisciplinary communication, they have yet to emerge as a polished mode of primary scholarship.

Genres of Audio Academia

In keeping with the foregoing disclaimer, outlining the genres of audio academia is a somewhat speculative practice, as examples are not exactly bountiful, especially for some types of content. Even in cases where many examples exist, since this short chapter is not intended as an annotated bibliography, only one or two examples of a genre are cited. Instead, the following list blends description with a bit of prescription—one scholar's admittedly idiosyncratic dreams for the audio-based scholarship of the future. And while I am disclaiming, I might as well note that while this list conceives of audio production as a communicative art, it does not include sound art per se, as "art for art's sake." The genres below all involve the crafting of—and/or communication of—research-based arguments.

Audio Journals. As already mentioned, I am not aware of a regularly appearing, audio-only journal featuring article-length original scholarship. I have heard casual discussions about the potential creation of such a journal for the field of sound studies or radio studies—for example, at a meeting of the Great Lakes Association for Sound Studies. There are "one-off" projects that we can look to for inspiration, however, such as *Provoke*, a Duke University–based collection of audio articles edited by Mary Caton Lingold, Darren Mueller, and Whitney Trettien. In one of those articles, Kevin Gotkin, Corrina Laughlin, Alex Gomez, and Aaron Schapiro argue for what they call "susurrous scholarship," which "translates written academic articles into sound pieces, playing with access and address in knowledge production" (http://soundboxproject.com/project-sonifying.html). While this is a powerful idea that is taken up again later in this chapter, the imperative for a scholarly journal to produce *original* scholarship militates against its use in that context. Another possible model is a special issue of *[in]Transition* edited by Northwestern University's Jacob Smith and Neil Verma, titled *Audiography: Recording as Academic Tool*. As these examples show, we are in a very early and necessarily reflexive stage of audio journal production, in which a central research question consists of what audio academia should sound like and what its practices should be.[2]

Audiobooks. Although one of the more venerable genres on this list, the potentials of the audiobook have been underutilized by academics and academic presses. In my survey of the genre, I identify three types of scholarly audiobooks. The first is the already-published academic book, subsequently recorded as an audiobook by a commercial audiobook production company. An example of this is Nicole Starosielski's *The Undersea Network* (2015), which was published in print by Duke University Press and in audiobook format by Audible.com. This arrangement has the benefits of high-quality voice talent, production values, and distribution but relies upon its profitability in the eyes of commercial audiobook vendors. Sadly, such commercially produced academic audiobooks are relatively rare. A second type is the conversion of a published book to noncommercial audio by the author. As of this writing, ethnomusicologist Benjamin Tausig is in the process of converting his Oxford University Press book *Bangkok Is Ringing* (2019) into an *open-access audio* version that features the sounds he recorded during his fieldwork in Thailand. Such projects may be premeditated or retroactively converted from written book to sound.

A third type is the "natively audio" audiobook, a monograph-length project conceived of as a sound project from start to finish. Author Jacob Smith and his editor, Mary Francis, have blazed a trail in this direction with *ESC: Sonic Adventure in the Anthropocene*, an ecocritical study of a golden age radio drama. Published as an open-access audiobook on the Fulcrum platform by University of Michigan Press, this book remixes excerpts of the CBS Radio series *Escape* with contemporary sound art, original music, and Smith's insightful commentary, providing a truly innovative new model of what a book can be.

Audio Lectures. Audio lectures seem to play second fiddle to video lectures, which is somewhat odd, given the fact that lectures are often quite boring visually. Nevertheless, audio lectures can be found in various free and paid platforms such as massive open online courses (MOOCs), YouTube, iTunes U, and The Great Courses. Compared to traditional audiobooks, audio lectures have the advantage of being written to be heard and are often easier to parse than bound prose read aloud. On the other hand, the efficacy of lectures is one of the biggest controversies in higher education, in which proponents and detractors "frantically cite a bunch of studies with anecdotal data and limited conclusions as gospel truth" (Gannon 2018). In any case, a challenge for the audio lecturer is to use digital audio in ways that stimulate the senses and provide space for reflection and response, enabling a kind of parasocial interaction between speaker and listener.

College and Community Radio. Just as terrestrial commercial radio has moved into the podcasting space (creating podcast versions of popular local morning shows, for example), so have independent, community, and college radio stations taken advantage of the web's ability to archive and expand the reach of their once-ephemeral local content. Radio stations have production facilities, know-how, and established audiences that scholars can benefit from. Miami University's *Stats and Stories*, a discussion-based show funded by the American Statistical Society, uses the university's radio facilities and journalism faculty talent to explore the relationship between statistics and current events. College and community radio have long served as platforms where academics can communicate with local audiences and intervene in local issues. A show like *Stats and Stories* has the sensibility and professional feel of local NPR-affiliate programming but uses podcasting to extend the genre's temporal and geographic reach.

Audio Documentary. Another public-facing genre is the stand-alone audio documentary, formatted either as a single show hosted on a website or a multipart, single-season podcast series. A series I executive-produced, *I-69: Sounds and Stories*, serves as an example of both a collaboration with community radio and an audio documentary series. In this project, I led a team of Indiana University undergraduate students in an ethnographic study of a controversial new interstate highway that was to bisect many small communities in Southern Indiana. Through field recordings and interviews, the team documented the sonic character of this rural region and its meaning to local residents, thus arguing for the human value of a soundscape soon to be overlaid with highway noise. This student-produced series won the Best Use of Radio Sound award from the Indiana Associated Press and allowed undergraduates to intervene in a hot-button local political issue.

Podcasts. Although any of the genres discussed in this chapter could potentially be distributed as a podcast through an RSS feed, some scholarship will be most legible to audiences as fitting within the podcast genre: a serialized episodic or scheduled release of audio files via RSS feeds delivered to a listener's device(s) of choice (Hansen, this volume). As a genre of limited-run or multiseason program, hosted on its own website, a podcast usually delivers a consistent format and type of content, though the differences between podcasts can be vast. If, as a simple thought experiment, we think about the huge variety of fiction and nonfiction podcast offerings and then try to imagine academic versions of these diverse shows, we can get a sense of the podcast's enormous potential for moving scholarship beyond traditional genres and modes of delivery.

Two Types of Scholarly Podcast

Currently, there are two main kinds of scholarly podcasts. First, there are polished and public-facing programs meant to translate scholarship to a broad audience; usually these shows are produced by public radio entities or commercial startups (often staffed by former public radio producers), although some are produced by universities and not-for-profit entities. Podcasts such as *Radio Lab, Invisibilia, Freakonomics, Science Vs.,* and *The Infinite Monkey Cage,* and various podcasts produced by the Vox Media group use a "high-fi, mid-register" combination of high production values and accessible, often narrative-driven exploration of academic ideas, bringing them to life in the earbuds and minds of nonexperts. Such podcasts bring great benefits to the academy and the public alike and are arguably equaling or surpassing American radio's past educational achievements. One drawback to this genre is that it relies upon journalists' abilities to comprehend and translate the work of academics. Moreover, while these shows may be useful to scholars in other fields, their appeal to experts would likely be limited, except, perhaps, as an undergraduate teaching aid.

Second, there are podcasts made by scholars for other scholars and those with specialist interests. Most often these are unfunded, roughly produced dialogs between scholars in the same or similar fields, with the most common subgenre being Skype-based interviews about recent books. These podcasts tend to emphasize the quick circulation of new ideas *within* the academy and therefore generally use a "lo-fi, hi-register" style in which low (sometimes terrible) production values and specialized language prevail. The podcasts of the New Books Network (NBN), with titles such as *New Books in Intellectual History*, *New Books in Genocide Studies*, and *New Books in Sound Studies*, exemplify the genre. NBN is largely unfunded, its hosts are unpaid and unpolished academics, its editing is nonexistent, and its microphones are often those that came with the scholars' laptops. In other words, NBN provides an important service of intra- and interdisciplinary communication but probably appeals only to more passionate and erudite fans of a given subject. While there are exceptions, such as the high-production *Aca-Media* podcast of the Society for Cinema and Media Studies and the heterogeneous and experimental productions circulated in the sound studies podcast *Sounding Out!*, for the most part, lo-fi/high-register, non-narrativized discussions of theory, methods, and findings rule in scholar-facing podcasting.

"Third-Way" Podcasting

I am in favor of opening up a space between the two aforementioned genres of scholarly podcasts—"a third way" that draws upon the strengths of both. The premise of this work is that scholarship—and particularly sound studies—can and should be done *in sound*. In contrast to most scholar-facing podcasts, which are usually interviews with authors *about* their work, the third-way podcast may stand on its own—either as the sonification of preexisting scholarship or as an original work produced in the audio medium. Such podcasts potentially allow scholars to use the affordances, aesthetics, and evidentiary power of sound mentioned earlier to make arguments that are different from those found in written work. This kind of podcast could also blur boundaries, allowing the scholar to communicate aurally with expert, interdisciplinary, and public audiences alike while bypassing editorial and aesthetic filters of intermediaries such as public radio broadcasters.

The podcast I produce, *Phantom Power: Sounds about Sound*, attempts to enact such a third way. Drawing inspiration from polished, public-facing shows such as *Radio Lab*, *Phantom Power* takes audio production seriously as a way of communicating humanistic inquiry and findings. Each episode is painstakingly produced and features original sound design, music, and interviews with sound scholars, writers, artists, and musicians. Like "hi-fi, mid-register" podcasts, our best episodes find ways to *narrativize* contemporary sound scholarship and sound art. Sometimes we begin with a mysterious sound, for example, and tell the story behind it. However, like scholar-facing podcasts, we do endeavor to get "into the weeds" of academic arguments and controversies, producing a program that is stimulating to experts.

We have a few strategies for bridging the gaps between these audiences and making a show that is useful to experts yet compelling and intelligible to laypeople. The first is the aforementioned practice of narrativization. Finding "the story" is an essential element for NPR producers like Ira Glass and Jad Abumrad, and so many podcasts have an "NPR" narrative sensibility that it can feel oppressive at times. However, it is worth remembering that two different podcasters can tell the same story with completely different narrative styles—and taking risks with temporality, narration (or lack thereof), and sound design can make an episode stand out. On *Phantom Power,* while not all episodes have presented compelling stories as a through-line, I have found that the best episodes often do. In fact, I would rather explore one of a scholar's minor works that has an interesting story and audio attached to it rather than her most impactful publication, if it does not. An example of this philosophy in action is our episode "Test Subjects," in which Mara Mills discusses a little-cited work of hers about "audio inkblots," recordings used to diagnose psychological disorders in blind people. With its surprising history and compelling archive of haunting sounds, this "minor work" from Mills was an ideal way to explore the interplay between media technologies and disability—a theme that runs through her most widely cited publications.

A second strategy is simpler to do but easy to forget to implement. I do not shy away from using expert language, but I do try to remember to define specialized terms and gloss scholarly identities when I "name-drop." It takes only moments to define "affect" or to describe Luc Ferrari's sound piece *Presque Rien,* but it is easy to forget to do so. Yet these little moments of explanation make all the difference in terms of inclusion for nonexperts.

Another useful strategy has been to cohost our show, using a loose, dialogic style. During the first two years of the show, poet and performance artist cris cheek appeared as a cohost. For each episode, either

I, cris, or freelance producer Craig Eley served as the main producer, doing the interviews and editing the sounds and music. cris and I then listened to a rough cut of these productions together and recorded verbal framing and reactions, working off of an outline that listed moments or concepts we wished to emphasize. We would then create a final edit that blended the narrative with our framing and reactions. The usefulness of this approach is that one of us would play the expert while the other stood in for the audience, reacting and asking questions. It didn't hurt that cris and I have differing areas of expertise, so our questions were often quite genuine. Speaking to one another forced us to put complex concepts into informal speech, which is often easier for listeners to parse than scripted language. We would also like to think our dialogues were sometimes funny, though listeners' mileage may vary.

As one can see, the production expertise and time investment required in a third-way podcast can be considerable. The practices outlined above require far more pre- and postproduction work than a simple interview with a scholar—in fact, doing the interview is the easy part. Because of this, we have not always followed our own best practices. For example, some of our shows did not feature a dialogue between cris and me simply because we fell behind schedule and were unable to record and edit one. In fact, just recently, cris decided to leave the podcast because it was taking so much time from his other scholarly and creative efforts. Currently, I am producing episodes without a cohost and weighing the increased speed of working alone against the benefits of finding a new cohost.

The question of time weighs heavily on the third-way podcaster, because it is far from certain that the many hours of production labor will be apparent to or deemed worthy by institutional gatekeepers such as tenure and promotion committees. In fact, one irony of the third-way podcast is that its attention to production quality and audience accessibility might actually undermine its claim to status as "serious scholarship." What Jason Mittell (2020) has written about the challenges facing videographic criticism applies equally to podcasting: "most scholars are not trained to conceptually engage with moving-image media as a mode of scholarly rhetoric, and academic fields have not reconciled how to position such work as part of systems of research, professional development, and peer-review." The technological barriers to audio and video humanistic scholarship have largely fallen away. The barriers that remain are constructs of academics' knowledge, aesthetics, and folkways.

Ultimately, it may be this interplay between institutional values and questions of aesthetics, genre, argumentation, and audience that will either enable audio academia to thrive or prevent it from escaping the margins. Gatekeepers will have to learn not to confuse the format or genre of a scholarly work with its erudition and contribution to the field. Producers will have to learn how to master "new" digital practices and skillfully integrate them with academia's best traditions. Recent peer-reviewed podcasts and podcast dissertations and theses are splendid examples of this approach. By serving as a sortable database of sonic scholarship, PodcastRE—and audio archives more generally—could play a key role in this evolution of audio academia. Not only does PodcastRE provide countless examples of audio that teachers, students, and researchers can use, but it can also provide the raw material for new, remixed sonic compositions. Ideally, PodcastRE will keep a record of audio academia's growth by archiving and rendering findable content such as the many shows mentioned in this chapter—helping audio academics learn from their past while generating future sounds.

Notes

1. Although we are fortunate to have *Sounding Out*, the sound studies blog and monthly podcast.

2. While this book was in press, I learned of The Amplify Podcast Network, Canadian scholar Hannah McGregor's collaboration with the Wilfrid Laurier University Press, which resulted in the first-ever peer-reviewed podcast series, McGregor's "Secret Feminist Agenda." Amplify's mission of generating institutional support and standards for academic podcasting is essential and exciting.

Works Cited

Austin, John L. 1962. *How to Do Things with Words.* London: Oxford University Press.

Bateson, Gregory. 2000. *Steps to an Ecology of Mind.* Chicago: University of Chicago Press.

Bianchi, William. 2008. "Education by Radio: America's Schools of the Air." *TechTrends* 52 (2): 36–44.

Edgar, Amanda Nell. 2019. *Culturally Speaking: The Rhetoric of Voice and Identity in a Mediated Culture.* Columbus: Ohio State University Press.

Gannon, Kevin. 2018. "Lecture-Based Pedagogy and the Pitfalls of Expertise." *The Tattooed Professor.* January 16. https://www.thetattooedprof.com/2018/01/16/lecture-based-pedagogy-and-the-pitfalls-of-expertise/.

Good, Katie Day. 2017. "Listening to Pictures: Converging Media Histories and the Multimedia Newspaper." *Journalism Studies* 18 (6): 691–709.

Good, Katie Day. 2020. *Bring the World to the Child: Technologies of Global Citizenship in American Education.* Cambridge: MIT Press.

Kachka, Boris. 2019. "'The Capitalists Are Here!': Are We in a Podcast Bubble?" *Vulture.* March 18. https://www.vulture.com/2019/03/are-we-in-a-podcast -bubble.html.

Keeler, Amanda. 2017. "'A Certain Stigma' of Educational Radio: Judith Waller and 'Public Service' Broadcasting." *Critical Studies in Media Communication* 34 (5): 495–508.

Lakoff, Robin Tolmach. 2012. "The Triangle of Linguistic Structure." In *A Cultural Approach to Interpersonal Communication,* edited by Leila Monaghan, Jane E. Goodman, and Jennifer Meta Robinson, 135–40. Malden, MA: Blackwell.

McLuhan, Marshall. 1964. *Understanding Media: The Extensions of Man.* New York: McGraw-Hill.

Myers, Mary E. 2016. "The Hoosier Schoolmaster of the Air." *Journal of Radio & Audio Media* 23 (2): 213–28.

Mittel, Jason. 2020. "What Is Videographic Criticism?" *Scholarship in Sound and Image.* http://sites.middlebury.edu/videoworkshop/what-is-videographic-cri ticism/.

Ong, Walter. 2002. *Orality and Literacy: The Technologizing of the Word.* London: Routledge.

Purdy, Leslie N. 1980. "The History of Television and Radio in Continuing Education." *New Directions for Continuing Education,* no. 5: 15–29.

Saussure, Ferdinand de. 2011. *Course in General Linguistics.* New York: Columbia University Press.

Searle, John R., Ferenc Kiefer, and Manfred Bierwisch, eds. 1980. *Speech Act Theory and Pragmatics.* Vol. 10. Dordrecht, Holland: D. Reidel.

Shepperd, Josh. 2018. "Public Broadcasting." In *A Companion to the History of American Broadcasting,* edited by Aniko Bodroghkozy, 211–36. Hoboken: Wiley Blackwell.

Smith, Jacob. 2019. *ESC: Sonic Adventure in the Anthropocene.* Ann Arbor: University of Michigan Press. https://www.fulcrum.org/concern/monographs/rx9 13r17x?locale=en.

Smith, Jacob, and Neil Verma, eds. 2019. *Journal of Videographic Film & Moving Image Studies* 6 (2). *[in]Transition.* http://mediacommons.org/intransition /intransition-audiographic-6-2019.

Spinoza, Benedict. 1970. *Ethics.* New York: Simon and Schuster.

Starosielski, Nicole. 2015. *The Undersea Network.* Durham, NC: Duke University Press.

Tausig, Benjamin. 2019. *Bangkok Is Ringing: Sound, Protest, and Constraint.* Oxford University Press.

Wilce, James. 2012. "The Grammar of Politics and the Politics of Grammar: From Bangladesh to the United States." In *A Cultural Approach to Interpersonal Communication,* edited by Leila Monaghan, Jane E. Goodman, and Jennifer Meta Robinson, 141–51. Malden, MA: Blackwell.

ELEVEN | The Feed Is the Thing

How RSS Defined PodcastRE
and Why Podcasts May Need to Move On

SAMUEL HANSEN

Since the word "podcast" was coined in 2004 (Hammersley 2004), the term has come to signify two related ideas: (1) a piece of on-demand audio, downloadable or streamable to computers or mobile devices, and (2) an on-demand internet radio-style show that recurs over time. Neither of these definitions, however, captures the full nature of the term. By forcing podcasts to be collections, or a single piece, of audio, the word fails to capture how podcast feeds can feature everything from videos to PDFs to PowerPoint presentations. These definitions are not only incomplete; they also manage to be overly broad. Further, by allowing a podcast to encompass all types of on-demand audio, the definition drags in things like streaming audio that may have much in common with podcasts but are still fundamentally different in many ways, especially their lack of a podcast feed.

A narrower, and more specific, definition is possible if we look at podcasts from a technical standpoint. Podcasts are much more specific than "on-demand audio" or even "a downloadable audio file." Technically, I am arguing that the definition of a podcast is, instead, a collection of downloadable files, of any format, served with accompanying metadata via an open updatable internet feed, primarily RSS. While other definitions of the term "podcasting" in this collection rightfully and successfully show the value of foregrounding the cultural and stylistic elements of podcasting, in this chapter I explore what we can learn from this technical point of view and from the claim that it is the metadata and the open feed that separate a podcast from other media files on the internet.

I use this technically driven definition of podcasts to inform this chapter. It begins with a close examination of the structure and functionality of the RSS feed and explores how RSS, more than anything else, shaped the data available in the PodcastRE collection. Specifically, I examine the structural affordances required due to how easy it is for a podcast author to modify an existing RSS feed and how the lack of a fixed set of agreed-upon podcast RSS fields led to a wide-net metadata capture approach for our database. Then, drawing on examples found while constructing the PodcastRE database, I consider how the current RSS standard has constrained the questions that PodcastRE is able to answer—in particular, how the lack of certain fields such as "Network" and "Contributor" stop PodcastRE from being able to answer questions that require the aggregation of related works. Finally, I explore the current state of RSS and its related corporately controlled namespaces. This exploration drives an argument about why, for technical, metadata, and openness reasons, it may be time for podcasts to move to a new open-feed standard, such as a JSON Feed.

Defining Podcasts

When starting an archive, it is very important to clearly state precisely what the archive will be collecting. I admit that when I started working with PodcastRE, I assumed this would be the easiest part of my job. If I had thought back to my own past and the number of conversations it took me—most of which took place while I was working as a podcast producer—until my father truly understood just what podcasts are, I should have realized that a podcast is actually a rather complicated concept. And I was no longer just a listener or a producer trying to explain what a podcast was to my father; I was now working on a podcast archive, a position that calls for a definition with much more rigor. That is when things got complicated, because any attempt to define the term raises a number of questions: Are they downloadable audio files available via subscription (OED Online)? Or are they downloadable audio and video files available via websites (Dictionary.com)? Maybe the definition should be the wonderfully mid-2000s statement "Podcasting combines the freedom of blogging with the technology of MP3s" (Watson 2005, para. 3). There is also, of course, the conflation of podcasts and other on-demand audio, such as the series available through Audible (McGinley 2018). All of these definitions turn out to be problematic in some way for PodcastRE.

A couple of the definitions are simply too broad for us to be able to capture as an archive. If podcasts are any on-demand audio, then we simply have no way to capture them without paying for subscriptions to all the boutique distributors such as Audible or Pinna, and not all such services allow for the downloading of files, making archiving even more difficult. Stretching podcasts to be any audio or video file available for download from a website also would have made our jobs with PodcastRE impossible. The universe of downloadable audio and video files is so enormous that it would be unworkable to capture a meaningful cross-section in an archive. Even if such a thing were possible, it would require either an unsustainable amount of manual labor searching for web pages containing the audio and video files or building a script that could identify all web pages with downloadable audio and video files and download them until our server space ran out. The inclusion of the idea of "downloadable via subscription" in the first definition does seem to solve the breadth problem—it constrains the total universe and limits the amount of work—but then it gets too specific with its focus on audio. Even expanding it to audio and video would still be too specific, as a quick look at the current PodcastRE archive shows. There are .jpg, .pdf, and even .ppt files downloaded and stored in PodcastRE. This is because of producers like those of LearnOutLoud.com that often share the images discussed in their *Art History Podcast* and the *US Citizenship Podcast*, providing slides for the lessons they cover in each episode.

Looking at the ways in which all of these definitions are problematic helps us come to a definition of podcasts that we have pursued for the PodcastRE archive. From the "too broad" category, we know there had to be some limiting factor that would allow us to actually collect a meaningful subset of podcasts in a way that does not require a lot of manual labor. From the "too specific" category, we know we should not limit the type of files archived to audio and video but also allow for supporting files. Our examination also showed that the files should be provided in a subscribable manner. Thus, for the purposes of PodcastRE's collection infrastructure, we defined podcasts as: a collection or series of primarily, but not necessarily exclusively, audio or video files that are available for download through a subscribable feed.

However, while downloading and storing files are important aspects of the PodcastRE project, having a server of files would be of little use without their accompanying information—the metadata—about those files and where they came from. The centrality of metadata for podcast distribution and consumption meant a slight revision to our working definition of a podcast: a collection or series of primarily, but not necessarily exclusively, audio or video files and the metadata for the series or collection that is available for download through a subscribable feed. Admittedly this was really just a long and overly academic way of saying podcasts are just shows that use RSS to distribute episodes and show information, which is really how many people think of them anyway. There are reasons, both technical and prospective, to use this definition, but a discussion of RSS is required before delving into them.

A Podcast History of RSS

Known by many names, Resource Description Framework (RDF) Site Summary, Rich Site Summary, and Really Simple Syndication, RSS was first published as a specification on March 15, 1999 (RSS Advisory Board n.d.). Based on XML and developed by two Netscape developers, Ramanathan Guha and Dan Libby, RSS was created so that the Netscape home page, "My Netscape," could be refreshed with new content from web pages that used the specification (Hines 1999, para. 9). Over the next couple of years, RSS went through multiple iterations until December 25, 2000, when Dave Winer and UserLand Software released RSS 0.92 (RSS Advisory Board n.d.). It was this version of RSS that is most important in the history of podcasting, as it was the first version that included the <enclosure> tag. Concocted by Winer, with strong prompting from Adam Curry (Winer 2001, para. 1), RSS was a way to deliver high-quality multimedia files over the internet without the quality and wait-time issues that plagued early streaming. The first use of an <enclosure> tag was to distribute a set of Grateful Dead MP3 files (para. 44), presaging its dominant use in the years to come.

RSS continued to develop for the next decade, with RSS 2.0 first being released on August 19, 2002, and then finally being frozen as a specification with version 2.0.11 on March 30, 2009 (RSS Advisory Board n.d.). Since then, the only updates that have come to podcast RSS feeds have come in the form of XML namespaces, which are ways of adding outside specification elements to XML documents (Bray et al. 2009, para. 1). The most commonly employed namespace used in podcast feeds is controlled by Apple, but now that Google has become a player in the podcast directory world (Bergen 2015, para. 2), their namespace is becoming more widely used as well. For those interested in seeing a sample RSS feed that illustrates the potential options for podcasters, Daniel J. Lewis has published a sample feed on GitHub (Lewis 2020).

RSS and Its Metadata Impact

This brings us back to the technical reason why it is important in the case of PodcastRE to define podcasts as being a feed of downloadable files and associated metadata. In order to work at the scale we wanted, it was very important that PodcastRE would be able to run with limited human intervention. This meant that not only did we need to be able to download podcast episode files in an automated fashion, but we also needed to gather the metadata we would be storing automatically. In other words, for PodcastRE, the elements available through the RSS specification, and its associated namespaces, are as important as the podcast episode files themselves and define the possible universe of metadata for the podcasts archived in PodcastRE.

This is not to say, however, that each podcast has a fully realized metadata universe. A major reason for this is the relatively sparse number of elements that are required for a feed to be valid. In fact, an RSS feed technically needs the presence of only four elements to be valid: the <channel> parent element with associated <title>, <link>, and <description> elements. This would be a feed without content, though, as it would contain no <item>s (Winer 2003, para. 13). For an <item> to be valid, it needs only a single "child" element to be present (para. 57). For an RSS feed to be considered a podcast feed by our above definition, it would also need to have at least one <item> that included an <enclosure> element pointing to a file available for download. In order for a feed to be accepted into directories like Apple Podcasts, Spotify, or Google Play, more elements are required, such as <image>, <language>, and <itune s:author> or <googleplay:author> ("Validate Your Podcast" n.d., para. 4; "Add a Podcast Using an RSS Feed" n.d., para. 13), but the required elements represent only a small portion of the available universe of podcast feed metadata. Even among the more widely used elements such as <description> and <itunes:summary>, there is overlap in coverage, so which element is used varies from podcast to podcast. This made it nearly impossible to define an authoritative list of elements to store, and therefore PodcastRE's metadata collection policy became analogous to casting the widest net possible in order to capture nearly all available RSS and podcast namespace elements. In the end, this extreme flexibility of RSS element use meant that, in most ways, the breadth of metadata coverage is not determined by RSS or directory requirements or even by our archival policies; instead, it comes down to the element use choices of each podcast feed's author (i.e., each podcaster or producer who is creating and maintaining the RSS feed).

RSS feed authors are not just responsible for decisions that determine whether there is either complete or noncomprehensive use of metadata elements. Since authors fully manage their own RSS feeds and the entry of their own metadata, they are directly responsible for the depth and quality of the metadata as well. This aspect of podcast metadata cannot be stressed enough. With the exception of a few of elements like <googleplay:category> and <itunes:type>, there are almost no controls on what podcast authors put (or can put) into the various elements. Even fixed-format elements like <pubDate> that seem rather self-explanatory (i.e., the date on which a podcast episode was published into a feed) can end up being used by authors to mean something very different. For example, in *The Reith Lectures* podcast from the BBC, there are many <pubDate>s before 1950, long before podcasts were a new format, as instead the show uses <pubDate> to mean the day the lecture was originally aired. Another important aspect of authors being in full control of podcast feed metadata is that they are capable of changing any element they wish. In fact, it is entirely possible for a podcast author to change something as fundamental as the title of an episode, or even the title of their whole podcast, at any time. This changing of already published metadata is actually a rather common practice, so much so that it was a major factor in the design of PodcastRE's data model and scripts (Morris et al. 2019). These data model and script design decisions have made it possible to track these metadata changes over time in the PodcastRE database, and a search of the database yielded many interesting examples. Some podcasts slightly alter their title for branding reasons— *Bookworm* (https://podcastre.org/podcasts?id=pod984), added their network and became *KCRW's Bookworm* (https://podcastre.org/po dcasts?id=pod2972); SEO, *Highest Self Podcast* (https://podcastre.org /podcasts?id=pod2787), added some terms and turned into *Highest Self Podcast: Modern Spirituality, Ayurveda, Conscious Entrepreneurship, Mind-Body Balance* (https://podcastre.org/podcasts?id=pod4758)— while others enact more drastic changes, like the podcaster who ended one podcast and started another in the exact same feed: *Ding-Donger with Matt Braunger* (https://podcastre.org/podcasts?id=pod1242), morphed into *Advice from a Dipshit with Matt Braunger* (https://podca stre.org/podcasts?id=pod5020).

Constraining PodcastRE's Answers

No matter how well thought out or interesting a research question is, it is the quality and quantity of data and metadata stored in an archive that defines the domain of what it can answer, not the question itself. Since the metadata we store in PodcastRE is the same metadata from the RSS feeds, it is the quality and quantity of the RSS author-created metadata that directly constrains the types of questions PodcastRE will be able to answer going forward (as well as the answers it provides). Many of these constraints stem straight from the lack of controlled vocabularies and validation. That constraints would arise is not surprising, given research showing that for searches in the University of Pittsburgh's library catalog, around 25 percent of hits were lost when its controlled vocabulary was not leveraged, even though they added tables of contents, summaries, and abstracts to the searchable text (Gross et al. 2015, 31). And this was a replication of a previous study that showed 35.9 percent of hits were lost without a controlled vocabulary, table of contents, summaries, and when abstracts were not added (Gross and Taylor 2005, 223).

To see the impact of the lack of controlled vocabularies on PodcastRE specifically, all a user has to do is look at the keywords stored in the database. Say a researcher wants to study podcasts about entrepreneurship. If they search "entrepreneurship" today, they would find 135 podcasts, but if they searched "entrepreneurial," they would get 30, and "entrepreneur" would find 323. There is not a complete overlap for any of the searches either, so no single term would capture all of them, which would not be the case if there were a controlled vocabulary for podcast keywords such as those assigned to articles in commercial academic databases. And if "entrepreneurship" were the term they had chosen, that is a loss of at least 58 percent of hits, which is still better than "entrepreneurial," which lost at least 90 percent. This lack of controlled vocabularies directly plays into the validation, and quality, issues as well. Specifically, none of those searches would surface the podcast *23 Shots of JD*, https://podcastre.org/podcasts?id=pod6508, as the author of that podcast has used the misspelling "entreprenaur" as their keyword. All of this means that a researcher using PodcastRE to study entrepreneurship podcasts would have to do a significant amount of work to develop their search and would still likely miss podcasts no matter how thorough their search term lists, as there is always another misspelling.

Then there are the research questions for which metadata elements simply do not exist. The two most glaring examples of this are the "Network" and "Contributor" fields. It is easy to imagine future researchers being interested in how the podcasts from Maximum Fun compare to those of Earwolf or wanting to explore how podcast producer Mira Burt-Wintonick's sound design and storytelling strategies changed over time on shows like *Wiretap*. But there are no elements in RSS or in the podcast namespaces that allow an author to directly indicate their network or producers, editors, and sound designers. No RSS elements means no metadata for PodcastRE to store and therefore little ability to facilitate this type of research via searches of the archive. Over the years, podcast authors have used work-arounds such as listing credits in the <description> element or including the network name alongside the podcast author's in <itunes:author>. Again, however, neither of these have been done often or consistently enough across podcasts to be a reliable way of determining contributors or networks. Given a tremendous amount of labor hours and computer time, it might be possible to identify contributors by auto-transcribing all of the audio files and then running named-entity recognition (NER) on the results and to find out networks by training a machine learning algorithm against all of the possible places the information could be, from <itunes:author> to <link> to <description> to the RSS URL itself. Obviously, both of those scenarios are quite unlikely to come to pass, and in order for PodcastRE to realistically answer questions such as these, there would need to be new elements in the feed.

That will likely be a long wait, especially for the <network> element, as Apple and Google have figured out a way to get network information without having to make the information open as it would be in an RSS feed. They manage this through their submission platforms, where networks can submit the feeds for all of their shows under a single account and therefore be linked together in the directories. This makes podcast network information a value-add for them. While neither Apple or Google is making money from its directories, they are making money from the platforms that the directories are a part of—iOS, Mac OS, Android, Google Play, and Chrome OS—and therefore they would be unlikely to add an element to their namespaces that would make data open that they currently have locked down.

Three Possible Futures

The conundrum with Apple's and Google's namespaces is a great illustration of the issues that arise from podcasting's current reliance on major corporations for its metadata standards. This is not to say podcasting should not be grateful for the work that Apple in particular has done around podcast metadata. Ever since RSS 2.0 froze in 2009, Apple has added many highly useful fields, such as <itunes:season> and <itunes:episode>, but they are a publicly traded company, which means they have motivations beyond simply fulfilling the wishes of the podcasting community. And while this issue seems to be related to only very specific standards and metadata minutiae, it is very much related to two broader questions that many in the podcasting community are asking, from networks to advertisers to independent podcasters alike: What will podcasts look like in the future, and how can money be made from them? While there are many possible answers to these questions and therefore many possible futures for podcasting, let us look at three of them that present a range of possible effects on archiving efforts like PodcastRE.

The easiest scenario to imagine is that nothing really happens. Apple and Google will continue to add new elements to their namespaces when they have a need, but podcasting will mostly look like it does now. If that is what happens, PodcastRE will be largely unaffected. It will need to be updated with new database fields for any new elements, but the scripts as they are now will continue to harvest podcast episodes and expand the archive.

It is also easy to imagine a second scenario, in which there is a move away from the definition for podcast discussed at the beginning of this chapter to one much more akin to on-demand audio. This could take many forms; the two commonly mentioned on the popular podcasting newsletter *Hot Pod* are the YouTube and Netflix walled garden models (Quah 2015; 2016a; 2016b; 2017; 2018a; 2018b; 2019). In the YouTube model, there would be a large free-to-use ad-supported centralized location where everyone goes to either upload or stream their podcasts. In the Netflix model, there would be many paid services that would provide podcasts from specific networks and creators with whom they have licensing agreements. Just as with video, it is unlikely to be an either/or situation but instead a hybrid of the two models. No matter what model prevails, though, if either becomes the dominant means of distributing podcasts, PodcastRE would need significant reconfiguring. It is most likely that these models would not permit the downloading of episodes, but even if downloading were still possible, it would likely require significant manual labor. This is not to mention that the current PodcastRE data model would be unlikely to match the new platforms' metadata schemas. Work would be needed in order to continue the research that

PodcastRE has made possible, as corporately controlled walled gardens are notorious for regulating who gets access to data about their services and how much data is made available in the event researchers are lucky enough to gain access (boyd and Crawford 2012, 674; Parks 2014, 360).

That brings us to the least likely scenario but the most promising way forward: podcasting transitions away from corporate-controlled namespaces to new, open standards. This could mean a consortium of players in the podcast community coming together to create a new XML namespace that can be regularly updated according to the needs of podcasters, developers, listeners, and directories. While this would be an important shift, it would still tie podcasting to a frozen specification. A more forward-looking version of this change would be a transition from RSS to a totally new feed standard, specifically a JSON Feed (Simmons and Reece 2017). JSON is a language-independent structured data format similar to XML with many benefits from a technical standpoint. Notably, it is more compact, can be parsed more quickly, and is human readable. The JSON Feed specification is also easily extensible without namespaces, so when new elements are needed, they can be added with much less fuss. There is even a podcast application, Breaker, that already supports JSON Feed (Berlin 2017, para. 1), with more coming (Cox 2017, para. 3). This future would require a moderate amount of development for PodcastRE, including adding JSON Feed support to its harvesting scripts and modifying the data model so that it can handle its extensibility, but since JSON Feed is still an open standard, archiving would be able to keep moving forward. Transitioning podcasting to a completely new feed standard is a daunting task that would require the buy-in of everyone from podcasters to application developers to the eight-hundred-pound gorillas of the podcast distribution world: Apple, Spotify, and Google. To facilitate this transition, migration paths for implementation would have to be made available for the distributors, and the cost in both cognitive and economic terms would have to be minimized for the listeners and podcasters (West 2007, paras. 27–29). In the end, all would see the benefit, as podcasting would be in a more technically beneficial position, having moved away from a long-frozen specification to a smaller, faster, more extensible one. Most importantly, podcasting is one of the last keepers of the promise of the open internet in a world of ever more walled gardens, and by moving from RSS to JSON Feed podcasting, it would be able to move forward while still keeping its promise.

Beyond the technical aspects, a move to a new open-feed standard would be in keeping with the ideal of podcasting, which first drew me to the medium. When I began as a podcaster, it was because it was a way for me to share my love of mathematics with the world in a free and open manner. There were no gatekeepers keeping me out, no one to tell me mathematics audio is too niche a topic. There was just a technology that allowed me to distribute my shows to whomever decided to subscribe and listen. This is my story, but there are a lot of other related, but still distinct, podcasting stories out there that archival projects such as PodcastRE are attempting to ensure can be told and heard in the future. If podcasts move away from these open-feed options, projects like PodcastRE will likely fall apart, and the stories and histories they hold will be much more difficult, if not impossible, to tell.

Works Cited

"Add a Podcast Using an RSS Feed." n.d.. Podcast Portal Help. Google. Accessed February 23, 2019. https://support.google.com/googleplay/podcasts/answer/6260341#episode.

Bergen, M. 2015. October 27. "Google Brings Podcasting to Play Music, Swinging at Apple's Dominance." Accessed February 23, 2019. https://www.recode.net/2015/10/27/11620066/google-brings-podcasting-to-play-music-swinging-at-apples-dominance.

Berlin, Erik. 2017. May 29. "Breaker Adds Support for JSON Feed." *Breaker* (blog). Accessed February 23, 2019. https://blog.breaker.audio/breaker-adds-support-for-json-feed-eddbd4afd0f3.

Bray, Tim, Dave Hollander, Andrew Layman, Richard Tobin, and Henry S. Thompson. 2009. "Namespaces in XML 1.0," 3rd ed. W3C Recommendation. December 8. http://www.w3.org/TR/2009/REC-xml-names-20091208/, W3C Recommendation.

boyd, danah, and Kate Crawford. 2012. "Critical Questions for Big Data." *Information, Communication & Society* 15 (5): 662–79. https://doi.org/10.1080/1369118X.2012.678878.

Gross, Tina, and Arlene G. Taylor. 2005. "What Have We Got to Lose? The Effect of Controlled Vocabulary on Keyword Searching Results," *College & Research Libraries* 55 (3): 212–30. Accessed February 21, 2020. https://doi.org/10.5860/crl.66.3.212.

Gross, Tina, Arlene G. Taylor, and Daniel N. Joudrey. 2015. "Still a Lot to Lose: The Role of Controlled Vocabulary in Keyword Searching." *Cataloging & Classification Quarterly* 53 (1): 1–39. https://doi.org/10.1080/01639374.2014.917447.

Dictionary.com, s.v. "Podcast." Accessed February 23, 2019 from https://www.dictionary.com/browse/podcast.

Hines, Matt. 1999. "Netscape Broadens Portal Content Strategy." *Newsbytes.* March 15. Accessed February 23, 2019 from from http://link.galegroup.com/apps/doc/A54120248/ITOF?u=umuser&sid=ITOF&xid=377f452d.

Lewis, Daniel J. 2020. "Podcast Test Feed." GitHub. 2020. Retrieved February 21, 2020. https://github.com/theDanielJLewis/podcast-test-feed.

McGinley, Ciara. 2018. December 19. "Audible Reveals Its Top Podcasts of 2018." Accessed February 9, 2019. https://www.goodhousekeeping.com/uk/news /a25584539/audible-top-podcasts/.

Morris, Jeremy Wade, Samuel Hansen, and Eric Hoyt. 2019. "The PodcastRE Project: Curating and Preserving Podcasts (and Their Data)." *Journal of Radio & Audio Media* 26 (1): 8–20.

OED Online, s.v. "Podcast." Oxford University Press. Accessed February 23, 2019 from http://www.oed.com /view/Entry/273003.

Parks, Malcolm R. 2014. "Big Data in Communication Research: Its Contents and Discontents." *Journal of Communication* 64 (2): 355–60. Accessed June 28, 2019. https://doi.org/10.1111/jcom.12090.

Quah, Nicholas. 2015. "The Netflix-YouTube-Twitter-Starbucks of Podcasting." *Hot Pod* 37. August 18. Accessed June 28, 2019. https://hotpodnews.com/hot-pod-the-netflix-youtube-twitter-starbucks-of-podcasting/.

Quah, Nicholas. 2016a. "Will Any of the Companies Trying to Build the You-Tube of Podcasting Succeed?" *Hot Pod* 78. July 5. Accessed June 28, 2019. https://hotpodnews.com/hot-pod-will-any-of-the-companies-trying-to-build-the-youtube-of-podcasting-succeed/.

Quah, Nicholas. 2016b. "Will the Next Wave of Audio Advertising Make Podcasts Sound Like (Yuck) Commercial Radio?" *Hot Pod* 89. September 27. Accessed June 28, 2019. https://hotpodnews.com/hot-pod-will-the-next-wave-of-audio-advertising-make-podcasts-sounds-like-yuck-commercial-radio/.

Quah, Nicholas. 2017. "Panoply's Pinna Might Just Be the First Really Interesting Attempt to Get People to Pay for Podcasts." *Hot Pod* 136. October 17. Accessed June 28, 2019. https://hotpodnews.com/panoplys-pinna-might-just-be-the-fi rst-really-interesting-attempt-to-get-people-to-pay-for-podcasts/.

Quah, Nicholas. 2018a. "True Podcast Love, in All of Us Command: This Is How Canada Listens to Podcasts." *Hot Pod*. April 10. Accessed June 28, 2019. https://hotpodnews.com/true-podcast-love-in-all-of-us-command-this-is-how-canada-listens-to-podcasts/.

Quah, Nicholas. 2018b. "A True 'Netflix for Podcasting' Experiment." *Hot Pod*. May 14. Accessed June 28, 2019. https://hotpodnews.com/a-true-netflix-for-podcasting-experiment/.

Quah, Nicholas. 2019. "Where Are We Now on the Subject of Subscription-Driven Podcasts?" *Hot Pod* 213. June 11. Accessed June 28, 2019. https://hotpodnews.com /where-are-we-now-on-the-subject-of-subscription-driven-podcasts/.

RSS Advisory Board. n.d.. RSS History. Accessed February 23, 2019. http://www .rssboard.org/rss-history.

Simmons, Brent, and Manton Reece. 2017. "JSON Feed Version 1." Accessed February 23, 2019. https://jsonfeed.org/version/1.

"Validate Your Podcast." n.d.. Podcasts Connect Help. Apple. Accessed February 23, 2019. https://help.apple.com/itc/podcasts_connect/#/itce5b9b0782.

Watson, Stephanie. 2005. "How Podcasting Works." March 26. HowStuffWorks.com. Accessed February 9, 2019. https://computer.howstuffworks.com/internet /basics/podcasting.htm.

West, Joel. 2007. "Seeking Open Infrastructure: Contrasting Open Standards, Open Source, and Open Innovation." *First Monday*. June 4. https://doi.org/10.5210/fm.v12i6.1913.

Winer, Dave. 2001. "Payloads for RSS." TheTwoWayWeb.com. January 11. Accessed February 23, 2019. https://web.archive.org/web/20080214205403/http://www.thetwowayweb.com/payloadsforrss.

Winer, Dave. 2003. "RSS 2.0 Specification." RSS 2.0 at Harvard Law. July 15. Accessed February 23, 2019. https://cyber.harvard.edu/rss/rss.html.

TWELVE | The Spotification of Podcasting

JEREMY WADE MORRIS

It's not a podcast if it's not platform agnostic.
—Josh Kinal, podcaster 2019

A few months before Spotify, the Swedish streaming music giant, started selling shares publicly on the New York Stock Exchange, CEO Daniel Ek released a letter outlining his company's values and visions. Like most pre-IPO letters, it was filled with rhetorical flourishes and grand sentiments like "We really do believe that we can improve the world, one song at a time" and "We're working to democratize the industry and connect all of us, across the world, in a shared culture that expands our horizons" (Ek qtd. in Fagan 2018). But the letter was also notable for the clues it gave about Spotify's aspirations beyond music. Even though most users know Spotify as a music service that emerged in 2008 as the feels-like-free alternative to the rampant downloading and file sharing that marked the early 2000s, the service has increasingly been expanding into other areas of audio culture. As Ek himself noted, "Music has just been the beginning. . . . What started out as an application and grew into a platform must now become a global network." The goal, Ek outlined, was to "take the lessons we've learned in music and apply them across culture" (Ek qtd. in Fagan 2018).

One of the areas of culture in which Spotify has been most active in applying its lessons from music has been podcasting. This statement likely seems less surprising now than when I began writing this chapter, given Spotify's recent high-profile acquisition of two major companies in the podcasting ecosystem and their exclusive distribution deal with

popular podcaster Joe Rogan. The purchase of Gimlet Media—a network of highly produced podcasts—and Anchor.fm—an app/service
that allows users to easily make, upload, and distribute podcasts—made
noise for its price tag of over $230 million (Sweney 2019), but it was actu-
ally just the latest of Spotify's forays into podcasting. The company had
quietly added podcasts to the platform in 2017, and they have since made
a series of exclusive deals with podcast producers to host and distribute
shows specifically (and solely) on their platform. While they were late
to include podcasts on their platform—at least compared to Apple and
Google as well as a raft of podcast-specific platforms that have been in
this space for over a decade now—Spotify is now clearly eyeing podcasting as a potential path to adding new listeners to their service, one that
is significantly cheaper than trying to pay hefty fees to music labels for
licensing popular songs.

On the surface, this seems like a relatively innocuous business strategy. Streaming services like Spotify want to provide listeners with popular
audio content, so they add podcasts to their services. However, the inclusion of podcasts as part of streaming services that also include music,
audiobooks, and other audio content represents a significant infrastructural shift for podcasting. This shift may make it more difficult for lesser-
known and niche podcasts to stand out in these spaces, and that could
have consequences for how users conceive of podcasts as a format. This
shift will also have significant repercussions for the preservation and
archiving of podcasts and for the ability of media historians to do the
historical work required for documenting the emergence and growth
of this powerful audio format. Accordingly, this chapter examines this
shift toward "platformized" podcasts, looking specifically at the case of
Spotify and what might be called the "spotification" of podcasting. It
pays particular attention to the role that open technologies like RSS and
XML have played in creating a vibrant environment for audio. It investigates the logics that Spotify deploys for podcast display and discovery
on its platform and argues that the spotification of podcasting may represent a welcome push toward more user-friendly and mainstream consumption of podcasts but, in the process, might threaten the very format
these companies hope to popularize. In other words, the spotification
of podcasting may make podcasts more ubiquitous than ever, but this
added visibility might undermine some of the format's earliest promises
of accessibility and diversity of voices. Although I do not mean to falsely
assume that what is happening with Spotify is automatically also happening to all other digital distribution services, I do think a term like

"spotification" helps us uncover specific developments that are worth considering for podcasting broadly as well as for other media, such as video streaming and digital news distribution.

A Brief History of RSS

Samuel Hansen's chapter in this volume covers the technical history of RSS (or Really Simple Syndication or Rich Site Summary), so I won't repeat the details here. Most research on early podcasting (Berry 2006; Sterne et al. 2008; Bottomley 2015; Markman 2011) similarly reviews how RSS emerged and how it allows users to subscribe to shows that are then delivered to a variety of listening devices when new episodes are published online. Although it's not particularly useful to define a medium solely by its technical characteristics—since referring to, say, television or radio as simply the broadcasting of electromagnetic radio waves or the screens and boxes in our homes excludes all the practices, aesthetics, and evolving conventions associated with those media—it is hard to argue against the idea that RSS is one of podcasting's essential elements, one that logistically shapes the flow and use of the format. Even though RSS originated as a web technology for distributing writing and other text-based content, the ability to add "enclosures" and to syndicate the delivery of audio files made RSS an ideal means to distribute internet-based audio content. There were certainly a fair number of experiments with online audio distribution before the development of RSS (see Bottomley 2020), and numerous devices on which to store and transport audio (e.g., iPods, MPMan, Diamond Rio, etc.), but the technology that put the "cast" in podcasting is, undeniably, RSS.

On the one hand, RSS is simply a format, a technical set of instructions for how to distribute content. On the other hand, no format is "simple"; it is also a set of ideas about how web content *should* be distributed. Formats affect the "look, feel, experience and workings of a medium" (Sterne 2012, 7). They are a distillation of multiple competing perspectives and decisions—including industrial policies, technology design, and sedimented habit—that are reduced to code (8). They are also the things that disappear through inattention in favor of "attention to the phenomena, 'the content' that they represent for users' edification or enjoyment" (Gitelman 2006, 6). The people building RSS saw it as an open and accessible technology, one that would give users "significant control over where and how they interacted with any given business or publication on the web" (Target 2019). Like so many Web

2.0 era technologies, it was meant to give users agency and power (Bruns 2006), both in their choice of what to consume and in their ability to become their own broadcasters. Of course, we can, and should, debate how open, accessible, and diverse this vision of the technology was for various groups of users; it was still very much steeped in the Californian Ideology—Richard Barbrook and Andy Cameron's (1995) critique of the blind faith tech-utopianism that pervaded Silicon Valley in the mid-1990s and that persists to this day in other pockets of digital culture. We cannot ignore that many users did not enjoy the same privileges, access to technology, and luxury to speak and create as those hailing RSS and podcasting's promises (Markman 2011; Markman and Sawyer 2014; Wang, this volume). But in the rhetoric of podcasting's histories, and even in contemporary imaginings, RSS represents "a wistful symbol of defiance against a centralized web increasingly controlled by a handful of corporations" (Target 2019). Because of its largely open framework, and the decentralized system of distribution it affords, RSS still represents, for many, the vision of a personally curated and more authentically unfiltered stream of information and content.

It would be inaccurate to say that anyone can create and use RSS feeds or that anyone who can will suddenly have a podcast that will be on equal footing as the most successful podcasts out there. But there are countless online resources to support podcasters in setting up RSS feeds and plenty of podcasting services that offer RSS functionality to give podcasters a wide range of distribution options. The fact that podcasting's infrastructure, for the last fifteen years, has relied so heavily on RSS feeds has made the entire ecosystem more accessible and less susceptible to concentration. In the words of one nostalgic commentator, RSS represents "the unfiltered view of the open web, and the chance to make your own decisions about what you find there" (Barrett 2018). Media scholar John Sullivan (2019) has even called RSS an "anti-platform," noting how it helps subvert traditional logics of platformization.

The Platformization of Podcasting

Despite the idealistic rhetoric around RSS, however, the technology has also been criticized for being complicated and user-unfriendly; surveys on podcast usage consistently point to a significant percentage of users who are put off by the technical demands of finding and subscribing to new shows (Van Dyke 2017; Jacobs 2018). There are some who argue that the word "subscribe" is misleading and unnecessarily complicated for older users; others think it results in simply too much content that one eventually feels guilty about (Corbett 2018; Goldstein 2019; Misener 2019; Hilton 2019). RSS is regularly singled out as a key barrier to more widespread adoption of podcasting for being too confusing or not feature-rich enough (Sernovitz 2008; Crichton 2018), despite the fact that it is far less obtuse than, I would argue, Facebook's privacy settings or figuring out how to not "reply all" on an all-staff email.

Put another way, the very features that makes RSS an open-source technology that supports user agency and choice, and that allows for the wide-scale distribution of a multiplicity of voices and perspectives, are the same features that make it unfriendly and too time-consuming for some users or not useful and profitable enough for many producers. RSS's status as a relatively open "anti-platform"—a keystone technology in making the podcasting landscape more distributed and accessible— has also rendered it more distributed and complicated. Paradoxically, this has created the opportunity, or at least the perception of an opportunity, for larger platforms and podcast distributors to imagine alternate ways of presenting and distributing podcasts.

Even if RSS acts as an anti-platform, there are, of course, "platforms" in the podcasting space. While the term "platform" is now widely and loosely used by a number of companies, research in platform studies has tracked how newer uses of the term lean heavily on its metaphorical and figurative connotations (i.e., a platform from which to speak, socialize, and share opinions) compared to its more computational roots (i.e., "a programmable infrastructure upon which other software can be built and run, . . . or information services that provide APIs so developers can design additional layers of functionality") (Gillespie 2017, n.p.; Gillespie 2011, van Dijck et al. 2018). Platforms are not simply intermediaries; they are also active agents that engage in moderating, shaping, and influencing not just the content but the very relationships users and content producers can have with the content that appears on platforms (Gillespie 2018).

As Sullivan notes, podcasting's "platforms" tend to focus on three primary points in the circulation chain: "storage, discovery, and consumption," with some of the larger platforms like Google or Apple engaging in all three (Sullivan 2019). And while literature from platform studies is relatively new and allows us to see platformization as "the penetration of economic and infrastructural extensions of online platforms into the web, affecting the production, distribution, and circulation of cultural content" (Nieborg and Poell 2018; van Dijck et al. 2018), platformization in podcasting is not necessarily new; there have been podcast aggregators, informal podcast networks, and influential distribution directories since podcasting's earliest days. However, the rising presence of newer, well-funded, and more populous platforms like Spotify in podcasting and its ever-deepening insinuation into all facets of podcasting make podcasters (and the podcasts they produce) increasingly dependent and contingent on the affordances, policies, and business models of the platform providers. RSS may allow anyone to distribute podcasts from anywhere, but if the primary platforms that people seek out to consume podcasts start downplaying or shifting away from RSS, this could have a significant impact on the mechanics of distributing podcasts. More important, it could affect the possibilities podcasting presents as a new mode of communication.

Without question, Apple has been the central "platform" for podcasts. For two decades, Apple has provided a podcast discovery engine (iTunes/Apple Podcasts), software for facilitating listening (the Podcasts App), and hardware for consuming podcasts, which it has done since podcasting's early days (Sullivan 2019). But although Apple occasionally bans content and podcasts (e.g., Alex Jones's InfoWars podcasts), and its podcast charts significantly shape the discovery process for emerging podcasts, the company has generally taken a hands-off approach to industrializing, professionalizing, and monetizing podcasts, at least when compared to, say, YouTube's approach to video or even Apple's approach to its iOS app store. Part of this is because of RSS. As Hansen argues in this volume (see also Sullivan 2019), the open and accessible nature of RSS has helped make podcasts ubiquitous and free, making it difficult for one platform to come along to monetize specific shows or throttle circulation. If Apple bans a show or tries to limit access to it through their platform, podcasters can always submit their material to other distribution sites or simply host it from their own websites. That said, Apple's hands-off approach to monetization and their relative slowness in developing new tools for producers to mine listening statistics have created an opportunity for other companies, like Spotify, to articulate a different vision for how podcasts might be displayed, discovered, and consumed. This different vision is a heightened form of platformization we can call spotification.

The Spotification of Podcasting

If podcasting has long had "platforms" and been undergoing a steady shift to platformization, the term "spotification" signals a shift in how podcast platforms operate. In his 2013 book, *Online File Sharing,* Jonas Andersson Schwarz introduces the term "spotification" as a pithy description of a trend he was witnessing "among commercial operators to harness the once unbridled user agency and force it into walled gardens" (112). In describing industrial reactions to digitization, Schwarz deploys the term "spotification" to describe how companies like Spotify, though not limited to Spotify, designed user-friendly interfaces and feels-like-free services to create platforms that seemed like a continuation of the rampant file sharing of the late 1990s and early 2000s despite the fact that they re-commercialized content in new ways and imposed new restrictions on when and how (and for how much) consumers could access digital content. As Spotify's presence has continued to grow globally, and as it has started to draw in other forms of audio content onto its platform, spotification has become a handy description for the ways in which platforms are slowly encroaching not just on other media types but also on specific cultural practices. Patrick Burkart and Susanna Leijonhufvud (2019), for example, use the term to reflect on how public service media are increasingly delegating some of their activities and practices to private streaming companies, including Spotify, such as providing access to historical local music and housing official repositories for digitized analog collections. Spotification, here, is used "critically to name the quest for software-based 'solutions' to complex issues," whether those issues are public media distribution in the era of streaming platforms or longer-term media preservation in the interests of national culture (174).

Spotification, then, is shorthand for a particular kind of encroachment that platforms engage in where access to vast stores of media content serves as the carrot for drawing users into a more restrictive, contingent, and liminal relationship with the very media they seek to use. Similar tendencies have been noted in terms of Facebook's or Google's centralization of control over web content (McChesney 2014; Vaidhyanathan 2011) before the term "platformization" came into fashion. But platformization extends these critiques by considering the impact not just on the amount of information available but also on the very shape and experience of that information, given the contingent relationships platforms create between creators, their content, and users. The spotification of podcasting, then, is not just a technical feature update (i.e., Spotify adds podcasts to its list of audio content), but it is also a cultural reimagining of how podcasts should be distributed.

Spotify's interface, on the surface, does not seem like a particularly drastic shift from Apple or Google podcasts. In the "Browse" tab, users

can now select "podcasts" as a category to explore, along with other categories ("Genre & Moods," "Charts," "New Releases," "Discover," "Con-
certs," and more), and podcasts are now recommended on users' main
home pages. Like their music playlists, these recommendations rotate
and often refer to current media or cultural events (when I conducted
this research in the spring of 2020, I was being served categories like
"Trailblazing Women behind the Mic" for the week surrounding International Women's Day, "Podcasts for Bachelor Nation" when the popular ABC TV show *The Bachelor* was airing, etc.)

The "Podcasts" tab is then further subdivided into various recommendations ("What's Trending") and categories ("Education," "Comedy," "Music"), which mimics other podcast aggregator sites, if slightly
less comprehensively. These recommendations are also based on listening history (e.g., "12 Gripping Audio Dramas" or "10 Celebrity Interview
Podcasts"). Following the links to an individual show or episode brings
you to a list of playable files where a user can click Play and listen to
their selection; it mimics finding and playing a song on Spotify. There's
no need to worry about subscribing or downloading a file, though there
are also no controls to skip forward easily by 10 or 30 seconds or play at
double or half speed, like many podcast apps now provide. Spotify does,
however, remember your place in the podcast so that users can listen
fluidly across devices.

In terms of its offerings, Spotify draws on a similar index to Apple Podcasts and other aggregators, and they recently opened up the ability for
anyone to submit feeds to the service. Like Apple Podcasts, Spotify does
not host content on its own servers (at least in most cases) and instead
merely draws its streams from existing RSS feeds online. Although there
is no publicly available quantitative data comparing Spotify to other
podcast indexes in terms of number, variety, or diversity, searches in the
interface suggest the service is relatively comprehensive for more popular and professional podcasts, while many of the more amateur podcasters have only recently begun adding their shows to the platform.

In a move that is slightly different from Apple or Google, Spotify has
invested heavily in developing its own original content and pursuing
exclusive licenses, with podcasts such as *Dissect, The Joe Budden Podcast,
Mogul, Amy Schumer Presents*, and a project with Barack and Michelle
Obama, which are, in theory, available only on its platform (Holt 2019;
Roettgers 2017). Although some of these original shows have different levels of exclusivity—many, like *Joe Budden* or *Mogul* were "exclusive" for only a specific release window before becoming available on

other platforms—Spotify's recent exclusive deal with Joe Rogan is a definitive push to intensify exclusivity. These efforts in some ways mirror the earlier attempts by companies like Midroll, Earwolf, and Howl. fm to create premium paid service models through exclusive content and subscriptions, so Spotify's moves here are neither entirely new nor wholly unprecedented (Bersch, this volume). Spotify's model, however, introduces new wrinkles: the company still makes the majority of the podcasts it offers available through its free, ad-supported tier, and its paid tier offers access to a much larger world of audio beyond podcasting. Spotification, then, is not just about putting a price on podcasts or about offering exclusive content. Rather, it's the manner in which features such as those are presented to users and normalized as conventions of podcasting.

It remains to be seen whether, with the acquisition of Gimlet, Spotify will take more than these initial tentative steps and build a more robust model of delivering exclusive original content as, say, Netflix has pursued. Both Spotify and Gimlet Media have indicated that there will continue to be a mix of exclusives and windowed shows (Carman 2019a). It is also unclear as of this writing whether companies like Luminary—whose model depends on a highly restrictive paywall (Carman 2019b)—or other premium efforts will find enough success to turn listeners away from the already available and ubiquitous free platforms. Spotify's model is one that offers both free, ad-supported memberships as well as premium memberships, but at the moment, the availability of, and access to, podcasts is not affected regardless of the level of membership tier. Regardless, these various paywall and premium models have obvious implications for amateur and everyday podcasters, since platforms will most likely promote their original podcasts and will recommend and pursue licenses with shows that have received visibility and popularity elsewhere, making it more difficult for less-established podcasters to break through, find an audience, and create a sustainable audio project.

But while the threat of an all-exclusive/paywall model is frightening, Spotify's purchase of Anchor suggests it is still very much interested in—or at least invested in seeing what the next few years will bring for—everyday, amateur, user-generated podcasts. Spotify's direct overtures to podcasters, in the form of offering them the ability to submit shows directly to the service and access to some of the back-end data analytics Spotify collects, suggests Spotify still sees everyday, amateur podcasters as a potential form of growth (Spotify 2019). Spotify may not promote, recommend, or feature amateur and emerging shows with the same level of support as they do with their original or sponsored content, but, like YouTube, the App Store, and other platforms, Spotify loses little by providing a platform for the distribution of user-generated content and waiting to see which shows bubble up in popularity.

Ultimately, however, the question of whether Spotify has more or less diversity in its content offerings, or whether it surfaces more or less new and interesting perspectives than other platforms, is perhaps a red herring. Spotify regularly claims to be expanding the variety of musical artists a listener listens to (Erlandsson and Perez 2017); they will likely make the same claim for podcasts. While scholars and the popular press can continue to debate whether this truly represents greater diversity or a more democratic environment for podcast production and access, we are perhaps better off focusing on what their podcasting features and interfaces changes cover over: the semantic and infrastructural shift away from the logic of the subscription and RSS feeds and toward the logic of the stream.

Spotify is the biggest and most popular example of a new breed of interfaces and services that replace RSS feeds with other forms of display—such as custom players, direct streams, etc.—to create a "lean-back" listening experience that relies more on automated recommendations and promotional placements for podcast discovery. Apple Podcasts is by no means a perfect interface, and its user-friendly design also downplays the mechanics of RSS. But by allowing users to subscribe to content and download an audio file, Apple Podcasts still highlights the connection to the original file location and provides user affordances that come with possessing a file. This means users can save the podcast in their library; they can move it to the device of their choosing; and they can even edit, remix, and incorporate it into other creative projects. It also, importantly, highlights the connection to the podcaster, since RSS also serves as the delivery mechanism for all the contextual metadata that podcasters embed in their shows and episodes (things like its title, date, producer, genre, a description of its contents, carefully selected keywords, etc.).

Spotify, on the other hand, erases this connection entirely. The only data that accompanies a podcast is the purely consumer-facing data, such as the title of the episode and show, the length of the show, the date of publication, and the show summary. There are links to share the podcast with friends (via social media and other means), but there's no obvious way within the platform to trace back to the location from where this podcast originally came or to read more data from the RSS feed. Like many platforms, the interface is built to keep users within the platform rather than lead them outward.

Spotify does promise podcasters some analytics metadata, including listener metrics such as total listens and episode performance, listener demographics, location, engagement, and more. However, because Spotify generates these through the platform, "stats from Spotify [are virtually enclosed, and] listens won't appear in the analytics offer by a regular podcast host and won't be measured by services such as Podtrac" (Washenko 2018). Spotify's presentation of podcasts, as with music, is meant to encourage in-platform listening, which makes sense and seems obvious in the commercial sense: the company wants to become both the source for podcasts and the source for data about podcasting. But considering podcasting's history and supposed claims to openness, Spotify presents a technical infrastructure designed to promote what Kate Lacey describes as "listening in" (2013). The ability to listen out, to make connections back to the podcast and its original space and place on the web, is made more difficult by the interface and its features. This gives podcasters less autonomy and agency over the presentation of their creative output and less ability for them to connect with listeners and fans.

Spotification is not simply a strategy for corporate companies. Some public radio institutions are increasingly pursuing a similar strategy. In the early part of 2019, for example, the BBC began removing many of its own podcasts from third-party platforms and instead offering them exclusively within their own custom-built, native app *BBC Sounds*. Most notably, the BBC removed their content from across Google's product lineup (i.e., Google Assistant, Google Home, Google Podcast Store, etc.), citing frustration with how Google appeared to be directing users searching for BBC podcasts to play episodes through Google rather than through *BBC Sounds* (Cridland 2019). Like their proprietary web player, the BBC iPlayer, the *BBC Sounds* app allows the BBC to track user data and control the circulation of BBC content, whereas Google was offering users other (and, as some users might argue, better designed) options for their listening experiences. Rather than seeing their content as something for wide distribution across multiple platforms, the BBC was seeking to direct users to a particular kind of consumption experience, one that they could exert some kind of exclusive control over and derive exclusive benefits from.

Spotification, then, is not just meant to critique an era where podcasts are no longer available for free. As noted, companies like Luminary and various other premium subscription models are testing just how much audiences will tolerate in order to avoid advertisements or gain access to high-profile, exclusive content. While these models on their own seem to fly in the face of podcasting's original ethos of a freely accessible and supportive format for the distribution of culture, spotification is not simply an assessment about whether or not creators (or platforms) should be able to charge for content. Rather, it is meant to call attention to the supposedly "technical" solution Spotify is presenting for the perceived problems in podcasting—that RSS is too complicated and not user- or producer-friendly—and to highlight the very real cultural shifts their interface design and service model spark for how podcasts can and should be accessed and experienced. It's not just that previously "free" shows like *Love and Radio* will now cost users a monthly fee on Luminary, or that future exclusive episodes of *Reply All* may require users to sign up for a Spotify account, though these are, for many, already significant costs that will make barriers to access higher. But it's also that users' relationships with these shows will now be mediated through these platforms and will thus require users to accept and use all the platform requires of them. While arguably this has been true of iTunes and the other platforms for podcast discovery and playback, the reliance on RSS and on open technologies has provided users (and podcasters) far greater agency and control over the terms of their listening.

Conclusion: Spotification and Preservation

The spotification of podcasting also brings obvious implications for media historians and for efforts to preserve podcasts. RSS feeds are central to the collection strategy upon which the PodcastRE database is built (Hansen, this volume), and the data that comes along with the XML files has allowed us to create advanced search and visualization features that allow users to search podcasts beyond popularity, curated charts, or automated recommendations (Noh, this volume). As platforms move away from these technologies and increasingly create exclusive content that relies more on ephemeral streams than on traditional podcasting technologies, the ability to find and preserve this content, at scale, becomes progressively more challenging. Put simply, we would not have been able to build the PodcastRE database and preserve over 2 million audio files were it not for the accessibility and openness that RSS offers. A move away from RSS means a move away from a technology that has allowed new forms of sociality (i.e., a burgeoning format that holds the promise of diversifying our sonic worlds), new avenues for research (i.e., projects like PodcastRE), and even new commercial opportunities (i.e., the healthy and robust market around podcast apps, advertising, services, etc.). For PodcastRE, it might be possible to create updated but similarly functioning scripts as those we have for automating podcast identification and ingestion from the Apple Podcasts listings. But the process will be far more contingent and platform-dependent, given how quickly these platforms change the features and functions of their services. As the interfaces and features for presenting podcasts become more dynamic, modular, and unstable, so too do the podcasts themselves.

In many cases, public institutions charged with preserving cultural history are, in light of funding cuts, having to rely more on streaming services like Spotify as repositories of cultures. As Burkart and Leijonhufvud note, countries like Sweden have already seen a "deliberate substitution of public and analog storage and retrieval functions" to private companies like Spotify, revealing what they call "an incipient morphing of Swedish public service radio into a co-branded, extended services provider" (2019, 180). Rather than ensuring that use of various cultural artifacts—historical gramophone records, in Sweden's case—remains open and public, the outsourcing of these responsibilities to streaming services trades short-term access and convenience for longer-term uncertainty about the future ability to find and use these goods, especially given that they are now primarily available via a company that is essentially an "advertising platform which also distributes music" (181).

If spotification represents a move away from, or a reining in of, open technologies like RSS and toward closed and proprietary platforms, then researchers should be concerned not just for the impacts on users and everyday listening experiences but also for their abilities to conduct research on media artifacts. Even beyond the specific usefulness of these open technologies for PodcastRE and preservation, RSS has undeniably helped podcasting flourish. While it may present users trying to add their first subscription with a slight learning curve, and while it may not provide incredibly detailed (some might argue, invasive) listening data and metrics for producers, there currently exists a vibrant listening landscape full of aggregators, apps, amateurs, professionals, podcasters, and listeners, all of which rely on, and benefit from, RSS and XML and the abilities they afford for almost anyone to self-publish and self-syndicate. The move away from RSS, evident in Spotify's interface and its approach to podcasting more generally, is also a move away from these early promises and hopes.

For the many podcasters who would argue, like Josh Kinal (2019), that "it's not a podcast if it's not platform agnostic," spotification responds instead by asking us to envision what it means for podcasting to be platform-dependent. So when Daniel Ek's IPO manifesto ends with the claim, "We really do believe that we can improve the world, one song at a time," it is difficult to be as optimistic as he is. While the music lover in me appreciates the lofty sentiment, podcasting has long promised to improve the world, one voice at a time. Counter to this sentiment, the spotification of podcasting—the attempts to try to move podcasting away from the ethos of its original technologies and toward new, more convenient and user-friendly platforms—represents an important shift that seeks to redefine how users conceive of podcasts. The spotification of podcasting thus potentially represents the narrowing of voices, a further enclosure around an audio culture that has the potential to be open and accessible.

Works Cited

Barbrook, Richard, and Andy Cameron. 1995. "The Californian Ideology." *Mute* 1 (3). http://www.metamute.org/editorial/articles/californian-ideology.

Barrett, Brian. 2018. "It's Time for an RSS Revival." *Wired.* March 30. https://www.wired.com/story/rss-readers-feedly-inoreader-old-reader/.

Berry, Richard. 2006. "Will the iPod Kill the Radio Star? Profiling Podcasting as Radio." *Convergence: The International Journal of Research into New Media Technologies* 12 (2): 143–62. https://doi.org/10.1177/1354856506066522.

Bottomley, Andrew J. 2015. "Podcasting: A Decade in the Life of a 'New' Audio Medium: Introduction." *Journal of Radio & Audio Media* 22 (2): 164–69. https://doi.org/10.1080/19376529.2015.1082880.

Bottomley, Andrew J. 2020. *Sound Streams: A Cultural History of Radio-Internet Convergence.* Ann Arbor: University of Michigan Press.

Bruns, Axel. 2006. "Towards Produsage: Futures for User-Led Content Production." In *Proceeding of the 5th International Conference on Cultural Attitudes towards Technology and Communication.* School of Information Technology, Australia, 275–84, edited by Fay Sudweeks, Herbert Hrachovec, and Charles Ess.

Burkart, Patrick, and Susanna Leijonhufvud. 2019. "The Spotification of Public Service Media." *Information Society* 35 (4): 173–83.

Carman, Ashley. 2019a. "Spotify's Grand Plan for Podcasts Is Taking Shape." Tech News. *The Verge.* March 5. https://www.theverge.com/2019/3/5/18243729/spotify-podcast-strategy-gimlet-media-anchor-purchase.

Carman, Ashley. 2019b. "Podcast Wars: $100 Million Startup Luminary Launches Tuesday without *Reply All* or *The Daily*." Tech News. *The Verge.* April 22. https://www.theverge.com/2019/4/22/18510897/luminary-podcast-app-launch-the-daily-gimlet-media-spotify.

Corbett, Rachel. 2018. "Should You Tell People to 'Subscribe' to Your Podcast?"

Company blog. RachelCorbett.com. October 30. https://rachelcorbett.com .au/grow-your-podcast-audience-subscribe/.

Crichton, Danny. 2018. "RSS Is Undead." Tech News. *TechCrunch* (blog). April 7. http://social.techcrunch.com/2018/04/07/rss-is-undead/.

Cridland, James. 2019. "The End of Open: BBC Blocks Its Podcasts on Google." Tech News. *PodNews*. March 25. https://podnews.net/article/bbc-blocks-go ogle.

Erlandsson, David, and Jomar Perez. 2017. "Listening Diversity Increases Nearly 40 Percent on Spotify." *Insights* (blog). November 2. https://insights.spotify .com/us/2017/11/02/listening-diversity-spotify/.

Fagan, Kaylee. 2018. "Spotify's 35-Year-Old Co-Founder Wrote an Emotional Letter to Investors Promising to Make Users 'Empathize' with Each Other and to 'Feel Part of a Greater Whole.'" *Business Insider*. February 28. https://www.bu sinessinsider.com/spotify-ceo-daniel-ek-letter-to-investors-2018-2.

Gitelman, Lisa. 2006. *Always Already New: Media, History and the Data of Culture*. Cambridge: MIT Press.

Goldstein, Steven. 2019. "'Subscribe' Is a Bad Word for Podcasting." Company blog. Amplifi Media. April 14. https://www.amplifimedia.com/blogstein/20 19/4/14/subscribe-is-a-bad-word-for-podcasting.

Hilton, Nick. 2019. "Are There Too Many Podcasts?" Company blog. Pod Culture (on *Medium*). April 2. https://medium.com/pod-culture/are-there-too -many-podcasts-e743ba49a452.

Holt, Kris. 2019. "Spotify Continues to Expand Its Lineup of Podcast Exclusives." Tech News. *Engadget*. June 14. https://www.engadget.com/2019/06/14/spo tify-podcast-exclusives-riggles-picks-rob-riggle-sarah-tiana/.

Jacobs, Fred. 2018. "Will Podcasting Ever Go Mainstream?" Company blog. Jacobs Media Strategies. June 14. https://jacobsmedia.com/will-podcasting -ever-go-mainstream/.

Kinal, Josh. 2019. "It's Not a Podcast If It's Not Platform Agnostic. Remember That. Repeat That. It Will Be Important in the Future." Social Media. Twitter—@sealfur (blog). March 30. https://twitter.com/sealfur/status/111188 2381999263744.

Lacey, Kate. 2013. *Listening Publics: The Politics and Experience of Listening in the Media Age*. Cambridge, UK: Polity Press.

Markman, Kris M. 2011. "Doing Radio, Making Friends, and Having Fun: Exploring the Motivations of Independent Audio Podcasters." *New Media & Society* 14 (4): 547–65. https://doi.org/10.1177/1461444811420848.

Markman, Kris M., and Caroline E. Sawyer. 2014. "Why Pod? Further Explorations of the Motivations for Independent Podcasting." *Journal of Radio & Audio Media* 21 (1): 20–35. https://doi.org/10.1080/19376529.2014.891211.

McChesney, Robert W. 2013. *Digital Disconnect: How Capitalism Is Turning the Internet Against Democracy*. New York: The New Press.

Misener, Dan. 2019. "Feeling Overwhelmed by the Sheer Number of Podcasts? It's Not Just You." Company blog. Pacific Content. *Medium*. January 11. https://blog.pacific-content.com/feeling-overwhelmed-by-the-sheer-numb er-of-podcasts-its-not-just-you-d46b37a8fdcc.

Nieborg, David B., and Thomas Poell. 2018. "The Platformization of Cultural Production: Theorizing the Contingent Cultural Commodity." *New Media & Society* 20 (11). https://doi.org/10.1177/1461444818769694.

Roettgers, Janko. 2017. "Spotify Launches Showstopper, Other Exclusive Podcasts." Entertainment News. *Variety.* February 23. https://variety.com/2017/digital/news/spotify-original-podcasts-1201994875/.

Schwarz, Jonas Andersson. 2013. Online File Sharing: Innovations in Media Consumption. New York: Routledge.

Sernovitz, Andy. 2008. "Why Are RSS Feeds so Complicated?" *Damn, I Wish I'd Thought of That!* (blog). September 26. https://damniwish.com/why-are-rss-fee/.

Spotify. 2019. "Spotify for Podcasters (Beta)." Podcasting Platform. Spotify Website. June 27. https://podcasters.spotify.com.

Sterne, Jonathan. 2012. *MP3: The Meaning of a Format.* Durham, NC: Duke University Press.

Sterne, Jonathan, Jeremy Wade Morris, Michael Brendan Baker, and Ariana Moscote Freire. 2008. "The Politics of Podcasting." *Fibreculture*, no. 13. http://thirteen.fibreculturejournal.org/fcj-087-the-politics-of-podcasting/.

Sullivan, John L. 2019. "The Platforms of Podcasting: Past & Present." *Social Media + Society* 5 (4). https://doi.org/10.1177/2056305119880002.

Sweney, Mark. 2019. "Spotify Buys Podcast Firms Gimlet and Anchor." Technology. *The Guardian.* February 6. https://www.theguardian.com/technology/2019/feb/06/spotify-buys-podcast-firms-gimlet-and-anchor-streaming-profits-music.

Target, Sinclair. 2019. "The Rise and Demise of RSS." *Motherboard: Tech by Vice* (blog). *Vice.* January 9. https://www.vice.com/en_us/article/a3mm4z/the-rise-and-demise-of-rss.

Vaidhyanathan, Siva. 2011. *The Googlization of Everything.* Berkeley: University of California Press.

van Dijck, José van, Thomas Poell, and Martijn de Waal. 2018. *The Platform Society: Public Values in a Connective World.* Oxford: Oxford University Press.

Van Dyke, Dave. 2017. "2017: Podcasting's Breakthrough Year." Press Release. Bridge Ratings Media Research. http://www.bridgeratings.com/2017-podcastings-breakthrough-year.

Washenko, Anna. 2018. "Spotify Opens Its Podcast Section to All Podcasters with Spotify for Podcasts." Tech News. *RAIN News* (blog). October 2. https://rainnews.com/spotify-enters-podcast-hosting-business-with-open-uploading-platform/.

THIRTEEN | Preserve This Podcast

A Podcaster-Led Preservation Strategy

DANA GERBER-MARGIE, MARY KIDD,
MOLLY SCHWARTZ, AND SARAH NGUYỄN

Podcasts as Ubiquitous yet Vulnerable

Podcasts, simply put, are audio files distributed over the World Wide Web, and because of this, they are at high risk of disappearing (i.e., becoming unfindable or unlistenable). This is happening at the same time the industry is expanding and reaching millions of listeners daily (Edison Research 2020), which may falsely lead some to think that podcasts will be around forever. Podcasts feel ubiquitous because they are distributed via Real Simple Syndication, or RSS feeds, on the web, which allow professional and independent podcasters alike to reach audiences widely for little or no cost. Smartphones and the relatively small size of MP3s, the format of all distributed podcasts, make podcasts portable. However, web content is known to disappear at a rapid rate: one study found that "links appear to die at a steady rate . . . and you can expect to lose about a quarter of them every seven years" (maciej 2011). Another study found that "rates of link rot can be high as 50%" even in "highly curated regions of the web" related to scholarly publishing and jurisprudence" (Summers 2018). There is even a term specific to the podcast industry, "podfade," that describes why podcasts decay so rapidly after they are first published (Friess 2006).

There are a number of initiatives underway approaching the issue of disappearing podcasts, many of which approach the issue from an institutional or top-down level, such as the Library of Congress's 2020 initiative to selectively collect podcasts (*PodNews* 2020). This chapter focuses on *Preserve This Podcast* (PTP), a unique public service effort to educate and train independent or "indie" podcast producers how to take digital preservation action throughout their production work. In order to carry out these efforts, PTP created a comprehensive curriculum that addresses how and why digital loss occurs and provided solutions in the forms of easy preventive steps that podcasters can take to stem this loss. The curriculum considers the distributed, proprietary, platform-independent ecosystems that podcasters are enmeshed in and seeks ways to teach podcasters how to organize, back up, and create metadata for their files that can be easily integrated into existing production workflows. PTP's approach focuses on centering creators and follows what is sometimes referred to as a "personal digital archiving" methodology to preservation (Ashenfelder 2013). Podcasting prides itself on being a relatively low-barrier, no-gatekeeping broadcast medium, so the PTP project aims to reflect this same spirit by keeping its lessons low-cost, approachable, and incrementally achievable.

Overview of the Grant Project

In January 2018 the Metropolitan New York Library Council (METRO), a nonprofit organization providing research, programming, and organizational tools for libraries, archives, and museums, received two years of grant funding totaling $142,000 from the Andrew W. Mellon Foundation. The grant project, titled "Preserve This Podcast: A Podcast Tutorial and Outreach Project," was funded as an outreach campaign to teach independent podcast producers about preservation issues that could potentially affect their own digital audio files. These issues, long known to professional archivists, are caused by digital products (i.e., files, software systems, platforms) being rooted in global systems of capital. This relationship between digital files and the market put creative legacies at risk for sudden obsolescence, digital file decay, viruses, and third-party, state, or governmental seizure, mismanagement, or manipulation. With four core team members, PTP produced a five-part teaching podcast miniseries, an accompanying educational booklet or "zine," a website, and a quantitative analysis from survey data about behaviors or notions harbored by indie podcasters about preservation. These were promoted over a series of workshops hosted around the United States and through additional conference talks. The mission for all interactions was to promote preservation strategies in an approachable, accessible, and affordable way.

PTP was conceived of by three archivists who have experience in either audio preservation projects, podcast production, or both: Mary Kidd (New York Public Library), Molly Schwartz (formerly the Metropolitan New York Library Council, currently at *Mother Jones*), and Dana Gerber-Margie (University of Wisconsin–Madison and co-founder of *Bello Collective*). Coming together as both archivists and audio enthusiasts, the project founders recognized that most podcasts produced independently had little or no long-term preservation support and were thus in imminent danger of disappearing. Additionally, they recognized that podcasts as a mass cultural medium provided inherent research value. They drew parallels between podcast loss and another well-known preservation crisis affecting VHS tapes, once popular among amateur, independent or home moviemakers, whose playback machines and parts are deteriorating and no longer being manufactured. Similarly, some of these VHS tapes are now considered important for their alternative documentary value and have been digitized by major collecting institutions to lengthen the lifespans of their contents (Landau 2014).

Once the grant funds were secured, the core PTP team was expanded to promote, research, project-manage, and produce curriculum deliverables. These individuals included Sarah Nguyễn (University of Washington Information School) as project coordinator, Jeremy Helton as community relations manager, Allison Behringer as editorial consultant, Dalton Harts as audio engineer, and Breakmaster Cylinder as composer. The team was built in this way, to include professionals established in both the archiving, preservation, and podcasting universes, in order to reach as many indie podcasters as possible. This chapter outlines the major deliverables of the PTP project and how those deliverables were informed by the curriculum.

PTP Deliverables

Podcasters Survey

PTP hypothesized that podcasters were likely unfamiliar with issues affecting digital files, and data from a broad survey distributed to podcasters confirmed this and more findings. In collaboration with data analyst Jacob Kramer-Duffield, PTP designed and distributed a survey to gauge podcaster individual and institutional behaviors on file management, storage/backups, and metadata. The survey was distributed between September and December 2018 and promoted widely over social media, listservs, Facebook groups, and through press releases to major podcast news sites. A total of 556 self-selecting podcasters and podcast professionals from over a dozen countries participated in the survey. More than half of survey respondents self-identified as either independent podcast producers working on their own show (62%) or freelance producers working for shows (23%). The survey results, published on PTP's website (http://preservethispodcast.org/), strongly suggest that independently produced podcasts are at greater risk of loss compared to those produced in institutional settings. This should signal a warning to both creators, who should take extra precaution protecting their podcasts, and collecting institutions, who should consider prioritizing acquiring podcasts created by independent podcasters. The survey suggested that indie podcasters are more likely to be less engaged with performing preservation measures than those working for an organization or company: 46 percent of those who are working as part of an organization reported backing up all files, including the raw tape and draft cuts (that potentially harbor important research value), while only one-third (33 percent) of independents reported doing so. This statistic alone substantiated PTP's outreach efforts targeted toward indie producers.

Despite institutional affiliation increasing the likelihood of respondents having a better understanding of preservation practice, the survey also shows that these institutions are not communicating their preservation strategy, if they have one, with their producers. Of the respondents who make podcasts for a larger organization, 58 percent of them said that they are not aware of their organization's backup strategy, and 27 percent said their organization has no system in place. Even among users who are backing up all of their files in uncompressed formats within an organization, 28 percent of them are doing it without knowing the organization's backup strategy. One respondent put it plainly: "The backups I make, I make with the intention that if something happens during a podcast's production . . . I will have another copy. I don't know that I've thought much about storing them for the long term. If I leave my position, I don't think they have a plan in place to maintain the files." (PTP and Kramer-Duffield 2019, 15). Although PTP did not target institutionally affiliated producers specifically, these findings suggest that the lessons put forth by PTP could be used by podcasters to build awareness towards or advocate for preservation measures at an institutional level.

Core Curriculum

The first year of the PTP project focused primarily on creating a core curriculum centered on key concepts from archival practices and podcast production. The curriculum in turn was used to create a set of exercises and lessons that were expressed through the teaching zine, podcast, and workshops in year two. The curriculum was a collaborative effort between PTP and several professionals working in areas of community or personal digital archiving, as well as audio, broadcasting, and digital preservation.

The final curriculum focuses on four concepts: (1) file and folder organization, (2) storage and backups, (3) metadata and RSS feeds, and (4) how to introduce novices to these concepts in ways that were understandable, approachable, and practical. Approachability was an important aspect of teaching preservation to novices; without this aspect, the curriculum had the potential to fail to reach listeners by creating financial, knowledge, or resource barriers. For example, oftentimes, the sheer numbers of files and folders can overwhelm a lone podcaster just embarking on a preservation project. The PTP curriculum reckons with this through its lesson "Get Organized!" which prompted podcasters to write in as much detail as possible their entire production workflow, and after, identify what files are being produced at each step. This exercise provides a framework through which podcasters can take stock of their files, and then organize them using hierarchical folder structures. By taking these steps, podcasters can know what they have, and decide what it is they want to save, which can have important downstream effects in saving podcasters time and money. For example, if a podcaster decides they want to save only master edit files and purge raw unedited files, they will effectively decrease the cumulative file size of their legacy, which could translate into saving dollars on long-term storage.

The Preserve This Podcast Podcast and Zine

PTP made use of the creative mediums of podcasts and zines to equip producers with the knowledge and tools needed to save their files, communicating in the language of podcasters' practice. The PTP podcast series, produced by Schwartz, tapped into elements such as documentary-style storytelling, behind-the-scenes interviews, and a cliffhanger or two to make the experience of learning about preservation captivating, memorable, and enjoyable. The podcast successfully garnered over 5,800

downloads (Mink 2020) and incorporated the stories of three indie podcasters, each of whom was featured being guided by PTP team members
through curriculum exercises on organization, backups, and metadata.
Featured podcasts and podcasters included:

- *Historically Queer*: Community historian Alice Y. Hom presents stories of queer activism by people of color through the years.
- *An Arm and a Leg*: Reporter Dan Weissman delivers revealing and entertaining stories about the spiraling cost of health care in America.
- *Spirits*: History geeks Amanda McLoughlin and Julia Schifini take
  a boozy look at mythology, legends, and folklore from around the
  world, offering fresh takes on classic tales.
- *The Oldest Profession*: Comedian Kaytlin Bailey details the storied history of the world's oldest profession and the sex workers who shape
  society.

Throughout each episode, the producers shared their anxieties, fears,
and eventual successes in following the PTP's preservation protocol. By
listening to "real-life" podcasters complete the lessons from start to finish, PTP demonstrated to their listeners that their preservation curriculum could be done on an individual basis.

The podcast works in tandem with a workbook or "zine," written and
illustrated by Kidd, that prompts listeners to turn to specific pages within
it; in turn, the zine references certain episodes of the podcast. The zine
provides readers with a visual and tangible component to exercises that
can be taken home and worked on independently. Rooted as a medium
that arose to disperse information in a grassroots fashion, early zine
creators worked independently of big publishing companies (Thomas
2018), a content-creation approach that echoes the current work of indie
podcasters, who often work against the grain of big syndicated media.
The zine proved to be a highly successful teaching tool within the PTP
context, showing that "sixty-four percent of . . . respondents to [the PTP
post-workshop survey] felt the zine was the most effective way of learning
about preservation" (Mink 2020).

Workshops

The launch of the *Preserve This Podcast* podcast coincided with scheduling a nationwide series of thirteen workshops in which PTP team members taught the curriculum in group settings. For each workshop, par-

ticipants were guided through each lesson, first by listening to relevant audio clips from each episode and then by performing the related exercises as a group. At the end of each exercise, participants were given the space to ask questions, share results, and provide anecdotes that tied together lessons with their own production workflows. These workshops often saw producers and archivists engaging with each other for the first time and allowed for representatives from these disparate fields to learn more about each other's practice.

The workshops were especially important for the PTP team, as they helped the team become more intimately familiar with the myriad approaches to podcast production and how some of these approaches, through no fault of the podcaster, created obstacles to sustaining long-term preservation of podcaster legacies. PTP observed that indie producers, especially those working solo or on small teams, wear many hats. Producers could also be editors, graphic designers, file and folder organizers, project managers, accountants, tech support, marketers, and disaster recoverers—and they are often performing these tasks on top of day jobs while maintaining family/social lives and individual mental and physical health (Niemeyer 2018). This demanding list of duties and responsibilities means there is often little time to focus on personal preservation practices or that it often takes a backseat to more pressing and immediate concerns.

Preserving Podcasts: A Unique Preservation Challenge

What It Means to Lose a Podcast

Although podcasts are contemporaneous to us, the systems used to create, distribute, or listen to podcasts are constantly changing, upgrading, or being replaced, and each one of these events adds a new layer of distortion to past content. This has happened before with analog media, such as VHS tapes and CD-Rs. Although podcasts hardly resemble plastic cartridges or iridescent disks, they, like previous analog formats, depend on a complex network of systems and platforms to render themselves discoverable, accessible, and listenable. In this sense, podcasts are arguably more volatile, since many podcast files are hosted on paid subscription third-party platforms whose viability depends on for-profit advertising structures. Many podcasts (and the resulting incomes they generate for podcasters that are in part used to pay to use these platforms) are capitalized through ad revenue. The machines that host and play podcasts are rooted in physical and magnetic mechanisms, and these, too, are sub-ject to deterioration, disasters, neglect, rent, or even foul play. While the metaphor of "the cloud" suggests eternal ubiquity, the material reality of hosting platforms is built on rooms of fallible servers, drives, cooling systems, and other machinery.

The magnitude of podcast loss can be measured by the *loss of references* to the original files. The podcast files of some of the earliest podcasts may still exist somewhere (on a hard drive in a closet or a computer on a shelf of a thrift store), but no references exist, such as a URL pointing to the audio file location on a host server or to the original RSS XML meta-data file. Because podcasting is a medium defined by both files (namely, MP3s) and how those files are hosted and distributed (websites and RSS feeds), those who perform podcast preservation must address these as inextricable and not separate characteristics of podcasts (see Hoyt, this volume).

To treat podcasts simply as digital audio files risks decontextualizing them from the systems, networks, and websites used for their distribu-tion, description, and promotion, and also risks losing important contex-tual information about the creators themselves. RSS feeds are an espe-cially challenging component to podcast preservation, mainly because they are important and rich sites of descriptive, structural, and admin-istrative metadata (see Noh, this volume). Systems like podcatchers use RSS metadata to read and convey the structure of a podcast (i.e., which episodes belong to which seasons, where the episode audio file can be downloaded from, etc.). The RSS schema, created prior to publishing a podcast episode to the web, contains metadata on the podcast creator's original intentions when publishing their work for listener consumption. Preserving the RSS feed could be likened to how a web archivist might seek to preserve the source code underlying a website or piece of soft-ware rather than taking a screenshot.

Early on in the curriculum research, PTP discovered that some of the earliest-produced podcasts have already disappeared from the web.[1] According to a cursory sample taken by PTP of 125 shows chosen at ran-dom from the Internet Archive's 2005 Podcast Core Sample, about 87 percent of podcasts from the 2005 era are no longer available online (via general search engine query), and 98 percent of them are no longer available in Apple Podcasts (PTP Podcast Episode 1). For the majority of these podcasts, their RSS feeds are no longer maintained, their web-site URLs have expired, and their audio files are no longer playable. Although it is possible that their creators have taken steps to preserve these episodes on their personal backup devices or services, it is almost impossible to determine how many of these "lost" podcasts are maintained through individual efforts. Given the decentralized nature of podcasting, it is also nearly impossible to determine exactly how many podcasts have disappeared. However, the research PTP conducted is evidence that podcast loss has not just already happened; it is a sure possibility for podcasts produced now and in the future.

One question readers of this volume and users of the PodcastRE database should ask themselves is, How will future scholars look back and understand the earliest-produced podcasts? Even with efforts at the individual creator level, like PTP, and at the institutional level, like PodcastRE.org, this will be a near-impossible task, as many of the URLs and other file references to older podcasts are already broken; the websites, systems, and platforms that once rendered these podcasts are no longer supported and have long disappeared. The relics of the early podcasting landscape may well resemble shards of pottery and broken bone buried beneath the sediment of time.

Preserving the Preserve This Podcast Podcast

The PTP project relied on finite grant funding, which prompted the team to take a self-reflective approach to their curriculum and take the very lessons they taught to producers, and applied them onto their own podcast, website, and zine. Without taking these steps, the PTP project risked placing its own digital legacy at risk of disappearing. Here, PTP project coordinator, Nguyễn, led the research and implementation on a self-hosting solution.[2] This involved three major steps: First, they employed GitHub Pages, a free website-hosting platform to host both the PTP website (excluding the domain name) and the podcast's RSS feed. Second, they arranged for a 301 redirect (which is the podcast equivalent of a US Postal Service address forwarding service) to the new RSS hosted on their GitHub Pages site by notifying Simplecast, PTP's original RSS host.[3] Last, they uploaded all podcast episode audio files onto the Internet Archive, which now acts as their podcast's audio streaming server. The RSS feed was also deposited into the PodcastRE platform, acting as a backup for the GitHub Pages/Internet Archive instances and as way to make the podcast's metadata searchable and researchable within the PodcastRE data visualization and advanced search tools. The remainder of the auxiliary files remain on Google Drive, as PTP is still accessing these working records, but also backed up onto each team member's personal backup drive. While this particular setup allows listeners to access PTP episodes and resources for the foreseeable future, this system, like all of today's systems, faces precarity as rapid technological shifts continue. It is a truth that successful digital preservation relies as much on establishing systems as it does on maintaining them, and how PTP reckons with this over the longer term remains to be seen, especially given the precarity and availability of grant funding (a problem that is also central to the challenges PodcastRE.org faces).

Beyond Preserve This Podcast

In many ways, PTP preached not just preservation but also caution towards the volatility of third-party platforms within the lessons. Workshops prompted participants to ask certain questions of their podcast hosts, such as, "Do you offer RSS 301 redirects even after I stop paying the podcast hosting bills?" By empowering creators with preservation practices, PTP pushed podcast creators, podcast hosting companies, collectives, and radio and media stations to incorporate preservation as a fundamental production step.

The two-year grant was a whirlwind but a joy. The response from both podcast creators and archivists was overwhelmingly positive, suggesting the need for future iterations of PTP. This was made most evident in the project's final assessment report, authored by humanities and education researcher Meridith Beck Mink. Here, Mink qualifies PTP's success and urges the development of ways to extend the teachings beyond the grant (2020). The PTP team is committed to being a part of the podcasting community, cognizant of the ongoing criticisms for grant-funded archiving projects that enter and abruptly exit communities once funding is gone. While all of the project's products, materials, and resources are freely available online, it is important to remain aware of the issues that podcast producers will face for future preservation as the industry expands and formalizes. By making its resource and tools suite freely available on the web, PTP offers a preservation framework that may be repurposed, customized, or scaled by any individual or group looking to born-digital media.

The PTP project reached not only podcast creators but also engaged archivists and librarians, who were often mixed in with podcaster audiences at in-person and online workshops, suggesting that the PTP ethos may stand a chance to thrive on an institutional scale. Archivists and librarians were interested in learning more about podcasters and their production workflows, as well as the unique challenges posed in preserving podcasts on an institutional level. In response to this, PTP produced a guide to hosting one's own PTP workshop. Additionally, PTP has been engaged in several "train the trainer"–themed workshops, including one hosted by the Association for Library Collections and Technical Services (ALCTS) early in 2020. A guide to hosting one's own PTP workshop is freely available online (http://preservethispodcast.org/pages/diyw orkshop.html), but the team continues to connect with cultural heritage institutions on an ongoing basis to spread awareness of "train-the-trainer" opportunities. For both archiving and podcasting, the community relationships and local connections are paramount.

Podcast preservation has also resonated with some of the country's largest collecting institutions. In late 2019, the Library of Congress (LOC) announced it would start to collect podcasts (Mink 2020). For the time being, the LOC's broad podcast collection policy will focus only on active podcasts addressing specific subjects. This narrow scope will likely miss important, lesser-known or marginalized podcasts, or those podcasts that are not actively being maintained. Local libraries and archives might look to expand their reach into podcast communities and lead more locally focused podcast preservation efforts to close this gap. Expanding efforts by local librarians and archivists to collect podcasts is the way to ensure widespread preservation and access.

Beyond personal digital archiving and formal collection by libraries and archives, it is also crucial to expand digital preservation and file management to media companies, institutions, and organizations creating podcasts. This grant emphasized independent podcasters, but the survey results show that institutions need help putting preservation into their workflow too. Organizations that have employed staff and those that hire freelancers need to have documented procedures in place to clarify for everyone not only who owns the rights to the content but also make transparent which party is responsible for ongoing custodianship of the preservation work. The ongoing work aims to bring awareness to creators, whether freelance or on staff, by helping to fold the existing curriculum into podcast, journalism, sound studies, and other creative coursework. The team is also considering consultations for companies and media organizations looking for how best to define their overall preservation strategy.

Despite the podcast industry changing and evolving all the time, the lessons put forth by PTP will likely remain useful and relevant to podcasters looking to retain their creative legacies. Talking with podcast creators about their personal digital preservation inevitably returned hesitation that anyone would actually care about their work. As more people enter this field to produce works that are creative, crucial, momentous, educational, and entertaining, it is increasingly apparent that many people do, and will continue to, care that these works are preserved in a way that recognizes their contributions to our public soundscape.

Notes

1. Here is a sample of findings from the PTP Metadata Archaeology exercise. Workshop participants were instructed to search and compare podcasts existing in the Internet Archive's collection and Apple Podcasts. Many podcasts were missing from Apple Podcasts. https://github.com/mnylc/preservethispodcast /blob/master/assets/Metadata-Archaeology_2005PodcastCoreSample.csv.

2. In order to inspire other podcasters to either take similar steps or explore new, sustainable preservation approaches, documentation on how to follow this protocol is openly available on GitHub: https://github.com/mnylc/preservethi spodcast.

3. It is important to note that not all hosts provide this type of post-cancellation service, because they are not in the business of losing users and subscribers.

Works Cited

Ashenfelder, Mike. 2013. "The Library of Congress and Personal Digital Archiving." In *Personal Archiving: Preserving Our Digital Heritage*, edited by Donald T. Hawkins Medford, NJ: Information Today, 35. http://digitalpreser vation.gov/documents/lc-digital-preservation.pdf?loclr=blogsig.

Edison Research. 2020. "The Infinite Dial 2020." Edison Research. https://www .edisonresearch.com/the-infinite-dial-2020/.

Friess, Steve. 2006. "Podfading Takes Its Toll." *Wired News.* February 7. https:// www.wired.com/2006/02/podfading-takes-its-toll/.

Landau, Arielle. 2014. "Audio and Moving Image Collections, Facilities, and Workflows Assessment." New York Public Library. August 27. https://www.ny pl.org/blog/2016/09/01/audio-and-moving-image-collections-facilities-and -workflows-assessment.

maciej. 2011. "Remembrance of Links Past." *Pinboard* (blog post). https://blog .pinboard.in/2011/05/remembrance_of_links_past/.

Mink, Meridith Beck. 2020. "Preserve This Podcast: An Assessment of the 2018– 2020 Project." Project Report. January. https://preserve-this-podcast.gitlab .io/preserve-this-podcast-assessment/index.html.

Niemeyer, Liam. 2018. *What Does "Producer" Mean, Anyway? Medium.* August 31. https://bellocollective.com/what-does-producer-mean-anyway-3cf8747b c4d5,

PodNews. 2020. "US Library of Congress Starts Archiving Podcasts." *PodNews* newsletter. January 7. https://podnews.net/update/congress-archiving.

Preserve This Podcast, and Jacob Kramer-Duffield. 2019. "Podcast Preservation Survey Findings." Preserve This Podcast Project. February 5. http://preserv ethispodcast.org/assets/PodcastPreservation_SurveyFindings_Feb2019.pdf.

PTP Podcast. 2019. *Preserve This Podcast* Episode 1: "Time to Take Notice." *Preserve This Podcast.* March 21. https://archive.org/details/PreserveThisPodca stEpisode1.

Summers, Edward. 2019. "Appraisal Practices in Web Archives." *SocArXiv.* March 15. doi:10.31235/osf.io/75mjp.

Thomas, Susan. 2018. "Zines for Teaching: A Survey of Pedagogy and Implications for Academic Librarians." *Libraries and the Academy* 18 (4): 737–58. https://preprint.press.jhu.edu/portal/sites/ajm/files/Thomas.pdf.

FOURTEEN | Saving Podcasting's Contexts

Archive Collecting Strategies
and Media Historiography

ERIC HOYT

Podcasts are audio files, the metadata that describes them, and the RSS feeds that allow us to subscribe. But podcasting, as a practice, encompasses much more (see Sterne et. al. 2008). Live shows, newsletters, websites, and social media threads are all parts of the podcasting ecosystem. For listeners, podcasts can become companions for road trips, dishwashing, and mowing the lawn. And podcasts emerge from assumptions about what makes for a good story, what audiences want, and how to make money.

PodcastRE's data preservation plan—which requires ongoing, active maintenance and systems upgrades—will enable researchers fifty years from now to listen to millions of audio files and search their descriptive metadata (see Morris et al. 2019). But if researchers only engage with MP3 and XML files, they will miss important production and reception environments that are contributing the rise of podcasting as a vital and important media format. What else should PodcastRE be collecting to achieve our promise of "a searchable, researchable archive of podcasting culture?" How can PodcastRE, as well as other research initiatives and cultural heritage institutions, go about saving podcasting's contexts beyond just the data files and sound files?

In this chapter, I survey and appraise a range of sources that would alter the way future media historians interpret podcasting as a medium. Some of the examples are what archivists would label as "contextual metadata" or a medium's "significant properties" (see Marchioni et al. 2009 and Stepanyan et al. 2012). Others are more similar to the film and television paratexts that Jonathan Gray analyzes in his book *Show Sold Separately* (Gray 2010). All of them are collectible in some way. My goal is to move beyond merely a theoretical discussion and toward a pragmatic plan for PodcastRE's future development. Collectively, these sources provide a map to the norms of production and reception, as well as the intermediaries through which producers and listeners interact.

Table 14.1. Schemas for what could be collected and preserved from podcasting culture beyond the sound files

	Production Artifacts	Intermediary Artifacts	Reception Artifacts
Published	How-to guides Recording software tutorials Practitioner and show newsletters Podcast websites	Social media posts, replies, and discussions between creators and listeners (e.g., Reddit AMA with Roman Mars) Patreon and Kickstarter fundraising pages (e.g., Doughboys and The Best Show) Ticketmaster and StubHub listings for live shows Official t-shirts and merch Websites of distribution intermediaries (e.g., Apple, Stitcher, Soundcloud)	Newspaper reviews and think pieces Podcast recommendation newsletters and blogs Fan fiction and art (e.g., *Welcome to Night Vale*) Laptops, iPods, smart phones, podcasting apps, and other distribution and playback technologies. Headphones and ear buds
Unpublished	Internal email discussions Outlines, notes, and tape logs Budgets and schedules Network memos Equipment used to record podcasts Saved ProTools and editing software sessions Scripts	Contracts between podcast producers with advertisers, promoters, performance venues, and other third parties	Email, text message, and social media messages regarding podcasts shared on a peer to peer basis. Homemade costumes worn to live shows. Playlists, downloads subscriptions, and other expressions of listener preferences and habits.

Schemas for What to Collect

In an attempt to begin mapping out the artifacts of podcasting culture that go beyond the podcasts themselves, I created the table above.
The columns represent three overlapping categories in the podcast
ecosystem—production, intermediary forces, and reception. Each
category is then broken down between published sources and unpublished sources.

This schema is imperfect and incomplete, to say the least. A Facebook post could conceivably fall into any one of the categories. Additionally, I have collapsed the three frames of classification—artefactual,
informational, and folkloric—that Trevor Owens has usefully theorized
(Owens 2018). When I refer to *artifacts* in this essay, I am using the term
in its more general sense to describe objects, whether born-digital or
physical, that people created and that someone could conceivably collect (archivists would likely apply the term *records* to much of these).
Nevertheless, the schema is still useful as a starting point, especially for
the way it asks us to consider the artifacts that—even in our age of digital
abundance—are not published (or made public) and therefore become
more difficult for institutions to acquire. Historians have long utilized
unpublished manuscripts, stored at state archives or library special collections, as the building blocks of their work. If we want to offer future
historians sources that are comparable to the NBC Papers or United Artists Collection (both housed at the Wisconsin Historical Society), then
partnerships and accession strategies involving podcast producers and
networks will be essential.

In the remainder of this chapter, I will move through the various
categories/zones of the table, offer up examples, and reflect on what
they mean. No publication of this nature would be complete without
the standard acknowledgement and admission: we can't save everything.
This is why the appraisal (to evoke a term from the world of archives) of
podcasting's contextual artifacts is important, giving us a lens for assessing objects for their significance and fit within PodcastRE's collecting
mission. To complicate things further, the numbers of artifacts in the
above table will only expand as podcasting evolves (including through
the "Spotifcation" of the medium, as Morris discusses in his chapter in
this volume). There is tremendous breadth to what we might collect,
as well as many unknowns. But rather than letting this paralyze us, we
should use it as a starting point, much like a chatcast, to think and talk
through the possible directions that await. Applying the analytical frame-

work of appraisal to podcasting culture also allows media scholars to consider elements of podcasting beyond the MP3 file or RSS metadata that might still be central and relevant for understanding this media and its meanings.

Production Artifacts

There is much one can learn about a podcast's production context simply by pressing the play button. Podcasting is a highly self-reflexive medium. With the notable exception of scripted dramas, most podcasts will, at some point, reference aspects of the show's production process. Listeners of ESPN's *Baseball Tonight* podcast, for example, are familiar with the host, Buster Olney, commenting on another "baggage claim Monday" and recording the show at an early hour in the Atlanta or Houston airport. Chatcast hosts apologize for technology shortcomings when one of their guests chimes in via Skype or telephone rather than a studio microphone. And most live shows wear their production contexts on their sleeves, calling out the city and venue they are being recorded within. These self-reflexive moments serve to make the podcaster seem more authentic and relatable. But they also embed details about the show's creative, spatial, and temporal environments.

Nevertheless, even a research question as basic as—"why does this show sound the way it does?"—cannot be thoroughly answered simply by listening to the show itself. As Amanda Keeler's chapter on true crime podcasts and my co-authored chapter on vocal performance make clear, the production of podcasts is rooted in norms and assumption about what makes for a good voice, an interesting story, and an ethical mode of presentation. As such, guidebooks and tutorials are important sources we need to be saving for future historians to be able to unpack these assumptions. Jessica Abel's *Out on the Wire: The Storytelling Secrets of the New Masters of Radio* (2015) uses comic book form to present tips from Ira Glass, Jad Abumrad, and other public radio luminaries as they reflect on the creative process, from formulating a good idea all the way to sound editing (Abel 2015). Atlantic Public Media's website Transom.org features blog posts from some of these same producers that offer frameworks for writing, recording, and editing (see Transom 2016 and 2017). They also reflect on the importance of media forms that preceded podcasting, especially radio programs in the genres of news, talk, and drama.

The norms that inform podcasting production encompass traditions from multiple forms of media. However, the content produced by podcasters extends across media forms, too. The website developed for *Serial's* first season served up text-based and image-based assets, including JPEGs of the infamous Best Buy (architectural plans and hand drawings of the big box store are both featured). Audiences seeking a deep dive into the evidence surrounding the murder case, or those simply curious to see for themselves what host Sarah Koenig was describing in their earbuds, could visit the website as an ancillary experience to the podcast. In 2019, five years after the show's launch, the "Maps, Documents, Etc." webpage is still functional and it has been preserved by the Internet Archive's Wayback Machine (see Rogers 2017). Most documentary podcast websites don't offer this level of supplementary evidence, or this level of long-term access to the site after the show has ceased to be a cultural phenomenon. Malcolm Gladwell's website for *Revisionist History*, for example, provides a more straightforward list of episode descriptions with options for streaming, downloading, and subscribing to RSS. But the Revisionist History website also includes a 30-second video trailer for the show—worth noting (and saving) for the way it reveals how podcasting promotion uses the visual register within social media feeds to spread the word and generate interest.

If there is one type of podcasting paratext more ubiquitous than a show's website, it is the weekly podcast newsletter. The best show-oriented newsletters (not to be confused with trade or recommendation newsletters, which are discussed in the Reception section of this chapter) give audiences new insights into a show's production and the thought of process its creators. For example, just hours after NPR's *Pop Culture Happy Hour* (*PCHH*) podcast released its episode discussing 2019's most anticipated movie (*Avengers: Endgame*), the *PCHH* newsletter reached my inbox containing a short essay titled, "Spoiler Etiquette in the Age of 'Endgame'." Written by the show's host, Linda Holmes, the essay offers witty reflections on what sort of information is and isn't acceptable to share about *Endgame* and blockbusters in general. Holmes gives fans (and future media historians) a window into her strategies for framing and moderating potentially spoiler-rich movie reviews (Holmes 2019). Of course, the newsletter also served as a not so subtle reminder that the new episode of *PCHH* discussing *Endgame* was now available. Inexpensive marketing, more than any other factor, is the chief motive driving the majority of podcast newsletters, which frequently promote new episodes and encourage listeners to make donations within the span of a few paragraphs. Newsletters also offer another avenue for collecting data on listeners, especially helpful since the actual podcasts do not typically report back on consumer behavior after initial download. In early-2019, we set up a PodcastRE email address to systematically save podcast newsletters for their insights into both the production and marketing cultures of podcasts. Ironically, we are collecting the HTML and Javascript files that were designed to collect information about us.

Newsletters provide a window into the podcasting production process, but it's a carefully constructed window—designed to frame our impressions of the podcasters in a certain way and leave a great deal out of view. Negotiations over a host's salaries and whether or not to pay guests, for example, are generally not disclosed in a show's newsletter. Nor is the behind-the-scenes flurry of new scripts, outlines, and interview bookings that can occur when a breaking news story hits a few hours before taping. For future media historians to gain an accurate understanding of the podcasting production process, these types of unpublished digital artifacts need to be saved. Unfortunately, there is little evidence that this is currently happening. As Andrew Bottomley puts it earlier in this same book, "the quantity of documents being generated are vast—a multitude of daily emails, countless drafts of presentations or scripts, and so on—but the lack of a paper presence makes them all the more likely to end up locked away on a hard drive, abandoned in a closet, accidentally erased or deteriorating, or otherwise made inaccessible to researchers." The lack of a paper presence for these quickly produced and consumed digital artifacts is a big part of the challenge for saving unpublished production materials (Blouin Jr. and Rosenberg 2011).

The even bigger challenge, though, is rooted in the institutional cultures of producers and collecting institutions. Contemporary media corporations guard their internal records carefully. As more and more podcast producers and networks get bought out by large media corporations, the likelihood of researchers to be able to access unpublished production artifacts steadily decreases. The companies have no incentive to open up their internal records. It wasn't always this way. In the 1960s and 1970s, the movie studios Warner Bros. and United Artists made giant gifts of their unpublished records (including contracts, budgets, and executive memos) to universities in order to save money on their taxes. Since that time, the tax laws have been changed to eliminate deductions for self-created value (Carman 2014). There is no upside to opening up the records and a great deal of possible downside. What the media historian sees as a juicy primary source, the corporate attorney tends to regard as sensitive information that could damage an individual and/or the firm. However, not all hope is lost. Even if large media corporations decide not to share their manuscript collections, public media organizations and independent podcast producers might see the value in making their unpublished files accessible to future researchers—especially if archives signal their intent to collect in this area and their commitment to the preservation and stewardship of the files.

In prioritizing and accessioning the collections of podcasting producers, we should also learn from the mistakes, oversights, and erasures committed by cultural heritage institutions. Archivists and historians continue to grapple with decisions that their predecessors made—sometimes long ago, sometimes more recently—about whose collections were worthy of saving and studying. As a result of these assumptions and decisions, the stories of white men are much better represented at most American archives than the collections of women, indigenous communities, and people of color (Blouin Jr. and Rosenberg 2011). The chapters in this collection from Jennifer Hyland Wang, Sarah Florini, and Briana Barner are important for the ways that they write Black and amateur women podcasters into media history. They demand that PodcastRE and other archives think critically about implicit biases in our collecting policies. How can we devote our resources, ethically and equitably, in the acquisition and stewardship of new collections? Archives and researchers both have roles to play if we want the long pattern of silencing—the erasure of contributions by cultural producers from marginalized communities—not to persist into the future and simply become reproduced across new media formats.

Intermediary Artifacts

The history of podcasting would be incomplete if presented only through the published and unpublished artifacts created by producers. Intermediary technologies, services, and agents are vital in the movement of media and money across the podcasting ecosystem.

Apps are the most important distribution intermediaries, the hubs that connect podcasters to their audiences. We now take it for granted that these apps operate on mobile devices, but as Jeremy Morris and Eleanor Patterson have pointed out, podcatching software existed years before the introduction of the iPhone in 2007 and the iPhone's native "Podcasts" app in 2014 (Morris and Patterson 2015). If we can save the various iterations of podcast distribution software, then researchers will be able to understand the changing assumptions about the ways in which users were encouraged (or discouraged) to engage with podcasts. There are huge challenges involved in these forms of software preservation, which can take the form of maintaining aging hardware and operating systems, as well as the building of emulators (for cutting-edge work taking place in this space, see the Software Preservation Network). But, as a number of archivists have pointed out, capturing and preserving screenshots or videos are sufficient in many cases. It ultimately comes down to the anticipated research questions—yet another reminder of the way in which the work of podcasting preservation is inseparable from our ideas about what defines the form and its significance (Owens 2018 and Fino-Radin 2012).

Apps are worth the considerable effort of saving, in part, because of the ways they are encoded with changing ideas about podcasting's business model and what it is that listeners want. In their 2015 article, Morris and Patterson analyze program apps—a category that, just a few years later, is nearing extinction (Morris and Patterson 2015). The stand-alone program apps for *Radiolab* and *This American Life*, for example, were available for purchase through Apple's Apps Store and offered users free access to library episodes and other nifty features (Radiolab's app had a "MAKE" function that would record sound and upload it to the Radiolab team). Many of the customer reviews, however, express dissatisfaction with the program apps, finding them lacking when it comes to the core functions that users expect (e.g., the ability to search and sort episodes, the app remembering where you left off listening within a given episode, etc.). Most listeners currently use general podcatching mobile apps, especially Stitcher, Spotify, and Apple's Podcasts, as their preferred way to consume all programs—*Radiolab*, included. But these present conditions will likely change, too, and we need to become more systematic about saving podcasting's intermediary technologies.

Although developing and selling apps turned out to be a boondoggle for most podcast producers, other digital services have turned out to be hugely important for their livelihoods and the overall podcasting economy. Crowdfunding websites provide a vital revenue stream for independent podcasters. Countless podcasters have raised money for new shows (or subsequent seasons of existing shows) through Kickstarter campaigns. Roman Mars, for example, made headlines in 2012 when he raised $170,000 for the third season of his popular podcast, *99% Invisible* (Loker 2012). But since that time, a different crowdfunding website has emerged as the most important for sustaining the work of creators. Patreon allows fans to become "patrons" and contribute funds on a per month or per episode basis. Patreon is so widely used by podcasters (and YouTubers), in fact, that the website graphtreon.com (which is supported by its own Patreon patrons) provides a Top 50 chart tracking patron and revenue metrics.

The Patreon pages of podcasts reveal how this intermediary service has transformed the content of shows and the labor of podcasters. Take, for example, the Doughboys—a comedy podcast that focuses each week on a different chain restaurant. Any listener using Stitcher or Apple's Podcasts app could freely download the Doughboys' recently released episode profiling Chili's Too, a staple of large airport terminals. But only patrons of the Doughboys could enjoy the creators' bonus content; videos, access to live recordings, and other perks become accessible after logging into Patreon and pledging one's support. The bonus content is worth preserving, but the Patreon webpage that frames and controls access is even more important to save for what it reveals about the economics of podcasting and the relationship between the podcasters and their audience. This intermediary artifact speaks to what podcaster Caroline Crampton has called "the classic Patreon dilemma of wanting to ask listeners to support the podcast itself, but instead providing extra episodes and livestreams for which people paid. Making this additional stuff is a lot of work, and while the contributions might cover that effort, the core product—the podcast—remains something the creator has to do for free" (Crampton 2019). Future media historians will be missing a huge component of the political economy of podcasting if they are not able to look back at Patreon webpages, which speak to the medium's business models, the demands on producers, and the relationships between podcasters and their listeners.

Those same historians will also be interested to see how podcasters have interacted with their fans over social media—another important intermediary digital service in the podcasting ecosystem. Roman Mars and Jesse Thorn have participated in Reddit AMAs (Ask Me Anythings, online question-and-answer discussions), and many Patreon-supported podcasters, including the Doughboys, maintain their own subreddit threads for engaging with fans (Reddit 2014, 2015, and n.d.). Twitter has also played an important role in the podcasting landscape, though not always in the ways we might expect. In their research, Martin Spinelli and Lance Dann found that prominent podcasters were more likely to use Twitter "as a digital bulletin board on which they post information and messages" (i.e. updates about new episodes and upcoming live shows) than they were as a forum for "active two-way discourse" with their audience. To be clear, Spinelli and Dann also found examples of podcasters engaging a great deal with audiences over Twitter, especially those pod-casters trying to make a name for themselves and attract more attention (Spinelli and Dann, 48–60). But if social media posts are preserved as part of podcasting history—and they should be—then they need to be understood as intermediary services that attempted to accomplish a wide range of promotional strategies, not merely as documented interactions between producers and fans.

One final group of intermediary online services with data that would be valuable to save are the platforms that sell tickets to live podcasting shows. Ticketmaster, StubHub, and other ticketing services contain data fields that would be fascinating to track—including the show's title, per-formance date, location, and the range of ticket prices. The Kinomatics Project, led by Deb Verhoeven and Colin Arrowsmith, has productively used movie ticketing data to study the global flow of cinema (Kinomat-ics n.d. and see Verhoeven 2016). If we adopted similar methods for the study of podcasting, we could analyze the popularity of podcasting and particular shows in various regions, as well as draw comparisons between the successfulness of shows on iTunes, Patreon, and ticketing sites. All of this depends on saving and structuring the necessary data, which in turn depends on possessing access and the rights to save them.

No discussion of live podcast shows would be complete without men-tioning the t-shirts, coffee mugs, and other merchandise for sale in the lobby. These intermediary artifacts, which are generally also purchas-able via a podcast's website, are worth preserving, too. They will look great on display if podcasting ever gets its own museum—the way film, broadcasting, and recorded music have now all been memorialized. In terms of research value, the different t-shirts can tell us a great deal about the way the podcast producers present themselves and invite par-ticular relationships with their audiences. The official t-shirts for most NPR podcasts feature the show's logo against a solid color fabric. It's a fashion befitting most NPR podcasts—a polished production, meant to feel approachable and casual, steering clear of anything that might seem too divisive, controversial, or weird. The Crooked Media network takes things in a different direction; its "Friend of the Pod" t-shirt serves simultaneously as a mark of the wearer's *Pod Save America* fandom and partisan opposition to the Trump administration. And different yet is the merchandise for *Welcome to Night Vale*, which includes a Night Vale Community College sweatshirt, "Sleep Like There's Nobody Watching" t-shirt, and other clothing articles that are congruent with the tone and/or diegesis of the fictional town. The official apparel for *Welcome to Night Vale* and *Pod Save America* both point toward a depth of listener engagement that goes beyond most of what can be found within the NPR podcasting ecosystem (Topatoco n.d. and Crooked Media n.d.). It should be noted that fan art and other fan created works need to be part of our preservation agenda, too; the homemade costumes worn to *Night Vale* live shows and the fan art inspired by the series and shared tell us a rich story about audience engagement with *Night Vale* (Spinelli and Dann 2019, 60–65 and Rowser 2013).

Whether it's an app, Patreon webpage, or t-shirt, all of the examples of intermediary artifacts surveyed here are published in the most basic sense (i.e., they have been made public). As I noted in my discussion of production artifacts, however, it would be tremendously valuable to save unpublished items as well. The behind-the-scenes agreements of producers with networks, sponsors, concert venues, and other vendors would all hold a great deal of research value. Similarly, it would be great to save the emails and other correspondence between podcasts and the directories and distribution companies attempting to get listed and featured.

Some of these contracts and emails will be preserved and become accessible if podcast producers collaborate with archives and other collecting institutions. However, as the podcasting industry continues to grow, it's likely that some contracts will be saved through a different mode of archive-building. The history of media is, among other things, a history of legal conflicts. Lawsuits generate extensive documentation, and they transform private agreements into court exhibits that enter the public record (see McDonald et al. 2015). My research into the intermediary companies that distributed feature films to television stations in the 1950s would have been impossible if it weren't for lawsuits filed at both state and federal levels (Hoyt 2014). If future historians feel discouraged by the lack of contracts between producers and sponsors donated to archives, they should not give up hope. It's a sign that it's time to start poking around the Westlaw database, federal record repositories, and county court archives.

Reception Artifacts

Even in the absence of archival deposits, however, we sometimes learn the details of deals in the podcasting industry thanks to the reporting of journalists. Often, the same newspapers, magazines, and websites that report on industry deal-making also provide reviews and consumer guides, pointing listeners toward podcasts they should check out. These outlets may also include the work of critics operating at an even larger scale, identifying trends among podcasts and using them to make larger points about culture. All of these are examples of artifacts that fall within the *published reception* category of the grid that opened this chapter.

In surveying reception artifacts, it is useful to begin with journalistic works, if for no other reason than because they have been the traditional starting point for most reception studies into the histories of radio, television, and film. Journalists, to be sure, also occupy an intermediary role—mediating the public's understanding of people, events, and phenomena that lay out of reach for most of us. But because reporting and criticism expresses assumptions about quality and taste, and because those expressions are fixed in the form of published writing, journalism is a valuable historical source for researchers seeking to understand the reception of media forms. Before a newspaper or magazine can regularly review podcasts and answer the question of whether particular shows are good or bad, the news publication has to implicitly answer another question: is podcasting as a media format worthy of critical scrutiny? When a mainstream newspaper, like the *New York Times* or *Wall Street Journal*, discusses podcasts alongside films, theatre, and other established entertainment forms, it indicates that the medium has been legitimated by cultural gatekeepers and thought to be sufficiently interesting to the paper's readers.

Even without any intervention on PodcastRE's part, the *New York Times'* and *Wall Street Journal's* reports and critical commentaries on podcasting will probably remain easily retrievable for decades to come (both publications have done tremendous work in preserving their past articles and making them digitally searchable). A bigger priority for PodcastRE's preservation efforts are saving the specialized newsletters—generally existing exclusively in digital form—that offer reporting, guidance, and criticism on the podcasting landscape. These newsletters are different from the ones profiled earlier in this chapter in that they are not extensions of one particular show. Instead, the newsletters (which are generally also websites running blog software) attempt to survey podcasting landscape at large, helping readers make sense of a rapidly growing and changing medium. Bello Collective and Discover Pods are both newsletters/blogs that point listeners toward worthwhile new podcasts, curate playlists themed around genre (e.g. "indie fiction podcasts"), topic (e.g., midterm elections), national identity (e.g., "9 Irish podcasts you should be listening to right now"), or ideal listening conditions (e.g., "5 Great Road Trip Podcasts"), and provide updates on industry news and developments (Discover Pods 2018). The newsletters and their contents are especially valuable for studying podcasting reception. For example, by explicitly suggesting podcasts to match life experiences—a road trip, for example—curated playlists implicitly make a number of assumptions about podcast listeners (e.g., road trips require a certain amount of privilege—access to a car and gas money, at the very least—but they are also the favored mode of transport for those willing to spend more time in transit in exchange for spending less money, especially compared to air travel), and those assumptions can be useful for reflecting on the kinds of audiences both the newsletter and podcasting more generally appeals to.

For future scholars of the media industries, trade-oriented newsletters will also be essential resources. *Hot Pod*, edited by Nick Quah, is the U.S. podcasting industry's leading trade paper, and it's 200+ issues provide a chronicle of developments (both small and large) within the industry from 2014 to the present. However, like other media industry trade papers, *Hot Pod* serves other important functions beyond merely disseminating the news (see Hoyt 2022). These newsletters can also be seen as serving gatekeeping and scorekeeping functions, helping to express and convey community standards and expectations, and weigh in on cases where those standards and expectations have not been met. Take, for example, *Hot Pod's* reporting on Luminary's controversial launch. In discussing the producers and networks that demanded that Luminary remove them from its search index, *Hot Pod* was playing the roles of community gatekeeper (noting actions that went against the general community's standards and expectations) and scorekeeper (tracking the winners and losers within the controversy) (Quah 2018). *Hot Pod*, along with the more globally focused newsletters, such as *Podnews*, are important to save if podcasting historians want sources comparable to *Moving Picture World*, *Motion Picture News*, and the other trades that film historians regularly consult.

Another category of reception artifacts worth saving are the physical objects used by listeners to collect and playback podcasts. An iPhone 6 and earbuds would be an obvious starting place, but just the start of a much longer line of hardware and software that offer clues to podcasting's history. Before the streamlined process of downloading and playing back podcasts within the same mobile device, the processes for downloading podcasts, playing them back, and making them mobile were far more cumbersome. Desktop computers, external computer speakers, and MP3 players from Apple's competitors (like Microsoft's Zune) all deserve consideration, along with the apps and software mentioned in the previous section (Morris 2015). The compact disc and its associated technologies—especially CD burning drives, inexpensive CD-R spindles, and the black Sharpie marker—should not be overlooked either. Why hang on to so much e-waste? It's unlikely these devices will still be playable in the decades ahead. But as the materiality of digital media has become increasingly hidden to users, and as the apps we use close down certain ways for engaging with the media, there is value to highlighting the visible, material iterations of reception technologies and the range of choices they enabled. If curated together for an exhibit, the key would be to leave museum goers with a particular impression—not gratitude and reassurance by the superiority and ease of their technologies, but a sense of the way podcasting audiences have been encouraged to listen to the media in certain ways at certain times and, meanwhile, bent other technologies to serve their listening preferences.

However, studies of podcasting reception cannot end with newspapers, newsletters, and audio hardware/software. As the existing scholarship on podcasting has emphasized, the form's relationship with its audience—frequently discussed in terms of "intimacy"—is one of the defining aspects of the medium (Swiatek 2018 and Spinelli and Dann 2019, 69–97). This is just one reason why we need to be proactive and creative in finding ways to save artifacts that speak to the direct listening experience of audiences. Public posts on blogs, Twitter, Facebook, and other social media platforms are all among the published artifacts that would fit this description. Emails among friends and family recommending podcasts would be examples of unpublished sources.

The reality, however, is that most of our intimate experiences are never expressed in any material form that we can save. I can't think of Slate's *Slow Burn* podcast without recalling driving 400 miles to spend time with my sister in St. Louis, a city that she no longer lives in and that I don't know if I will ever visit again. *Slow Burn* is largely about what we choose to remember and record; in my case, the show brings to mind a specific person and place far removed from the first season's actual focal points (President Nixon and Washington D.C.). My hunch is that many podcast listeners have their own rich memories linking podcasts with a time, place, and person. The associations can form in peculiar ways, too. *Hot Takedown,* a data analytics-oriented sports podcast from FiveThirtyEight and ESPN, has existed in various iterations over the last few years, with some long hiatuses. Yet I've always seemed to find *Hot Takedown* and listen to it while performing mundane household tasks, like unloading the dishwasher and taking out the trash. Whereas *Slow Burn* has traveled hundreds of miles with me, *Hot Takedown* almost never leaves my house. This is, in part, the difference between a serialized documentary (a genre frequently recommended for road trips) and a topical sports podcast (a genre premised on speculating about games that will be played in a matter of days or even hours). But it's also a sign of the personal and haphazard ways in which we encounter, experience, and remember media texts.

One method for saving these sorts of podcast memories and personal associations is to do what I just did above: write them down. They would also work well as recorded oral histories, which could even be turned into podcasts with accompanying metadata that notes specific shows (Slow Burn), places (St. Louis), contexts (road trip), and people (sister). Some useful models for how we might approach this can be found through the work of scholars affiliated with the HoMER Network (History of Moviegoing, Exhibition, and Reception). Annette Kuhn and Jacqueline Maingard as well as Daniela Treveri Gennari, Pierluigi Ercole, and Catherine O'Rawe have gathered oral histories and analyzed existing oral histories to explore how cinema fit into the social fabric of people's lives in London, Cape Town, and Rome (Kuhn 2002, Maingard 2017, and Ercole et al. 2017). The integration of memory studies with media studies brings its challenges. As Annette Kuhn, Daniel Biltereyst, and Philippe Meers point out in their introduction to the special issue of the journal *Memory Studies* on this topic, "*how* people remember is as much a text to be deciphered as *what* they remember" (Kuhn et al. 2017). For this reason, more ethnographic research into contemporary podcasting audiences would provide a great point of comparison to the memories collected in oral histories. The widely read and cited annual Edison report captures quantitative changes (Edison Research 2019), but it leaves out the qualitative observations and analyses about media engagement that distinguished many of the foundational works of television studies (See Morley 1992, Seiter 1995, and Brunsdon 1997). Both ethnographies and oral histories depend on researchers putting in the work of documenting them.

Conclusion

This chapter has explored some of the many artifacts—beyond sound and metadata files—that archives should consider collecting in order to better represent podcasting's cultural and industrial contexts to future researchers. This is not an easy task, nor is my survey and schema of categories complete. But the perfect is the enemy of the good, and any work in this space is better than none. The surest sign of major progress will be when we open the Bello newsletter and read that a podcasting company has donated their collections of scripts, emails, contracts, and other documents to the Wisconsin Center for Film and Theater Research, UCLA Film & Television Archive, or some other collecting institution. Initiatives like the Preserve This Podcast project (discussed in the previous chapter) encourage podcasters to reflect on their own archiving practices and to ask questions about what should be saved for the preservation of individual files, shows, and episodes. How might we build on this work in a collective effort to save additional contextual materials as a necessary part of documenting the history of this important media format? For this to happen, podcasters and archives alike need to appreciate the value of the scripts, notes, contracts, communications, and other records they generate in the process of creating the final products that listeners enjoy over their earbuds and car speakers.

One of the things that stands out from the above survey (and preceding chapters in this collection) is podcasting's porousness as a medium. Podcasters borrow from past and adjacent practices across numerous media forms, technologies, and business models. On the reception side, podcasting is porous, too, embedding itself in places and memories that sometimes have very little to do with the ostensible topic of a given program. These qualities of podcasting owe a great deal to the medium's mobility. Producers roam the streets with digital recorders. As listeners, we carry podcasts with us across train rides, walks, and errands. The sounds move between earbuds and speakers, small and large. It's a spatially mobile medium. But for podcasting to be a temporally mobile medium—for us to be able to carry the podcasts and experiences of making and listening to them into the future—we need to save the texts and contexts of our dynamic and messy present moment.

Works Cited

Abel, Jessica. *Out on the Wire: The Storytelling Secrets of the New Masters of Radio.* New York: Broadway Books, 2015.
Blouin Jr., Francis X, and William G. Rosenberg. *Processing the Past: Contesting Authority in History and the Archives.* Oxford: Oxford University Press, 2011.
Brunsdon, Charlotte. *Screen Tastes: Soap Opera to Satellite Dishes.* London: Routledge, 1997.
Carman, Emily. "That's not all, folks!" Excavating the Warner Bros. Archives." *The Moving Image* 14, no. 1 (April 2014): 30–48.

Crampton, Caroline. "Making Money: Part One." *Hot Pod,* April 9, 2019. https://hotpodnews.com/making-money-part-one/.

"Crooked Media Merch Store." *Crooked Media.* https://store.crooked.com.

Ercole, Pierluigi, Daniela Treveri Gennari, and Catherine O'Rawe. "Mapping Cinema Memories: Emotional Geographies of Cinemagoing in Rome in the 1950s." *Memory Studies* Vol 10, no. 1 (2017), 63–77.

Fino-Radin, Ben. "Take a Picture, It'll Last Longer. . . ." Text. Notepad, August 28, 2012. http://notepad.benfinoradin.info/2012/08/28/take-a-picture/.

Garant, Robert Ben, and Thomas Lennon. *Writing Movies for Fun and Profit: How We Made a Billion Dollars at the Box Office and You Can, Too!* New York: Touchstone, 2011.

Gray, Jonathan. *Show Sold Separately: Promos, Spoilers, and Other Media Paratexts.* New York: NYU Press, 2010.

Hess, Amanda. "You Know Your History? These Podcasts Aren't So Sure." *The New York Times,* December, 15, 2017. https://www.nytimes.com/2017/12/15/arts/podcasts-revisionist-history-malcolm-gladwell.html.

Holmes, Linda. "Spoiler Etiquette in the Age of 'Endgame.'" *Pop Culture Happy Hour* Newsletter, April 26, 2019. Subscribe-able at https://www.npr.org/podcasts/510282/pop-culture-happy-hour.

Hoyt, Eric. *Hollywood Vault: Film Libraries before Home Video.* Berkeley: University of California Press, 2014.

Hoyt, Eric. *Ink-Stained Hollywood: The Triumph of American Cinema's Press.* Berkeley: University of California Press, 2022.

"I am Roman Mars, creator and host of 99% Invisible, a radio show and podcast about design with over 3,000,000 downloads per month and co-founder of Radiotopia, a storytelling podcast collective. AMA!" *Reddit,* October 26, 2015. https://www.reddit.com/r/IAmA/comments/3qbbnb/i_am_roman_mars_creator_and_host_of_99_invisible/.

"I, Jesse Thorn, started my own NPR show, and now I own a podcast network, a theme cruise, and a menswear blog." *Reddit,* June 18, 2014. https://www.redd it.com/r/IAmA/comments/28gye6/i_jesse_thorn_started_my_own_npr_sh ow_and_now_i/.

"Kinomatics." *Kinomatics.* https://kinomatics.com/.

Kuhn, Annette. *An Everyday Magic: Cinema and Cultural Memory.* London: I.B. Tauris, 2002.

Kuhn, Annette, Daniel Biltereyst, and Philippe Meers. "Memories of Cinemagoing and Film Experience: An Introduction." *Memory Studies,* 2017, Vol. 10 (1): 3–16.

Loker, Kevin. "At $170,000+, '99% Invisible' Becomes Most Funded Kickstarter in Journalism." *AdWeek,* August 12, 2012. https://www.adweek.com/digital/99-invisible-most-successful-funded-kickstarter-public-radio-journalism/.

Maingard, Jacqueline. "Cinemagoing in District Six, Cape Town, 1920s to 1960s: History, politics, memory." *Memory Studies* Vol. 10, no. 1 (2017): 17–34.

Marchionini, Gary, Helen Tibbo, Christopher A Lee, Paul Jones, Robert Capra, Gary Geisler, Terrell Russell, et al. *VidArch Preserving Video Objects and Context Final Report* (2009).

McDonald, Paul, Emily Carman, Eric Hoyt, and Philip Drake, eds. *Hollywood and the Law.* London: BFI/Palgrave, 2015.

McKee, Robert. *Story: Substance, Structure, Style and the Principles of Screenwriting.* London: Methuen Publishing, 2005.

"Media Archaeology Lab." *Media Archaeology Lab.* https://mediaarchaeologylab .com.

Mills, Andy. "Lessons Learned While Making A (The) Daily." *transom,* October 10, 2017. https://transom.org/2017/lessons-learned-making-daily/.

Mitchell, Mike, and Nick Wiger. "Chili's Too." *Doughboys.* Podcast audio. April 25, 2019. https://headgum.com/doughboys/episode-200-chilis-too-with-eva -anderson.

Morley, David. *Television, Audiences, and Cultural Studies.* Abingdon: Routledge, 1992.

Morris, Jeremy Wade, Samuel Hansen, and Eric Hoyt, "The PodcastRE Project: Curating and Preserving Podcasts (and Their Data)." *Journal of Radio & Audio Media* 26, no. 1 (2019): 8–20.

Morris, Jeremy Wade, and Eleanor Patterson. "Podcasting and its Apps: Software, Sound, and the Interfaces of Digital Audio." *Journal of Radio & Audio Media* 22, no. 2 (2015): 220–230.

Morris, Jeremy Wade. *Selling Digital Music, Formatting Culture.* Berkeley: University of California Press, 2015.

Owens, Trevor. *The Theory and Craft of Digital Preservation.* Baltimore: Johns Hopkins Press, 2018.

Quah, Nicholas. "A True 'Netflix for Podcasting' Experiment." *Hot Pod,* May 14, 2018. https://hotpodnews.com/tag/luminary/.

"r/doughboys." *Reddit.* https://www.reddit.com/r/doughboys/.

Rogers, Richard. "Doing Web History with the Internet Archive: Screencast Documentaries." *Internet Histories,* 1:1–2 (2017), 160–172.

Rowser, Jamila. "50 Pieces of Beautifully Strange 'Welcome to Night Vale' Fan Art." *Girl Gone Geek,* October 1, 2013. https://girlgonegeekblog.com/2013 /10/01/50-pieces-of-welcome-to-night-vale-fan-art/.

Seiter, Ellen. *Sold Separately: Parents & Children in Consumer Culture.* New Brunswick: Rutgers University Press, 1995.

Spinelli, Martin, and Lance Dann. *Podcasting: The Audio Media Revolution.* London: Bloomsbury Academic, 2019.

Stepanyan, Karen, George Gkotsis, Hendrik Kalb, Yunhyong Kim, Alexandria Cristea, Mike Joy, Matthias Trier, and Seamus Ross. "Blogs as Objects of Preservation: Advancing the Discussion on Significant Properties." *Proceedings of the 9th International Conference on Preservation of Digital Objects* (Toronto, ON, CA, October 2012), 219–225.

Sterne, Jonathan, Jeremy Wade Morris, Michael Brendan Baker, and Ariana Moscote Freire. "The Politics of Podcasting." *Fiberculture* 12 no 1 (2008), http://thirteen.fibreculturejournal.org/fcj-087-the-politics-of-podcasting/.

Swetala, Christopher. "Fact-check Yourself Before You Fact-wreck Yourself." *transom,* April 25, 2017. https://transom.org/2017/fact-check-fact-wreck/.

Swiatek, Lukasz. "The Podcast as an Intimate Bridging Medium." in *Podcasting: New Aural Cultures and Digital Media,* eds. Dario Llinares, Neil Fox, and Richard Berry. London: Palgrave MacMillan, 2018. 173–188.

"The Podcast Consumer 2019." *Edison Research,* April 5, 2019. https://www.ediso nresearch.com/the-podcast-consumer-2019/.

Townes, Jeff. "P-Pops And Other Plosives." *transom,* April 27, 2016. https://trans om.org/2016/p-pops-plosives/.

Verhoeven, Deb. "Show Me the History: Big Data Goes to the Movies!" in *The Arclight Guidebook to Media History and the Digital Humanities,* Acland, Charles R. and Eric Hoyt, eds. Falmer: REFRAME/Project Arclight, 2016. http://pro jectarclight.org/book

Verma, Neil. "The Arts of Amnesia: The Case for Audio Drama, Part One." *RadioDoc Review* 3:1 (2017).

"Welcome to Night Vale Store." *Topatoco.* https://topatoco.com/collections /wtnv.

Williams, Wil. "5 Great Road Trip Podcasts." *Discover Pods,* October 16, 2018. https://discoverpods.com/road-trip-podcasts/.

Audio Dispatches

Digital materials related to this title can be found on the Fulcrum platform via the following citable URL: https://doi.org/10.3998/ mpub.11435021

Dispatch 1. Adam Sachs on the growth of the podcasting industry

Dispatch 2. Reginold Royston on podcasting in Africa and the African diaspora

Dispatch 3. Tanya Clement on digital methods for sound analysis

Dispatch 4. Jonathan Sterne on sound studies, preservation, and historiography

Index

Page numbers followed by n indicate notes. Page numbers in italics indicate a table or figure.

radio documentaries, 72–75, 78
radio features, 74–76
Radio Journal, 12
Radiolab, 56, 71, 77, 189–90, 244
Radio Preservation Task Force
   (RPTF), 15, 44–45, 47n3, 79
Radio Research Project (LOC), 75,
   80n5
Radiotopia, 46, 56
.ram (RealAudio metadata), 43–44
rap music, 87
The Read, 85, 89–90
RealAudio, 31, 36, 43–44, 46
RealAudio metadata (.ram), 43–44
reality-based podcasts, 71–81; collabo-
   rational, 125–26; true crime, 124–34
Reality Check with Jas Fly, 85
Really Simple Syndication. *See* RSS
RealPlayer, 44
Real Talk with Jason Whitlock, 113, 114
"Rebirth in Barrow's Inlet" (LOC), 75
reception artifacts, 238, 239, 247–51
Reddit AMAs (Ask Me Anythings),
   245–46
Redick, J.J., 113, 122n5
references: loss of, 231
"Regional Series" (LOC), 75
reinvestigation podcasts, 126–27
The Reith Lectures, 200
Reply All, 92–93, 219
Report to the Nation, 75
research: early scholarship, 11–17;
   interdisciplinary approaches, 11–17;
   with PodcastRE database, 111–14;
   production studies, 38–40; sound
   studies, 11–17, 20, 157–62, 257
resonance, 154
Resource Description Framework
   (RDF) Site Summary. *See* RSS
Revisionist History, 71, 96, 241
Rhymes, Busta, 88
Ricciardi, Laura, 127
Rich Site Summary. *See* RSS
Ridgen, David, 125–26, 130, 134
Riggs, Marlon, 80n7
Rivers, Glenn Anton "Doc," 114, 122n5
Robles, Amy, 62

Rocket Mortgage, 98
Rogan, Joe, 209, 216
Rogers, Richard, 13–14
Roland Martin Reports Daily Podcast, 113
Roosevelt, Franklin Delano (FDR), 74
Rose, Charlie, 88
Rose, Tricia, 87
Rosenberg, William G., 14–15
Rottenberg, Catherine, 65
Rowan, Lisa, 57
Royston, Reginold, 12, 20, 257
RPTF (Radio Preservation Task
   Force), 47n3
RSS 0.92, 198
RSS 2.0, 198
RSS 2.0.11, 198
RSS feeds, 2–7, 47, 195–207, 220, 224,
   231; added fields, 203; as anti-
   platform, 211–12; history of, 198,
   210–11; metadata, 137, 199–200, 231;
   preservation of, 231; sample feed,
   198
Russo, Alexander, 57, 95

S. Anthony Says . . . , 113, 116, 120
Sachs, Adam, 20, 99, 257
sampling, 87
Sanders, Sam, 176n1
"Santa Man & Moriarity" (*Hollywood
   Handbook*), 101
Sassoon, Joanna, 135–36
scandals: Donald Sterling, 109–23, 113,
   171–72, 173–74
Schapiro, Aaron, 187
Schifini, Julia, 229
scholarly podcasts, 181–94
School of the Air (SOA), 183
Schudson, Michael, 128–29
Schulz, Andrew, 85
Schumer, Amy, 215–16
Schwartz, Molly, 9, 19, 224–36
Schwarz, Jonas Andersson, 4, 214
Science Vs., 189
Scott, A. O., 79
Screenshots, 35
Scripting News (Winer), 48n6
Sears, Roebuck & Company, 183

Printed and bound by CPI Group (UK) Ltd, Croydon, CR0 4YY

09/06/2025

14685641-0005